JAVA 2 NETWORKING

McGRAW-HILL JAVA MASTERS SERIES

Boone, Barry   *Java Certification for Programmers and Developers,* 0-07-913657-5

Chung, David   *Component Java,* 0-07-913690-7

Jenkins, Michael S.   *Java Abstract Data Types,* 0-07-913270-7

Ladd, Scott Robert   *Java Algorithms,* 0-07-913696-6

Moss, Karl   *Java Servlets,* 0-07-913779-2

Nelson, Matthew   *Java Foundation Classees,* 0-07-913758-X

Rice, Jeffrey, and Salisbury, Irving   *Advanced Java 1.1 Programming,* 0-07-913089-5

Savit, Jeffrey, Wilcox, Sean, and Jayaraman, Bhuvana   *Enterprise Java: Where, How, When (and When Not) to Apply Java in Client/Server Business Environments,* 0-07-057991-1

Siple, Matthew   *The Complete Guide to Java Database Programming,* 0-07-913286-3

Venners, Bill   *Inside the Java Virtual Machine,* 0-07-913248-0

To order or receive additional information on these or any other McGraw-Hill titles, in the United States call 1-800-722-4726, or visit us at www.computing. mcgraw-hill.com. In other countries, contact your McGraw-Hill representative.

Java™ 2 Networking

Justin Couch

McGraw-Hill
New York   San Francisco   Washington, D.C.   Auckland
Bogotá   Caracas   Lisbon   London   Madrid   Mexico City
Milan   Montreal   New Delhi   San Juan   Singapore   Sydney
Tokyo   Toronto

Couch, Justin.
 Java 2 networking / Justin Couch.
       p.   cm — (Java masters series)
    Includes index.
    ISBN 0-07-134813-1
    1. Java (Computer program language) 2. Computer networks.
 I. Title. II. Series: McGraw-Hill Java masters.
 QA76.73.J38C68   1999
 005.7′2—dc21   98-43479
                                                        CIP

McGraw-Hill

A Division of The McGraw·Hill Companies

1 2 3 4 5 6 7 8 9 0   DOC/DOC   9 0 4 3 2 1 0 9

P/N 0-07-134814-X   part of   ISBN 0-07-134813-1

Java™ is a trademark of Sun Microsystems, Inc.

*The sponsoring editors for this book were Simon Yates and Judy Brief, the
editing supervisor was Ruth W. Mannino, and the production supervisor was
Claire Stanley. It was set in New Century Schoolbook by Priscilla Beer of
McGraw-Hill's Professional Book Group composition unit in cooperation with
Spring Point Publishing Services.*

Printed and bound by R. R. Donnelley & Sons Company.

McGraw-Hill books are available at special quantity discounts to use as pre-
miums and sales promotions, or for use in corporate training programs. For
more information, please write to the Director of Special Sales, McGraw-Hill,
11 West 19 Street, New York, NY 10011. Or contact your local bookstore.

 This book is printed on recycled, acid-free paper containing a minimum
of 50% recycled, de-inked fiber.

CONTENTS

Contents

PREFACE

In writing this book, I wanted to convey my experiences writing networked Java applications to you, the programmer. There is a fine line between a highly technical book that simply spews forth a rehashed version of the specification and the Networking "For Dummies" style. Neither of these approaches appealed to me. Having spent a long time writing networked applications for all sorts of environments—from high-speed LANs to 16-K radio links—I felt my experience would greatly benefit the new programmer.

This book aims to pass on knowledge gained from real-world applications development in mission critical situations. Frequently, in development you don't have the time to sit down and implement prototypes of your system using a number of different techniques for comparison. Therefore, the book presents a common example used across most of the chapters, allowing you to evaluate the strengths and weaknesses of each approach when applied to a single task. Commentary in each chapter highlights these points, thus allowing you to compare for yourself the differing strategies without having to go out and do it all yourself.

A number of programmers start by copying examples from someone else and then modifying the examples to suit their needs (myself included). The examples I have included here try to produce code that would be suitable for such modification. In some cases, the code has come directly from working applications or has been included into work projects (minus any sensitive bits of course).

What This Book Is

First and foremost, this is a book of techniques for using Java in a networked environment—Java's Networking APIs—and making Java programs interact with the wider world of the Internet. The examples are all designed to be practical illustrations of the different networking techniques using code snippets and the cutting edge of Java's networking in Java 2.

By the time you have made your way through this book, I expect you to be familiar with all of Java's networking options and to be able to decide on the best one for any particular application. Networking is never a one-size-fits-all solution to a problem. You must really understand all of the options, both their strengths and weaknesses, and be able to apply the correct solution in any situation with the minimum of fuss. Therefore, the subjects that we do cover, we cover in depth.

What This Book Is Not

This is in no way a beginner's book. Nor is it a book that attempts to cover every single Java networking API ever in existence. For example, there is enough material on Servlets, CORBA, and JDBC to fill whole books on their own. I don't attempt to do these subjects an injustice by including a few pages on each of them. Instead, I try to focus on the core technologies behind them, so that you can deal with the choice of whether to use the high-level APIs or the more fundamental first principle's approach.

Against this, the book is also not a superbible of the APIs. We don't cover every single method and option in excruciating detail. This is a practical book. A lot of the time you will need 80 percent of the APIs to do the job at hand. We go to the 90 percent mark by covering a lot of the more advanced features of an API using practical examples. That last 10 percent is always a worry because for every implementation of Java, there are as many variations. What works in a particular fashion on a given platform is completely different on another, and we simply don't have the space to cover every single variation.

Finally, this book is not necessarily about backward compatibility. It makes no bones about being a Java 2 book. You won't find bits talking about how Java 1.0.2 does things, or even 1.1. Granted there are many common parts to the 1.1 APIs, we're about building cutting edge applications. Oh, by the way, that also means that Applets aren't considered a high priority in this book either. Real-world applications doing large, nontrivial tasks very rarely run inside a web browser, and besides, at the time of writing, there isn't a single web browser that supports Java 2 without the use of Sun's Java Plug-in.

How to Use This Book

If you know what and how networking works, then the first two chapters can be skipped entirely. The third chapter introduces you to the java.net package. As this package changes with every new major version of the JDK, it is wise to give this chapter a quick once-over before heading on with the book; things may have changed from what you expected.

Finally, hard-core programmers should start with Chapter 5. This contains the background information for the common project that is used throughout many of the other chapters. Having completed this chapter, feel free to wander to whatever chapter is of interest to you. Each is self-contained, and illustrates how to go about applying a technique to the given situation while covering as broad an area of the API as possible.

Requirements

All of the code to make all of the examples run is presented on the CD accompanying this book. It requires Java 2 to run and compile most of the applications. Some will run with Java 1.1 (such as the intro Serialization and RMI examples), but generally you should stick to the standard JDK 2. Most code examples probably won't run with Microsoft's Java VM either. Code has been tested mainly on Windows NT and Solaris boxes (Linux had not caught up with Java 2 at the time of writing).

There is some native code here. Thus, for Win32 machines you might want Microsoft's Visual C++ to compile it, while on Solaris machines the standard cc or GCC should do the trick for you. Batch files/shell scripts have been included to aid in the build process.

ACKNOWLEDGMENTS

Dion Mendel (mendel@ccis.adisys.com.au), proto-hacker extraordinaire, was responsible for putting together most of the content handler code presented in Chapter 10. Dion has since implemented a number of other image loaders based on the code presented in that chapter in the course of his day job. Also, he helped me out a fair bit with implementing the user interface part of the Telnet protocol handler. Sorting out the differences among HPUX, Solaris, and Linux proved to be quite a challenge for our Telnet client.

Much gratitude goes to Rich Burridge (Rich.Burridge@eng.sun.com) for the support he's given me during the JSDT development. He's withstood a barrage of questions and bug reports/suggestions from me right from the very start of JSDA (the predecessor to JSDT). Thanks Rich for all the help, for the code support and for checking over my handiwork in this book! We'll still beat you at the Cricket though....

Cameron Gillies (gillies@ccis.adisys.com.au), graphics guru, knows more about Swing and AWT than you could possibly imagine. Cameron wrote the front end for the shared whiteboarding example in Chapter 13 and assisted a lot in getting the other GUI code going. He's been the one almost entirely responsible for all of our graphics development work, and can turn anything into a slick, fast piece of work. He is able to make Swing code run as fast as native components!

Finally, thanks to all the guys and gals working with me on my project at work for putting up with all the late nights, weirdness, and swearing as we've gone through the project. We certainly have lived through interesting times! Stay tuned, there's more to come....

JAVA 2 NETWORKING

CHAPTER **1**

Introduction

Java™ as a language is still very young, yet one of its main selling points has been that it can be used in writing applications for the Internet. Its platform-neutral capabilities have been marketed very heavily in the push to establish the language as a serious choice for application building, not just for making web pages pretty. Any application that runs over the Internet must by definition use some form of networking. A network may be anything from the modem connected to your serial port operating a 300 baud to the fiber-optic cable using ATM at 625 Mbps in a router.

Java Networking Background

To help you understand some of the concepts of the Java networking philosophy, a little bit of background information is in order. Until the advent of Java, dealing with network programming in a language like C/C++ was regarded as a bit of a black art. The choice of options was frightening and usually involved several pages of code just to establish a single network connection.

As in other Java APIs, the original Java network interface design followed the KISS principle. Suddenly pages of setup code came down to three or four lines. Much of this resulted from the designers' removing just about all of the various options that a C programmer would have available. To ordinary programmers this was not a problem, as they seldom used the advanced features. Also, programmers were invariably engaged in learning a number of other APIs in the new language to accomplish their task.

Java 1.0

Java 1.0 gave the programmer the basics of networking capability. It provided the user with a method to make connections to other computers and listen for new connections. On top of this it layered some additional APIs for dealing with higher-level Internet-related protocols in the form of customizable Universal Resource Locator (URL) handlers.

Apart from these URL handlers, there was little choice about what sort of network connection you got. If an error occurred, you were notified of it, but many of the lower-level choices like connection timeouts were missing. It was possible to program around these missing parts, but it was a fairly messy process.

Life creating large-scale applications was also not particularly easy. The classes which provided the raw data handling capabilities (`Socket` and `ServerSocket`) were not extensible in the customary object-oriented way, having been declared `final` in their specification. Also limiting to the programmer was the fact that, if you did provide your own implementation of a raw socket handler (`SocketImpl` is covered in Chapter 3, "The `java.net` Package") for any application, you could only set it once. This limited what could be done within a single application very severely.

Java 1.1

Sensing that programmers wanted more control over their network connections, Sun Microsystems, Java's developer, added more control over the connections to the APIs with the release of Java 1.1. Introduced were the four most common options that programmers used (which are covered in Chapter 3, "The `java.net` Package," and Chapter 5, "Writing TCP Communications"). These options allowed the Java programmer to build networked applications that behaved more like their native code counterparts.

Also added was the ability to create your own customized network handlers at the much lower level of the raw data coming into the Java application, while still retaining the high-level URL handler capabilities. Also, the `final` status was removed and now application builders had the flexibility to create robust server applications and useful clients.

The third useful part added to the 1.1 specification is the ability to create multicast connections within Java code. Previously this needed to be done outside of Java in native code or was limited to the local-area network (LAN) that the machine was connected to. Multicasting makes it easy to accomplish a number of the tasks that we will be examining later on in the book. You can think of it as a very efficient way to enable broadcast-type transmissions over the Internet with little effort.

Java 2

Compared to the sweeping changes that Java 1.1 brought the core networking capabilities, the move to Java 2 was rather less significant. A few new classes were introduced, but functional changes were minimal on the surface. The only really major change was the new fine-grain security model, but in day-to-day application programming, it is not much of an issue.

In Java 2, the changes moved to the supporting APIs. APIs that relied on the core networking capabilities had a lot more functionality added to them. Now the extended Java networking family was starting to take shape.

Nonnetworking Additions

Perhaps the biggest improvement in expanding the networking capabilities of Java 1.1 didn't come from changes within the network API itself. The ability to turn an instance of objects into a series of bytes and then reconstruct it exactly from that series of bytes has created a lot of opportunities for new applications of Java networking. Now, you can pass an entire object over a network connection and build it again on another with minimal effort.

The ability to write out an object is called serialization and reconstructing it again is called (naturally) deserialization. The task of doing this is covered in Chapter 7, "Object Serialization," but at its most basic level it is extremely simple to enable. What it now allows you, the programmer, to do is forget about the underlying network connection details, and just worry about what data are to be passed around. Using object serialization techniques means that you can even include the object-oriented (OO) data encapsulation concepts into your data transfers.

Serializing objects has created a number of the Java buzzwords that you are probably familiar with in some way. Remote Method Invocation, better known as RMI, is built on the principle of object serialization. Some of the other higher-level APIs like the Java Shared Data Toolkit (JSDT) that I'll be introducing in this book also use RMI either internally, or the user may use it over the top of that API.

Layering the Networking APIs

Like all good designs, the Java networking APIs are provided in a series of layers of abstraction. The programmer can then decide at which level to work. This book shows a number of APIs which are based on the core Java networking capability.

To start you going, we'll consider the basics of the Internet view of networking. Java's basic networking capabilities are split between the `java.net` and `java.io` packages. Between these two packages, you are able to establish and communicate over a network connection and pass moderately complex data over it.

Once a network connection has been established, there are a number of possibilities for the programmer. You can define your own custom protocols, use an existing one (e.g., Network Time Protocol, or NTP, and Simple Mail Transport Protocol, or SMTP), or build a higher-level API on top of the basic services. Java provides a number of these higher-level APIs. At the bottom of the heap are the URL content handlers contained in the `java.net` package.

Next in line is RMI, which uses `java.net` and `java.io` to implement its functionality as well as a good deal of native code. RMI comes in a number of packages: `java.rmi`, `java.rmi.dgc`, `java.rmi.registry`, and `java.rmi.server`. RMI uses the networking facilities to pass references to Java classes over the network. Classes may return an instance of another class or an instance is passed as a method parameter, which is facilitated by the lower-level Java packages.

RMI still involves some amount of digging around in the weeds if you need to do complex tasks that involve more than one person acting on a remote object. At the next level up from RMI is another layer of protocols. JSDT, which has already been mentioned, is one such application of RMI. However, as you will discover in a later chapter, JSDT can use any one of a number of protocols to implement its functionality, depending on the situation. JSDT is primarily implemented using capabilities from `java.net` and RMI (`java.rmi`), and there are custom native code implementations.

Where to Next?

Now that you have a very brief introduction to the Java concepts of networking and how they fit together, we'll spend the rest of the book exploring each in detail. We'll follow the same lead established here: first deal with the low-level APIs and then move higher up the layers of abstraction.

In the next chapter we'll outline the fundamentals of the Internet Protocol, the heart of the Internet, and then provide an outline of the `java.net` package.

CHAPTER **2**

Internet
Networking
Concepts

In order to understand how Java networking works, first you'll need a decent grounding in some theory. For this chapter, you won't be dealing with any Java code. Instead you need to understand the whats and hows of Internet networking. If you already have an understanding of these concepts then you can skip this chapter and read on with Chapter 3, "The `java.net` Package."

From the Wire to the Application

Networking is all about getting some code on one computer talking to code on another machine. Frequently these two pieces of code are written in two different programming languages. The client machine may be written in Java on a Windows NT machine while the server may be written in C on a Unix machine on the other side of the world. You as the programmer don't want to be concerned as to how they get from your piece of code to the machine on the other end, just so long as they are both talking the same lingo. Making sure this happens correctly depends on a whole raft of standards, protocols, and other people's code.

In general terms there are usually five contributors to making this all happen:

- Physical standards
- Networking standards
- Protocol standards
- Transport standards
- Application standards

In most books you will find these concepts discussed in terms of yet another standard called the Open Systems Interconnect (OSI) model. This presents a seven-layer pyramidal structure defining the levels of interconnection for various parts of a network connection between two machines (particularly from an engineering standpoint). In discussing general communications systems, this is a great model for comparing two different architectures, but is a bit overcomplex for our discussions here. Instead, I'll base our explanations on the five areas defined above.

Networking is a universal thing. The basic voice phone system uses a network to distribute calls and yet computers can form a network over the top of that basic voice network. As you will see shortly, a computer is not the only device that may be connected to the Internet, so we need to speak in terms that are much more general. For the following sections I'll term a device as being any object that is capable of connecting to the Internet, and understanding the information sent to it.

Physical Standards

At the very heart of the network connection is the stuff that makes the network—that is, the physical connections between two machines. It is tempting to define this as being the piece of wire that runs between one machine and the next, but that is only part of the story.

There are many ways to connect computing devices together. Consider a mobile phone that can present email and a Cray supercomputer. The mobile phone uses wireless radio links to send data to the nearest base station, while the Cray will probably be connected with a piece of fiber-optic cable. Neither of these involves a copper wire connection, yet it is possible to send email from phone to the Cray and vice versa. Physical standards define the type of medium that a connection is made on and how communications take place on that medium.

A bunch of different standards define what sort of medium the connection is made between, and then what is used to propagate a message over that connection. Let's look at the familiar piece of (probably) blue cable hanging out of the back of your desktop machine. This is defined as Universal Twisted Pair (UTP) cabling.

UTP means that you must use a piece of copper cabling that has eight separate wires in it. These eight wires are required to be twisted together in a particular fashion. At the end of that cable is a plastic connector that must have a certain shape, and also must contain eight connectors. Each of these little tiny copper pads must match to a particular wire in the cable. Also, there are certain defined limitations on just how much of the cable is allowed to be untwisted (for example, only 5 mm in a category 5 cable). All of these are required by the UTP standard. In a similar fashion the mobile phone has a set of standards that says it is a wireless radio link and works at a certain frequency.

Back to our UTP cable example. Once you have everyone manufacturing the correct cable, and you can physically plug the cable from the back of one machine into the back of another, then you need to define how you are going to communicate information across that link. That is, you need to define how to represent a 1 and a 0. In UTP cable, this is done by changing the voltage on selected wires out of those eight required by the cable standard. How this is done is also defined by the physical standards. Our UTP cable operates at a voltage change of 0 to 5 V. The standard is how to represent information on the wire. Does + 5 V represent a logical 1, and is 0 represented by a voltage of zero, or is it the other way around? At what frequency (speed) does the change happen? This sort of UTP cable connection would be known as XBase 2, where X is the frequency of the line (10 or 100 Mbps).

NOTE: In electrical engineering terms, the signal sent might not represent just 1 and 0. In the case of wireless links, a single change may represent 2 or more logical bits of information.

Networking Standards

Once you have decided how to read a 1 and a 0 from the line, you need to define how to understand whether information is currently being transmitted for you to read. Some standards names familiar to you might be Ethernet, Token Ring, and ATM (Asynchronous Transfer Mode). These all define how to make a connection and send information from one device to another and are independent of the physical connection between them.

Until recently, Ethernet was typically run over copper cable like UTP or coaxial cable. Now, with higher speeds like those of Gigabit Ethernet, it is being frequently seen on fiber-optic cable as well. With this, you can see that the Ethernet standard is independent of the physical connection between two devices (the Ethernet standard originally was derived from a radio link research project).

Networking standards defined how to get the information onto the physical connection, and how to arbitrate between a number of devices all trying to access that connection, potentially simultaneously. Ethernet uses a broadcast-and-wait policy. First it looks to see if anyone else currently has any information being sent on the connection. If not, then it starts its own broadcast. If it detects any other incoming information while it is writing its own information, or within a certain set time limit afterwards, then it trashes its own information, waits a predetermined amount of time and tries again. All this is defined in the particular networking standard.

The networking standard must also define a particular addressing scheme to label each device connected to the physical link. This way, individual devices can directly address one another. If there were no addressing scheme defined, then a device would not know that the information was specifically destined for it. Although other, higher-level protocols also have addressing schemes, one is needed at this very raw level so that a device connected to the physical link can make a decision very early about whether to ignore or process the incoming information. It is very common that for one physical connection, there is probably more than one device attached to it (consider the mobile phone for instance). Even when a device is broadcasting the information to all devices on the network, it still requires a "special" address that says that all must listen to the information.

Protocol Standards

With one device able to directly address another, you then need to layer on some common way of adding some services on top that allow you to operate independently of the type of network connection. At this level, all you want to be able to say is "Establish me a connection to the device known as X."

If all the devices were based on the same physical connection, then you could just write everything using the capabilities directly available in the networking standards. However, what if the two machines were not on the same physical connection? The network standards know only how to deal with a device on the same physical connection. It is the job of the protocol standard to locate and connect to a device on a different physical connection. This could be anything from a device in the next room to one halfway around the world.

Terms you would be familiar with here are IP and IPX (Internet Protocol and Internetwork Packet Exchange, respectively). IP is the protocol of the Internet. Every router, computer, and device directly connected to the Internet must be able to speak IP.

NOTE: *IP is normally seen in conjunction with its mate TCP, as in TCP/IP. Strictly speaking, they are two separate entities at different levels in the scheme of networking. IPX provides some services of both protocol standards and the next level up in the transport level.*

The main job of a protocol standard is to enable connections between multiple different networks. It first makes sure that data on one network which is destined for another locates which path to take, and it then makes sure that the data are passed on to the next stage. Usually the devices that need to know most about this are routers. It is the job of the router to form the physical connection between networks and perform the appropriate massaging of the electrical connections between them to enable the information to pass onto the next network.

Transport Standards

Knowing how to get from A to B is only part of the story. You still need to actually establish a real connection for data to pass between two devices. This is the job of the transport standard. To a large extent, the transport standard is dependent on the underlying protocol standard, unlike the lower levels.

At the transport level, instead of talking about the pure device-to-device connection, we can now talk about an application-to-application connection. At the protocol level it is still mainly concerned with device-to-device communications, but now we can say that we want to communicate between two applications. This is probably the first time that you will encounter a set of general-purpose APIs for dealing explicitly with networked communications. These are represented by the `java.net` package in Java and have equivalent APIs in almost every high-level programming language.

So what does the transport level provide? Basically it is a method of establishing, controlling, and tearing down communications between two applications. Standards at this level are designed to provide a choice of different connection types with varying levels of reliability. You can request anything from a permanent connection that has 100 percent reliability, and maintains the order of everything sent, to a connection that sends something once, with no guarantee that it makes it to the destination.

The two ends of the spectrum are represented by the terms *connection-oriented* and *connectionless* services. In the realm of IP, these are represented by TCP (Transmission Control Protocol) and UDP (User Datagram Protocol). Connection-oriented services provide a permanent link between two applications and a guarantee that what you send from one end will arrive at the other. Connectionless services, on the other hand, never establish a permanent connection. Each item of data is given the destination address and is pushed out onto the physical connection. Once it reaches the physical connection, there is no guarantee that it will even make it to the destination.

Why would an application want to use a totally unreliable method like connectionless services? Basically, for speed. Setting up and tearing down a network connection is an extremely slow process in computing terms. For connections around the world, it may be 3 or 4 seconds before the connection is established. Data traveling over that connection is also much slower since there may be errors and the message must be resent. A lot of applications don't even care if the data doesn't reach the endpoint. For example, a program sending out position updates of the user every second does not care if one is missed because there will be another to follow a second later.

Application Standards

When you are designing your own application, the type of service to use is a major choice. If you are writing a client or server for an already existing service then the choice is easy—you must write for whatever that service is. And now you've entered the realm of the application standards.

There are a lot of predefined standards. FTP and HTTP are examples of services that you should already be familiar with. Each of these has a standard that you are required to adhere to if you want to communicate with an application that is different from the one that you are writing.

When it comes to writing your own system (both client and server), then the choice is much greater. Do you need speed or reliability? Whichever choice you make, you must then design the contents of the messages. Just to confuse the issue a little, this is usually referred to as a protocol. So, FTP stands for File Transfer Protocol, HTTP for HyperText Transfer Protocol.

After you have a connection between two machines (although this might not literally be the case in a connectionless service), you still need to define the actual content of each message that you send. Much of the time, this comes down to being a series of bits arranged in a certain order. Each bit has a meaning and is placed together into a series of bytes to form the message to be sent. At the other end of the design, you may well be reading a text string from the network connection and then acting on the command that has been sent. Believe it or not, this is the way that many of the standard Internet protocols work. HTTP, SMTP, POP and many others use text command strings as the protocol.

Understanding IP Services

The Java networking APIs deal only with IP-based networking. Therefore we need to understand exactly what you are getting in the services provided by the `java.net` package. So far in this chapter you have already been given an outline of how IP fits into the general scheme of things. Now we'll look purely at what Java can provide to you the programmer.

Java provides three basic services: TCP (connection-oriented), UDP (connectionless), and multicasting or mcast broadcast). Each of these will now be treated in turn to more accurately define what you the programmer can expect from each of these.

A Few More Terms

So far in this chapter, I've attempted to keep the jargon level down so that you get an understanding of the basic concepts. Now, in order to make my job easier further along in the book and for you to understand what others are saying, we need to define a few more terms. Many of the terms here you are probably already at least familiar with, so hopefully this should be more of a refresher for you.

A network connection is normally referred to as a *socket*. You can have listening, receiving, and sending flavors of sockets. Usually the term *socket* is tied to a TCP-type connection. However, it is also correct to use the term *socket* to apply to UDP or Multicast connection types.

Regardless of whether you have a permanent connection or not, each time information is sent, it must go in a discrete chunk. This chunk of information is termed a *packet*. Each packet must be self-contained in that it carries the address of the destination and the data that is to be sent to that destination. From your piece of application code, the data descends through the various levels that have been outlined previously. At each level that it goes down, that original piece of data that you put in your application code has more and more information attached to the

front of it. Each level adds its own header to the data. It does not technically become a packet until all of that information is transmitted at the
physical layer.

When sending data from one machine to another, you need to specify
the address of the destination. What happens if you have more than one
application running on the destination machine that is listening for
incoming network traffic? The answer is that IP includes a kind of sub-
addressing scheme as well. These subaddresses are known as *port* numbers.

Just as there are set protocols for a number of applications, there are
also set port numbers. In IP terminology, these are called *well-known
services*. Port numbers below 1024 are reserved for these well-known
services and should not be used by any application employing custom-
built protocols. However, since the port number is an unsigned 16-bit
value, then there are another 63,000 or so spare ports.

Understanding UDP

As I've just outlined, the simplest form of data unit is the packet. Once
it has left the sending device, the sender no longer has any control over
it. Information sent on a UDP socket is not that much different.

As you've seen earlier in this chapter, UDP is a connectionless service
built on top of IP. It is also a one-shot network connection. You create a
message to be sent, then create a UDP socket and tell it to send the message to the destination. Once you have sent it, the socket cannot be used
again. You will need to create a new socket if you want to send more
data.

At the destination end, the application will be listening for data on a
UDP socket as well. Since the data from a UDP transmission is, by
nature, a single packet, then we know that once we have received it, it
can be processed immediately. However, just as in sending data, if we
want to listen for more information on that same port then we must create a new UDP socket to replace the one that has just been used.

If you have been following the pattern, the next point should be reasonably obvious. If we need to create a new socket for each send and
receive, then communications can only be one way. That is, if the initial
sender wanted to know if an answer had been sent, then it too must create a listening UDP socket just like the receiver.

Once the receiver has been given the data, there may still be other problems. UDP does not include any form of error correction apart from what the lower-level standards may have included. Therefore it is possible that the data you receive may have been munged in some way. You will need to make sure either that your custom protocol has some error management built in, or that the application knows how to detect and ignore erroneous messages without crashing.

Understanding TCP

If your application really needs to have a reliable connection, then TCP sockets are the way to go for you. This connection makes sure that the data always gets to you in the same order that it was sent.

In a previous section, it was explained that data is always sent as a stream of packets. TCP provides you the appearance of a continuous stream of data. This means that if you are writing lots of data in one operation, internally the data will be divided into lots of bite-size pieces to send them off, and the low-level services at the other end will reassemble them into something meaningful. If an error occurs in just one of those packets, then the entire stream (that the user sees) of information needs to be stopped while the destination waits for the resend of the corrupted data. This can be a major source of delay for other services.

In some ways you can think of TCP being built on top of UDP. UDP provides a packet-by-packet transmission of data, and the TCP then looks at individual UDP packets and does the management on top of that. While in real life that is not necessarily the case, it gives you a reasonably good conceptual idea of how TCP and UDP relate together.

Contrasting to UDP again is the communication arrangement. It has already been mentioned that TCP is a connection-oriented service. That is, you establish a connection first before sending any data. This connection remains available until you explicitly close it and can have data sent along it at any time that you choose. This also means that you have a return path for data as well. A client sending data off to the server can listen for error messages or other information coming back along the already established connection with minimal effort. In fact, that is usually the point of establishing a TCP connection in the first place.

Another difference between TCP and UDP is the way in which an application deals with listening for new socket requests. In UDP you saw that it didn't really matter which end of the system you were on;

you had to do the same thing to listen for data whether you were the original requestor or the server. In TCP, the two actions are very different. When a server receives a request for a new socket connection, it must do something with it. A TCP connection is going to be permanent. If it is to keep listening for new requests, then it must hand off the new connection to another part of the program code and continue to listen.

For this reason there are three different types of TCP sockets. First, there is the *sending socket*. This is created by a client application that requests a service of a server. In it you specify what the destination address and port number is to be. On the server end, to deal with the problems mentioned in the previous paragraph, two additional socket types are needed. A *listening socket* spends its entire life listening for new requests and then notifying your application code that something has happened. Your application must then create a *receiving socket* to process the incoming data and to send replies along. Once the connection is established, the receiving socket and the sending socket are identical in functionality. The real differences come from the way that they are first created.

Multicasting

One subject area that has only been briefly touched so far is that of a deliberate broadcast to everyone. In networking terminology this is called *multicasting* but is frequently shortened to just *mcast*. Java 1.0 did not have multicast capabilities, but this was fixed with Java 1.1.

What a multicast socket does is create a socket on a particular IP address. Because it is broadcast, there is no "destination" as such, just applications that have decided to listen to that address themselves. It is quite possible for the broadcaster to be broadcasting into empty space. The IP standard has set aside a range of addresses for this application specifically, which cannot be used by standard TCP sockets.

Multicasting is built into the IP standard. When a client requests to join a multicast session, it is the job of IP and the routers to locate the nearest source of that IP address feed and make the appropriate adjustments to ensure that the feed reaches the client. This design makes multicasting extremely efficient in bandwidth usage, as the server only needs to create a single stream and the routers take care of the branching/filtering to individual clients on an as-needed basis.

NOTE: *Some routers do not support multicasting, and other alternatives may be required. The explanation of the alternatives are beyond the scope of this book.*

Internet Standards

Now that you have a handle on the underlying concepts, it is time to work through a few of the higher-level acronyms and protocols that you've noted. Contrary to popular belief, the Internet is more than just about the web. Already you have seen a number of acronyms, such as FTP and HTTP, introduced. The purpose of this section is to explain how all of these terms fit together to bring you a document displayed in your web browser. In the following discussion the term *internet* is used to describe both the Internet network and any private network that uses the fundamental technologies defined by the Internet.

Basic Internet Standards

The Internet relies on a number of fundamental protocols to make sense out of all the millions of computers. Generally speaking, most of these protocols are based on TCP rather than UDP connections. These basic standards allow all machines connected to the Internet and private intranets based on Internet technology to communicate, regardless of the host operating system.

Naming and Addressing   At the protocol standards level, you need to know how to address one machine from another potentially halfway around the world. The IP addressing scheme takes care of this, using four numbers that you usually see written in the following form:

203.27.111.67

This is a 32-bit address, and is divided into four octets, where going from left to right more progressively defines the machine that you are on. Typically, only the last number addresses a particular machine, and the first three are used to specify the network that the machine resides on. The format above is typically referred to as the "dotted quad," or "dotted decimal," notation.

NOTE: *An octet is the same as a byte in that it contains eight sequential bits. However, in the networking world the lowest order bit is numbered 1 and the highest order number 8. In general, for computing realms the numbers are 0–7 for a byte.*

IP addresses are assigned to companies that are publicly connected to the Internet, usually by an organization such as The Internet Assigned Numbers Authority (IANA). At the time of this writing, the new authority looks like it will be the Internet Corporation for Assigned Names and Numbers (ICANN). Blocks of addresses are assigned on a per-network basis depending on the number of machines.

There are different sized blocks depending on the requirements of the company. Under the current IP structure, the address blocks are broken into four classes: A to D. Class A belongs to all numbers below 127.0.0.0 and is generally assigned to really large organizations, such as the U.S. government. Each assigned network consists of three octets. Class B addresses range from 127.0.1.0 to 191.255.255.255. These specify smaller addressing ranges of only two octets per network. Class C networks range from 192.0.1.0 to 223.255.255.255, and consist of only a single octet per network (at most 255 addresses). From 224.0.0.0 to 239.255.255.255 addresses (Class D) are not specifically allocated to a network. Each individual address in this range belongs to a multicast channel. (This is explained in greater detail in Chapter 6.) Above 240.0.0.0 is not assigned for any purpose at this stage, and is generally referred to as Class E.

Several lots of these numbers have some special significance. That is, on the general Internet networks, you will never see the numbers 127.0.0.1, which is the address of the local machine, sometimes referred to as a *loopback device*. It is used for allowing IP communications to the local machine so that sockets and other systems may run without necessitating having a network card physically installed in the machine. Often, corporations also have large networks inside a firewall that presents only a minimal address to the outside world. For these networks, there is a set of addresses in each class type.

With the millions of hosts on the Internet, remembering all the numbers of your favorite sites can be a major problem. DNS, the Domain

Name Service, provides the name to IP addressing scheme. In the real contact between machines, only IP addresses are used, but for the majority of the time, names are used at the application level.

Routing and Network Management At the same level as IP addressing and DNS are a number of management protocols for dealing with hardware issues. You don't normally see these protocols as they are concerned with keeping the network humming along without your noticing it.

To ensure that two pieces of hardware can see each other, the Interclient Communications Management Protocol (ICMP) provides a number of services. Of this service, you are probably most familiar with the ping command that uses the ECHO REQUEST message of an ICMP packet. These typically very small packets are used to test various low-level functions of the hardware.

The key to keeping a distributed network going involves the routers. A number of different protocols are used at this level. RIP is the Routing Information Protocol that routers use to exchange information between themselves. Sending a message from one machine to another can be a fairly complex task. It is quite possible that every packet within the message may take a different path to get to the destination. RIP is used by routers to exchange status information to enable optimum path calculations for sending packets along.

When there are a number of public access points for large-scale connections such as ISPs (Internet Service Providers), the Border Gateway Protocol (BGP) is used to provide extra routing information. BGP is specifically designed to swap network reachability information between large routers. It allows one router to tell sibling routers what network addresses that it can see downstream from itself. That way, any other routers that need to contact those addresses know where to send the packets.

Routers are not the only pieces of hardware connected to the Internet. The classic Coke machine in a student dorm is just another device as far as the network is concerned. All these devices have something in common: a network connection and the need to be managed. The Simple Network Management Protocol (SNMP) is used to control and monitor anything that is connected to the Internet. Unlike the router protocols, SNMP deals only with configuration information such as who is connected and what sort of device is connected. The idea is to allow remote administration of the device using the protocol.

Applied Application Standards

You will never interact directly with most of the above protocols. This is the domain of the sysadmins. Also, for many of these tasks Java does not contain the needed methods and capabilities that are used within the protocols. We will turn to the protocols you are likely to deal with on a day to day basis both in your work environment and possibly in coding.

Mail and News   Above the basic issues of addressing between machines are a number of different ways of sending data between them. These take the form of many different protocols, several coincidentally ending with the two letters TP (for transport protocol). These form most of the fundamental background to almost all of your daily activities on the Internet and probably within your company's private networks. Two of the most fundamental are mail and news.

Mail is transferred with the Simple Mail Transfer Protocol (SMTP). SMTP has a number of extremely powerful capabilities, which unfortunately also get abused for sending spam. One of these is the ability to relay mail. Relaying is the feature whereby a single mail message with a list of recipients is posted to one mail server that is asked to take care of the process of distributing to the individual recipients. The ISP's machine cops the workload and the network bandwidth while the spammer gets away with minimal resources (and quite luckily with almost zero traceability).

The other major source of information for the average user is newsgroups. The Network News Transport Protocol (NNTP) is used to distribute feeds to the distributed news system. Unlike SMTP and email, where the communications are generally one to one, NNTP (and the surrounding news system architecture) is a distributed protocol that allows a news item posted on one machine to be delivered to every other news server in the world.

File Transfer   Apart from email, the next biggest use of the Internet is for the transfer of files. File transfer takes many forms; just viewing a web page is a file transfer action. File transfer actions are characterized by having a repository of many files from which one is transferred to a client machine.

The most widely known of these actions is the web application. This uses the HTTP protocol to transfer a file from the web server to the client machine, the web browser. The idea of this protocol is to display a text page at the other end in response to a request. All information is text encoded on the stream between client and server. There are many different possible actions, including sending files and information to the web server, for example, a CGI (Common Gateway Interface) request. This protocol ensures that for every request a file is always returned, even if that file says "nothing exists here" (the famous 404 File Not Found).

The File Transfer Protocol (FTP) is slightly different from the HTTP protocol. FTP is designed to transfer binary files in the most efficient form. Where HTTP must convert everything to text, FTP just sends the raw bytes. There are various other facilities in FTP that other protocols don't allow, such as being able to continue a download from partway through a file after a connection dropout. FTP also can perform other useful tasks such as changing DOS text file formats to Unix formats on the fly (using the binary or text mode).

Describing Information

Since many of the above protocols are text based (SMTP, NNTP, and HTTP), a large problem arises when you need to transfer binary data using that protocol. Also, you need some way of specifying where to find a file in a general way out across the Internet.

Location   Before downloading a file, you need to know where to find it. A number of different schemes are in use or under development by the Internet Engineering Task Force (IETF). The most familiar is the URL (Uniform Resource Locator), but there is also the newer Uniform Resource Name (URN). These two fall under the category of being Uniform Resource Identifiers. The general goal is to describe a resource that is needed in some way that includes all of the required information to fetch that object.

URLs are very common these days. For example,

http://www.vlc.com.au/intro.html

tells my application that it needs to contact the machine called www.vlc.com.au using the HTTP protocol, and download the file called intro.html.

However, what if you don't really want to specify where to look for a file, just that you want a particular resource? URNs are designed to act like a library system that says "fetch this resource but I don't care where it comes from." This gives the underlying system the opportunity to fetch the file from a local source such as a CD or disk if it exists, but go to a networked site if necessary. A URN defines a namespace identifier and a string defining the resource. An example is

urn:vrml:umel:/texture/wood.gif

where urn: defines that this is a URN identifier. Following the first colon is the namespace identifier, in this case defined by the VRML consortium's UMEL group, and finally a string that says "find the file /texture/wood.gif relative to the top of the current definition provided by the group."

NOTE: *The Web 3D Consortium (formerly the VRML Consortium) has a group called the Universal Medial Element Library Working Group doing a lot of implementation and development of the core URN system as well as distributed libraries and Java code to implement them. Check http://www.vrml.org/WorkingGroups/vrml-umel/ for more information on URNs.*

Type   Where text-based protocols work, the commands are typically written to the underlying networking stream using 7-bit US-ASCII characters. When you attach a binary document (say an MS Word file) the 8-bit binary is turned into the 7-bit characters needed by the protocol. Typically, this is done by UUEncoding (and the decoding called UUDecode) because of the system used for the encoding. The problem is knowing how to deal with the file once it reaches the receiving end. First, you need to tell the system how to interpret the file attachment. This is performed using the MIME type (Multipurpose Internet Mail Extensions) that describes the type of file.

MIME types use a two-part description of the content that is to follow: a major category classification and a minor type. These two are represented using two words separated by a slash '/' character. For example,

```
image/png
```

In this example, the major type is an image. That is, the data that follows (in terms of the protocol information) is to be interpreted as image data. The second part says that the type is in the PNG (Portable Network Graphics) format. MIME types are used extensively on the Internet. (The use of MIME types is covered in Chapter 7.)

Standards Information   All these protocols have standards associated with them. There are a number of different standards bodies, but for the majority of principles the Internet Engineering Task Force (IETF) is the governing body of everything Internet related.

Internet standards are defined as Requests for Comments (RFCs). Each RFC has a unique number associated with it. RFCs are interesting in that they are both genuine requests for comments (particularly in the early draft stages) and also a definitive standard for some part of the functioning of the Internet. Everything that has been talked about as standards in this chapter has an RFC associated with it.

To find out more about IETF go to http://www.itef.org/ and about RFCs go to http://www.rfc-editor.org/.

Summary

Hopefully by now you have a fairly firm understanding of how the various parts of the computer network infrastructure relate together. In particular, we have looked at the various options available to a programmer who is writing in an Internet standards-based environment. Although we've generally tried to stay jargon-free, that means that you haven't got the full picture. If you wish to explore these concepts in more detail, the side notes scattered through the chapter point to more technical information.

In the next chapter we are going to examine the practical implementation of this chapter in the Java language. All of the basic networking capabilities are contained in the `java.net` package, which includes all of the capabilities, plus more, outlined in the previous section.

The java.net Package

In the first two chapters it has been repeatedly stated that the `java.net` package is the core of all the Java networking. Unless you are writing network applications using only native code, then it will indeed be that. All of the concepts that you learned about in the previous chapter are contained within the classes presented in this package.

Within this package you will find classes that implement UDP sockets (`DatagramSocket`), TCP sockets (`Socket, ServerSocket`) and multicasting (`MulticastSocket`). Each of these represent a basic socket type and provide all the methods for dealing with the data that are sent or received as well as methods for controlling some of the properties.

On top of this basic networking functionality are classes for dealing with Uniform Resource Locator (URL)-based connections. A URL is a high-level abstraction defining a service that is to be requested. The URL contains all the information to make a request—the destination machine, a port number, and the request information. It may even include a login name and password if needed by the service type.

This chapter does not intend to give a detailed description on how to use every class, as this is covered in later chapters. Instead it gives you a quick overview of each class and some of its basic features and options.

Java Networking Implementation

Like the rest of the core classes in Java, the networking package at some stage must make the transition from the platform-independent Java API to platform-dependent native code. Networking services are always provided as part of the core of the operating system and thus any code to access it must do so in the operating system (OS)-defined way. Java, of course, tries to hide this all from the user, yet it needs to provide as efficient a crossover as possible.

The API provides a nice separation between the objects you use and the method of creating them. In most applications that you'll probably write there will never be a need to use anything more than just the basic classes. Java 2 also introduces permissions to the equation. Permissions are used to control on a fine-grain basis exactly what a given application, set of applications, or the entire system will and will not have access to on the system.

Utility Classes

The utility classes provide all of the background implementation and data representation for connections. A number of these classes are also used outside of the `java.net` package too.

Address Representation   Part of the `java.net` package is classes to represent and control networking addressing. The `InetAddress` class is the main interface to this capability provided by Java. `InetAddress` serves many different functions within the Java APIs even though all it represents is a particular IP address.

Because InetAddresses are used to represent an address of a machine on the network, there are certain validity checks to perform as well as some performance optimizations resulting from caching. For this reason there is no constructors for InetAddress. In order to create a new InetAddress representing a machine you must use one of the provided static methods.

One Name, Many Machines?   One of the features of the Internet's DNS services is the ability to represent one machine by many different IP addresses. The case where this is most prevalent is in the backbone hardware of the Internet itself—routers. A router sits in the middle of two or more connections to different sites and decides which of those connections to send the individual packets. For each connection, the route must have its own address. Thus, if the router is connected to five networks it will have five different IP addresses. However, only one name may be used to represent that machine to the world. If you did a lookup of that name you would be returned five different addresses. Computers are capable of the same feat by having multiple network cards in them. Machines configured this way are termed *multihomed*.

NOTE: *In recent years a number of operating systems and web server software (e.g., Linux and Apache) have implemented the opposite version of this—a single machine with many network names associated with the one IP address. This is termed virtual hosting and is the core of most large-scale ISP implementations.*

The `getByName` method returns the representation of that machine. If you are unsure whether that machine goes by several addresses, you can use the `getAllByName` method instead, which returns an array of `InetAddresses`. There is always one address that represents the primary address of the system. It is important to know which address this is because a socket created on a multihomed machine without specifying which address to use will use this default address.

`NetPermission/SocketPermission`   Java 2 introduces much finer-grained permission control on the sandbox. While the older versions provided very coarse capabilities, the new model provides very discrete control over all activities. The new model is based on Access Control Lists (ACLs). These lists are termed *policies*. A policy defines each specific capability in an externally defined file that can be changed at will. The most important difference is that Java can now have security control over applications just as much as applets. The particular activity and a list of actions that can be performed define each permission.

The `NetPermission` class is used to control the permissions used for all network activity. It is very general—either you have the permission to do something or not. Network permissions apply to all network activity even down to items as simple as resolving a host name from an IP address.

`SocketPermission` defines the activities that may be performed on sockets alone. It defines a permission on a per host basis allowing you to connect to one machine but not another. A typical example of this is the applet restriction of only being allowed to connect to the web server the applet was served from.

TCP Sockets

As mentioned above, there are two parts to the TCP socket implementation. Firstly there is the sockets themselves, then there is the OS-dependent implementation of them. First we'll look at just creating a basic socket.

`Socket`   `Socket` is the class that represents a clientside socket. Constructing an instance of this class automatically creates a connection to the named remote machine. The constructors include many different forms of the same request, most of which include the InetAddress of the destination machine. The alternative is to directly use a `String` representation of the name and the port number. Note that in all cases you need to have both an address and a port number to connect to on the destination.

In the earlier section on multihomed machines, the point was made that some machines have more than one IP address. Two variants of the constructors are available so that you can bind the socket on the local machine to one of those IP addresses.

There are also two variants of the socket constructors that take no address at all and are declared `protected`. These create unconnected sockets. Unconnected sockets may be used for a variety of purposes where you are creating your own socket implementations or subclassing the standard socket. Generally these are used so that your class initializes the static parts of the socket code such as the socket factory code and for use in the server socket code (more about these later).

Client sockets also define a number of options that can be used. The concept of sockets originally came from the BSD variant of Unix (the other being known as System 5, or SVR4 for System V Release 4). These came with a lot of different configuration options allowing you to control many aspects of the behaviors. Java 1.1 introduced these options to the Java socket implementation. Some of these options are available only on the client end of the socket connection.

The first option is SO_TIMEOUT, and it is set by using the `setSoTimeout()` method. Giving this method a value sets the time in milliseconds that the socket should block waiting for data. If nothing is received in that time an `InterruptedIOException` is generated. This leaves the socket still valid, but just says that nothing was received in that time. Internally, this is implemented by using the appropriate time-out method on the underlying input stream of the socket (that returned by the `getInputStream()` method). You might use this option if you want to wait for only a certain time for a value. For example, this might be used on an HTTP connection while waiting for a response from the server. If nothing is received during the allocated time, you assume the server has not responded and notify the user appropriately. This option needs to be set before the stream blocks for a `read()`.

Second in the list of options is SO_LINGER, which defines how long the socket should stay valid after you call the `close()` method on it. Sometimes, when there has been a lot of data on a socket connection, calling close might terminate the socket before it has had a chance to send all of the buffered data. This option allows the socket to linger on for some time after you've officially closed it so that it may clear that buffered data.

In some of your applications, you might wish to provide customized sockets. For example, you might wish to provide sockets that transparently encrypt data. You can do this by subclassing the socket class directly. Then, by overriding the appropriate methods you can return your own streams with the encryption and other options already built in.

`SocketImpl` At some point, the platform-independent Java code must meet the platform-dependent native code. You need to provide a specific Java implementation of the socket. This class is used as the base class of the real implementation of the socket. The `Socket` class defined above is just a language-independent way of representing a socket interface. `Socket` is a shell that calls the identical methods in the `SocketImpl` class. Generally this class is used to hide the platform-specific native implementation of socket handling. By subclassing the implementation abstract class and writing your own code, you could also create your own custom socket handler.

Apart from the methods that match the actual methods in the `Socket` class, there are also a number of extra methods for the lower-level control of creating a socket, binding it to ports, and other general control mechanisms. Any programmer that has done socket programming in either Win32 or Unix systems will be quite familiar with these methods.

`SocketImplFactory` If you want to create your own socket implementation, you will also need to create your own handler class for dealing with different socket types. This is done by using the factory design pattern. The factory, when asked to produce a socket, will do so but return only the abstract base class representing the real implementation.

Having created an implementation of this interface, you will need to tell the system that it exists. Both the `Socket` and `ServerSocket` classes have a `setSocketImplFactory()` static method allowing you to set the factory class. This method can be called only once per VM instance. Calling it more than once will generate an exception.

`ServerSocket` Having a client socket is only part of the system. You will notice in the definitions of the `Socket` class that there is no way of making the socket sit there to wait for incoming connections from other client machines. This is because the two tasks of accepting an incoming connection and creating a new connection are fundamentally different tasks at the native OS implementation level. In order to accommodate this, Java defines the `ServerSocket` class for dealing with the server side of the equation.

Compared to the "plain vanilla" socket, the server version has a less bewildering array of constructors. These are limited to making it listen to a particular port and also adding the capability to define how many connection attempts may be held in backlog before denying more connection requests. For the multihomed machines, there is a variant allowing you to specify which of the local addresses to bind to, which also includes the backlog argument. If this InetAddress is `null` the socket may accept connections on all of the addresses.

Specifying a backlog value is very important in high-performance or heavily loaded servers. The backlog is a way of controlling how many people are connected to a machine indirectly. The backlog queue is not a maximum number of connections in total, just the maximum number of connect requests that have not yet been fulfilled. If you have a server that has a lot of connections, generally the accepting code would have a higher execution priority. Too many connect requests mean the rest of the connections get starved of CPU time.

`ServerSocket` has a much smaller range of options available to it. It only maintains the SO_TIMEOUT option of the client socket. The difference between this and the client version is that the timeout is specified for how long the server should block waiting for an incoming socket connection with the `accept()` method.

NOTE: *The `accept()` method and other methods are covered in Chapter 5, "Writing TCP Communications."*

UDP and Multicast Sockets

TCP sockets implemented a "permanently" connected network connection. You'll remember from the previous chapter that there are another two variations of the socket club. These are the connectionless services—sockets that do not have any long lasting form of connection between sender and receiver. Both the multicast and UDP sockets form part of this group.

DatagramPacket   At the lowest level, there is a packet containing information. Both forms of unreliable connections require an encapsulation of the data and everything else they send, including the destination machine address. The `DatagramPacket` class represents this encapsulation.

Data are represented in the class as an array of bytes, which is always passed as an argument in the constructor. DatagramPackets are used for both the sending and receiving of data which means that the array you pass in is not required to contain data. It simply needs to exist so that data may be written to it. If you decide to change this array, there are always set and get methods for the data.

Some forms of the constructor also take an InetAddress that represents the destination machine when the packet is used to send data. The details of how this works are left for Chapter 6, "Writing UDP and Multicast Communications."

DatagramSocket   In the TCP socket implementation, there were two forms of the `Socket` class. UDP is different in that it uses the same class for both `receive` and `send`. What functions the class performs depends on how the DatagramPacket is constructed and which of the `send` and `receive` methods are called.

Like the preceding two socket types, this socket also has the SO_TIMEOUT option available. Another option provided is the ability to set the `receive` and `send` data buffer sizes. These function as hints to the underlying OS implementation about the network I/O buffers. Increasing these can achieve greater performance by allowing all the data to be stored at once and reducing the backlog of waiting data to be processed in the buffers. It is recommended that this should be set the size of the largest packet that is likely to be sent.

MulticastSocket   Built on top of the `DatagramSocket` is the `MulticastSocket` class. This class provides extra specific capabilities for dealing with mcast-specific issues. Where it differs from the `Socket` is how you connect to the group. As will be seen in Chapter 6, instead of nominating an address and port number in constructing the socket, it is done as a separate step. In multicast terminology, a particular IP address that is used for the socket is described as a group. The `join Group()` and `leaveGroup()` methods are used to control the socket interactions with the network.

NOTE: *Multicast sockets are not permitted to work in applets. Multicast sockets can be enabled in Java 2 by setting the appropriate permissions.*

Apart from joining and leaving groups, multicast sockets include the option to set a Time to Live (TTL) value. This value ranges from 1 to 255 inclusive and defines the maximum number of router hops that take place before the packet is dropped. These are optional as the class uses the `send` and `receive` methods of the DatagramSocket base class for normal operation.

NOTE: *As each packet goes through a router, the TTL value is decremented. Once the value reaches zero the router just drops the packet, not continuing to send it further along.*

DatagramSocketImpl Just like the socket had its own implementation class used to map to the native code, the DatagramSocket has its corresponding class. The class contains most of the same methods as its TCP brother; however, the difference is that there is no factory class this time. Internally the DatagramSocket uses the `Class.new Instance()` method to create a new instance of this implementation class.

Applied Networking Implementation

Now that you've been introduced to the basic networking classes, it is important to look at the other half of the `java.net` package. A rough generalization is that everything else is associated with URLs and connections using URLs. This is a big advantage of Java over most programming languages; the core networking library contains classes for directly dealing with issues that have sprung up because of the emergence of the web. Native compiled languages like C/C++ require third-party or custom-written libraries to do the same thing.

The classes presented in this section are built on top of the classes presented in the first part of the chapter. They use the capabilities of principally the TCP socket services to provide reliable connections.

URL Utilities

Dealing with these extended networking capabilities is broken into two sections—processing and connections. First we'll deal with the processing capabilities. The classes in this group are used to describe, load, encode, and decode URLs.

NOTE: *Chapter 2 introduces the basic concepts of URLs and MIME types that are discussed here. A detailed explanation of these classes in use is given in Chapter 10.*

URL   Obviously, the first cab off the rank when dealing with URLs is the class that is used to describe any URL—appropriately named URL. Although you are probably generally aware of what a URL is from using the web, it is actually a lot more capable than that use would indicate. A URL, as its name suggests, is a resource locater for any type of resource. The most common usage is for web pages (http://www.foo.com/...) and for downloading files (ftp://ftp.foo.com/...). However, URLs can be applied to almost any network services. For example, Netscape's early Java implementations in their browser included an implementation of a Telnet client that was expressed as the URL telnet://bar.foo.com/.

Creating an instance of the URL class requires you to pass in either a fully qualified URL or a base URL and a relative part. URLs are immutable objects once created. Once you have an instance of the URL, you can then query it for each individual part. General programming does not have much use for this sort of functionality, but it is really handy when you come to implementing your handling classes, which are covered soon.

NOTE: *URLs can be changed, but only by subclasses and by stream handler implementations calling the* set() *method.*

The URL class is also used to do the front end of all the hard work of connecting to the named resource. The OpenStream(), openConnection(), and getContent() methods are used for dealing with this and are covered later.

URLEncoder/URLDecoder   These two classes form a matching pair for dealing with information that is encoded onto a URL string. These days, almost every large site is based on a database of pages or some sort of query mechanism for generating a page. You can tell this by having a look at the name that appears in the Location text field, typically located just above the web page. This will generally look like this:

http://www.foo.com/somepage.pl?name=justin+work=vlc+value =%13

The role of these two classes is to translate to and from this string form to a readable string. The above example would then be represented as:

http://www.foo.com/somepage.pl? name=justin work=vlc value=<CR>

This is mainly of use when you are writing code that generates URL requests to a server—for example, to load a new page based on the information in a Java-based form. On the server end the decoder would be used to split the values up into more meaningful terms for processing code. (The decoder actually forms a large part of the Java serverlet extension API.)

FileNameMap   When loading a web page, the URL is only half of the story. The other half is the description of the content that is about to follow from that connection. The standard for this information is MIME types. You are probably aware of what these are through general web usage. They define a major group and minor type within that group for each different type of content. Most of the time this is automatically generated for you when the web server sends the file to you—it is part of the required header.

However, URLs may deal with more than just web (HTTP) connections. The idea of the `FileNameMap` class is to provide this mapping service for you when the information is not part of the underlying protocol. The interface defines a method where you are passed a filename and it expects a string in return, which defines the MIME type of the content. This is then later used either internally by the URL or by your calling code to deal with the returned comment from the URL connection.

Because the definition is an interface, this means that you will need to create your own implementation. When implementing this class, unless you know exactly every type of file that you will be dealing with, it is generally a good idea to get hold of the system one first—through `URLConnection.getFileNameMap()`—and add it to your own class internally so that you may draw on its definitions.

URL Connections

The second half of the URL-related classes deals with creating and managing the connections. Although the URL class contains methods for opening, managing, and obtaining data from a particular resource, it does not perform any of the functionality itself. These are handled by the classes described in this section.

URLConnection and Subclasses Most of the underlying network management is handled by the URLConnection class. It is responsible for taking the URL, finding the correct implementation class, managing that implementation class, and then returning the results to the user. It also provides many useful methods for querying the status of the connection.

URLConnection is the base class used to define any connections defined by a URL to any sort of object. It does not do anything itself. For example, the HttpURLConnection class extends the URLConnection abstract class to provide a connection handler for HTTP URLs. There are a number of other subclasses provided by default. In the standard JDK1.2 distribution, Sun includes protocol handlers for HTTP, JAR, FTP, file, gopher, doc, mailto, netdoc, systemresource, and verbatim. A number of these you are not likely to have heard of because they are used internally by Sun's implementation of Java and belong in the sun.net.www.protocol package.

URLStreamHandler/URLStreamHandlerFactory When you provide a subclass of URLConnection you have to make it known to the system somehow. Because URLConnection is an abstract class, you cannot just create a new instance of it. It is the job of the URLStreamHandler class to take care of this for you. The stream handler class is the class that is used to process a particular stream—everything from creating the connection, to processing the basic content, to closing everything down nicely at the end.

Like the URLConnection, you should never directly create an instance of URLStreamHandler. This is left to the URL class to take care of. The class goes through a large process of deciding which class to load for a given protocol instance by calling the URLStreamHandler Factory if one has been set. Thus the process is this: URL calls URLStreamHandlerFactory for a protocol handler; the factory creates a subclass of URLStreamHandler, then, when the openConnection()

method is called, `URLStreamHandler` creates an instance of the sub-classed `URLConnection`, which is what you are returned.

`URLStreamHandlerFactory` acts just like the other factory classes that you have seen so far in this chapter. You can set a subclass of this factory to find the stream handler that you require for any custom implementations. When the URL looks up a protocol handler, it first checks to see if the factory (if it has been set) contains the correct protocol handler; if not, it then checks in one of a number of packages, and failing that checks its own `sun.net.www.protocol` package for a stream handler. If all of these fail, there is nothing you can do.

ContentHandler/ContentHandlerFactory   As you are already aware, HTTP connections and a number of other protocols all rely on a MIME-type mapping for a file to determine what to do with the stream of bytes that has just been created. In Java, this is handled by the `ContentHandler` abstract class and its implementations and the factory class.

These two classes form the same pairing relationship as the previous classes. When a content marker (in the form of a MIME type) is encountered in the stream, the factory is queried for a content handler of the required type. The factory is then passed the incoming stream of content data and requested to produce an object from this stream. A typical example of this would be producing an image of a type not natively supported by Java.

Authenticator   The last class that we have to deal with in this chapter is `Authenticator`. Some URL connections might require authentication before you are allowed to proceed with an action. Typical examples are FTP and secure HTTP logins. The `Authenticator` class is an abstract class that you extend to provide the authentication capability. It sits in the middle of the stream and when authentication is required, gets called to provide the appropriate message or interaction with the user.

In normal programming, this class is not used very much. It might be used if you are implementing an FTP client, for example, but most URL connection work does not tend to become involved in the authentication. Typical tasks that you might perform with subclasses would be prompting the user for a password or providing a username. Sometimes this requires direct feedback to a user (such as requesting a password) but other times it might be more behind the scenes, such as providing a port number.

A closely related class to this is `PasswordAuthentication`. It provides a username/password combination that is passed to the `Authenticator` subclass on request.

Java Security Arrangements

No discussion about Java and networking is complete without looking at security aspects. Indeed, security is paramount to networked programs, in terms not only of the data traveling over the connections, but also of the making and breaking of those connections.

Java 2 introduces a much more fine-grained control mechanism than previous versions. Instead of the all or nothing approach of applications versus applets, now everything is treated the same. The VM uses a policy file that is located on the local machine to determine what code is permitted to perform each action.

Controlling Code Access

For every instance of the VM on your machine, there will be a global default policy file. Typically, this file resides in the lib/security directory where the Java Runtime Environment (JRE) is installed, in a file called `java.policy`. Inside this file is a list of each piece of code defined by location and what it is permitted to do.

A typical set of permissions looks like this:

```
grant codeBase "file:${Java.home}/lib/ext/*" {
  permission Java.security.AllPermission;
};
```

The first line says grant the file defined by its code base in the given directory the following permissions. If you wanted to grant all code signed by a particular digital certificate, you would change the word `codeBase` to `signedBy` and then follow it by a comma-separated list of the signer names. You can mix and match these two keywords if you want greater control as well.

After the open bracket, there is a list of each permission that you wish to grant. In the above example this gives the nominated code base the ability to absolutely apply everything it wants to your system. This is fine if it deals with the core classes from the JDK, but for general code it can be an absolute nightmare. A normal permission for a network connection may look like the following:

```
permission Java.net.SocketPermission "localhost:
1024-", "listen";
```

This says that a socket may listen on the local host for any port above 1024. The exact form of each permission is determined by the permission class itself, and usually can be looked up in the `javadoc` documentation.

Specifying Alternate Policy Arrangements

Under the default install arrangements, any code now conforms to the standard restrictions placed on applets—even if the code is a standalone application. Obviously this is a big change from the old ways, and is very likely to break old code running under the new VM security architecture. You need to know how to fix this situation. There are two choices: add permissions to the global file or specify an alternate arrangement.

The first and probably most obvious choice is to add new entries to the existing policy file. You can do this fairly simply by using the cut and paste of existing entries and digging around in the `javadoc` for the specific permissions that you need to add.

If you need greater control than this, then you will probably want to create a separate policy file. To create an alternate file, you simply need to write exactly the same stuff as you would for adding it to the current file. There's not even a restriction on the name of the file. Once this is completed, you need to specify on the command line the alternate policy file by defining the property `java.security.policy`. The location of the security file is required to be a fully qualified URL. For example:

```
c:\>Java -DJava.security.policy = file://some_dir/
mypolicy SomeClass
```

The policies defined in this file are now used in preference to the standard system settings, although there is no need for you to specify all the permissions for all the system code.

NOTE: *Throughout the rest of the book, we will be assuming the default security setup. Notes are placed in each chapter where appropriate, thus highlighting the permissions that need to be enabled to make the code run.*

Summary

That finishes our tour of the `java.net` package. As you can see, there is a wide variety of tasks that can be performed. This chapter did not attempt to provide in-depth discussions of each class, as these will be covered in much more detail in later chapters.

Threading for Networking

Once you start building applications of any size that involve networking, you will quickly notice how they can start to interfere with a linear program code flow. The understanding of multithreading becomes essential to building a well-behaved, nontrivial application.

Multithreading Concepts

Why do you need to involve threads with a network application? Consider the following problem. You have a listening socket, and it finds a new request which results in a new TCP socket and a new instance of your class like this (minus all the exception handling):

```
ServerSocket listener = new ServerSocket(3000);
while(true) {
  Socket incoming = listener.accept();
  MySocketHandlerClass handler =
   new MySocketHandlerClass(incoming);
  handler.process();
}
```

Now what happens? It accepts the socket connection and processes the incoming data. What have we been saying about TCP sockets in the first part of the book? They are a semipermanent connection. That means that to process the data, our process() method will return only after the socket connection has been closed. This closure may be some minutes or even hours down the track. In the meantime, the while loop has not yet executed its next accept() call. We've effectively stopped the application from working. What we need is a quick way to send off the incoming data into its own processing loop and return as soon as possible to listening for new connections. This is why you need to understand multithreading.

What Are Threads?

A thread is a piece of code that can act independently of any other code within an application. The piece of code is usually started by another piece, but once it has been told to start executing as a thread, it will run independently of the original caller. Once a thread has been created, it will control its own destiny about when it thinks it should stop executing, unless there is some outside interference.

On a larger scale, consider any modern operating system. You can start multiple applications simultaneously and they will run all the time, regardless of which one you happen to be typing in at the time. Each of these applications exists as a separate thread within the operating system (usually called a process at this level). Creating a thread within an application has the same effect. As you will see later, the threading within an application may or may not be controlled at the OS level. The Java virtual machine (VM) may well take care of threading issues by itself.

After the VM creates a new thread, it may do whatever it likes with it in terms of deciding when it should be run. You could be in the middle of a method somewhere in thread A when the VM decides that it needs to stop thread A and start executing thread B. Sometime later, it finishes B and returns back to A again. This can be the cause of many programming problems that we'll explore later.

When you create a thread, it allows that piece of code to execute like it was standalone and had nothing to do with the rest of the application. If you have a look at the piece of pseudo Java code that was presented above, you can see where threading would immediately come in handy. It would allow our newly created handler class to process the incoming data separately from the loop that is listening for incoming connections.

Java is very different from any other programming language in that the ability to create a thread is included as part of the language. In other languages, threads were included by using operating system-specific code that was outside of the language itself. Using OO principles, you just label any class that you like as being a thread and then you can execute it from anywhere you like in your code. The Java virtual machine then looks after all the rest of the details such as organizing how it will run.

Besides the user's application, there may well be a number of other threads running at the same time. The VM must somehow divide the time up between all the threads requiring CPU time. The user can control to some extent just how much of the CPU time can be allocated to an individual thread. This is called the priority of the thread. The higher the priority, the more CPU time the thread gets. There is no fixed scheduling of priority such as X must have Y percent of CPU. It is all relative. If there are 3 threads all with the same priority, regardless of its value, they all share the same amount of CPU. For each thread, if there is a thread of higher priority needing CPU time, then that higher priority will get the time and the lower priority will not be run at all.

> **NOTE:**   *This is an oversimplified, idealistic view of threading. Depending on the implementation of threading used, not all processes of the same priority will get equal CPU share. This old style is called cooperative multitasking. The multitasking implementations of Win32 and Unix operating systems are termed preemptive multitasking. The MacOS and MS Windows 3.x use the old-style cooperative multitasking.*

Accessing Common Resources

Although threads are labeled as being independent entities when it comes to execution, they still need to share the machine with many other threads and even other applications. Also, since there may be a number of threads within an application, they may all be requesting to use the same resources. Somewhere in the middle, there will be a clash of wills as two separate threads try to access one piece of data.

Race Conditions   Say you have an application that is running as a turnstile counter counting the number of people entering and leaving a carpark. Our application has two threads as indicated in Figure 4-1— one for incoming cars and one for the outgoing cars. They both access a shared object called Counter.

```
public class Counter {
  private int count = 0;

  public void inc() {
    int n = count;
    n++;
    count = n;
  }
  public void dec() {
    int n = count;
    n—;
    count = n;
  }
  public int getCount() {
    return count;
  }
}
```

Figure 4-1
Parts of the carpark
turnstile counter
program.

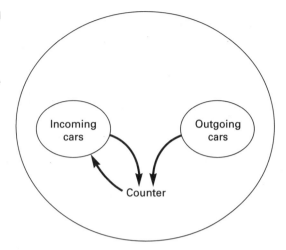

As a car enters the carpark, it increments the counter; as the car exits, it decrements it. Very simple. Threads are completely independent, so what happens if the incoming car thread gets interrupted halfway through the call to the `inc()` method? If the `dec()` method is called by the outgoing car's thread, then we end up with wrong values because the value n contains the original value of count, not the updated one from the decrement call. This is called a race condition, where the value of the output is highly dependent on the order in which the threads are run.

Obviously you wouldn't write the code like this with the intermediate variable, but the point is made. Multithreaded code does not normally contain such short methods and the possibilities of interruption are always significant.

Deadlocking In order to protect against race conditions, research over the years has produced a number of solutions. In all forms the result is to have some sort of shared variable that indicates whether a particular resource, be it a section of code or another variable, is available or not.

The result of this is another potential problem that you are likely to encounter in threading: two resources attempting to access two others. Each might grab one resource and then wait until it can access the other. If they both grab one each, then the code will form a deadlock situation where each thread is waiting on the other to release the other resource that it needs to complete. There is no escape from this once it occurs (at least at the VM level).

Implementing Control   Research over the years has produced a number of different solutions to the two problems mentioned above (and many more). The solutions have gone by a number of names:

- *Critical sections.* Parts of the code are labeled as a block that cannot be interrupted. If a thread starts to execute this section, then no other code can interrupt.

- *Semaphores.* A message-based system where each thread indicates that it wishes to access data and is placed in a queue to access it. Code cannot pass into the next section unless it is allowed passed the semaphore.

- *Mutex. Mut*ually *ex*clusive sections, usually implied by a lock flag. Before a critical section is entered, a lock must first be granted. The lock is usually a boolean flag that is specifically requested. Mutex is an extension of the basic critical section concept. A mutex can be used to stop from running another piece of code that requires the same lock, even though they may never actually execute the same method or access variable.

- *Monitors.* Another variation on the mutex theme, monitors allow queuing but a particular lock variable must be specifically requested in order to proceed. That is, you just label the code as monitor-based and the underlying architecture takes care of whatever flag conditions need to be met.

Java implements the monitor concept. All you need to do is label a piece of code as mutually exclusive and the VM takes care of the rest of the details.

NOTE: *If you would like to know more about the theory of controlling resource contention issues, it is covered in almost any book/course on basic operating system design. An introductory online guide to this can be found at*

http://www.mcs.kent.edu/docs/mcsparlmach/encorec/encore.html

Look at the section titled Basic Parallel Programming Concepts.

Design Concepts

Once you've got the hang of writing Java threads, it can very quickly become too easy for you to do. Something taking too long? Throw it off into another thread. Shortly you will notice that your application is now running *slower* than before. What is happening?

There's an old cliché which says you can't get something for nothing. This definitely holds true for multithreaded applications. If everything is a thread, and all threads are supposed to be run at the same time (or at least appear that way), how do you change from one thread to another? This is the job of the VM.

At the very lowest level, the VM acts just like a normal computer. It has the currently running code loaded into local memory (on a CPU it is likely to be stored in the cache), and many of the variables are probably loaded into the registers. The VM decides that it is time to swap threads. Now, all that code needs to be unloaded out of the CPU, so all the register values have to be written out to the main memory, the current state of the thread needs to be saved, and the new code for the next thread needs to start running. Since the new thread code is not likely to be in the cache, you cop a big performance hit because that needs to be fetched, the thread state needs to be loaded, and finally the new thread is ready to run.

As you can see, swapping between two threads is quite a long task. This process is termed a *context switch*. Every context switch consumes some amount of CPU time where it cannot be executing your code. If you have many threads, you should be able to see how quickly the CPU can end up spending all its time just swapping code into and out of the VM rather than executing it. The end result to you is an application that runs exceedingly slowly—which is not the idea of using threads in the first place.

The choice of what to put into a thread and when is as individual as the application. Generally it is a good idea to use a thread for any task that is going to take very long periods of time to execute. A general rule of thumb that I work from is this: If it takes more than 3 seconds to get a response, a separate thread should be used. This is probably most noticeable when the "response" is determined by the screen update time. If you had a menu that caused a new image to be shown, and the `ActionListener` code directly loaded the image, then you would notice that, although the code is processing, the menu still appears on screen because it hasn't yet received the repaint command. A better solution is to put the image load in a separate thread that allows the ActionListener code to return as quickly as possible and allow a refresh of the screen. A couple of seconds later, the image appears. Even though your code is not executing any faster overall, it *appears* that the application is much quicker. And appearances are everything!

Java Threading

In Java, threading takes on a very OO role. You can make any object capable of being run as a thread simply by extending a class or implementing an interface. The choice of which you use depends on what you need to do. Both of these mark to the VM that the class is to be considered capable of running as a thread and that the appropriate steps need to be taken.

Executing a Thread

How do Java threads run? A simple enough question. Threading is core to the Java language and to the runtime environment (the virtual machine). First, the class needs to be declared to the runtime environment that it is capable of running as a thread. This can be achieved either by extending `java.lang.Thread` or by implementing `java.lang.Runnable`. Within both of these there is a `run()` method. This is the method called by the VM when the thread is to start acting independently.

Application code, if it wishes to operate as a separate thread, is required to override the run method, as this is the only one that will be called when a class is to start executing. Once this method exits, that is the end of the thread. If you want your thread to be something more than a simple calculation, such as code that is reading data from a network connection, then you will need to write some sort of looping code.

Unlike most other code that you write, it is OK to make an infinite loop in the run method. This is a good thing since you don't want the thread to exit until you have done everything that you want. In the case of some applications, this could be hours or even more. The run method is how the Java VM distinguishes one thread instance from another. It is called directly from the heart of the VM, not from your user application code.

Should you want to start a new thread from your code, you should not call `run()` directly. Remember that it is most likely that you've put an infinite loop in there, so, if you call it directly from your code, the call will never return and the application will hang at that point. Instead, Java provides another method—`start()`. Calling the start method of a class marked to be a thread is what signals to the VM to start running the class instance as a separate thread. Your thread class may override the standard start method to do some setup work, but you must remember to call `super.start()` as the last thing in the overridden method, otherwise the thread will never actually run.

Once the `start()` method has exited, the run method is called some time later by the VM. Just like standard code, your start method should never call `run()` directly. Always let the VM look after this. If there is some reason that you need to stop a thread, then there is always the `stop()` method. This is declared final so you can't override it, but it calls an immediate halt to the code in the run method.

NOTE: *Java 2 is declaring the stop method of Thread to be deprecated. There are a lot of inherently unsafe problems that arise from the Java implementation of multithreading. The crash halt of a thread requires complex coding that may never catch all conditions. The best way to write code is to use a flag to indicate that the thread should stop and call the* `interrupt()` *method of that thread to break any blocking code. The run method should check this and exit cleanly when needing to stop.*

`java.lang.Thread`

If you went searching through the Java API documentation looking for multithreading clues, then most likely you would run across `java.lang.Thread` first. This is one of the two options available. This is an abstract class that can be extended and provides the core requirements for threading. As soon as you extend the class, there is nothing else that you have to do to make it capable of being run as a separate thread, since it provides implementations of everything that is needed.

To make your extended class actually useful though, you will need to provide your own implementation of the run method. The default run method is empty, so as soon as your thread starts, it ends!

To construct and run a new thread you will need to do the following:

1. Write a new class that extends `Thread` overriding the run method.

2. Create an instance of that class in your Java code.

3. Call the start method on that thread.

This process is demonstrated in Figure 4-2.

Figure 4-2
A basic threaded
demonstration for a
class-extending
`Thread`.

```java
public class ThreadTest1 extends Thread {
  private int thread_number;

  // constructor takes an integer indicating what thread this is
  public ThreadTest1(int threadNumber) {
    thread_number = threadNumber;
  }


  ...
  public void run() {

    System.out.println("running thread " + thread_number);
    while(something_is_happening) {
      // do something here
      ...
    }
  }

  public static void main(String[] args) {
    // create a new instance of the class and run the thread
    ThreadTest1 test1 = new ThreadTest1(1);
    ThreadTest1 test2 = new ThreadTest1(2);

    // now run the threads
    test1.start();
    test2.start();
  }
}
```

The result of the above code sample should result in two lines print-ing out:

```
c:\test_dir\>java ThreadTest1
running thread 1
running thread 2
```

This indicates that the two run methods have been called. From now on it will be sitting in an infinite loop that you will need to kill using CTRL-C.

Notice that all we need to do to start the thread running is call the start method of each instance of the thread that we have created.

`java.lang.Runnable`

The other method of providing multithreading capability to a class is to implement the Runnable interface. This interface is also used by the Thread class itself and is really the heart of the threading capabilities of Java. `Runnable` is one of those series of interfaces like `Cloneable` and `Serializable` that mark a particular class as something special to the VM, outside the normal interface rules.

   `Runnable` requires only that you implement one method—the `run()` method. In this case, because you are dealing with an interface you must provide the method implementation. Apart from that, there is not that much difference in coding that you need to account for (although there are a number of other differences that will be covered shortly). You will still need to go through the same process as the previous section but with a few minor modifications, namely:

1. Write a new class that implements `Runnable`, providing the `run()` method.
2. Create an instance of the class in the Java code.
3. Create an instance of `Thread`, passing it the class that you have just created as part of the constructor.
4. Call the `start()` method on that thread.

If we now take the code sample shown as Figure 4-2 and modify it to use the Runnable interface, you will get the code sample in Figure 4-3. The interesting thing to note about this example is the main method. Notice that we've first had to create an instance of the class that implements `Runnable` and then create an instance of `Thread` passing it this class. This nominates to the threading class that the `ThreadTest2` is available to be run as a thread.

   Note also the last two lines of the main method. They show that there are two possible ways to then start the thread running. You can call it either directly on the interface that implements `Runnable` or from the thread that was created to run it.

Deciding Which Way to Thread

In the previous two sections you've been shown two possible ways of writing multithreaded code. Now the problem is choosing which way to go. The choice depends on what you need to do.

Figure 4-3
The implementation
of the thread demon-
stration using
Runnable rather
than Thread.

```java
public class ThreadTest2 implements Runnable {
  private int thread_number;

  // constructor takes an integer indicating what thread this is
  public ThreadTest2(int threadNumber) {
    thread_number = threadNumber;
  }


  ...
  public void run() {

    System.out.println("running thread " + thread_number);
    while(something_is_happening) {
      // do something here
      ...
    }
  }

  public static void main(String[] args) {
    // create a new instance of the class and run the thread
    ThreadTest2 test1 = new ThreadTest1(1);
    ThreadTest2 test2 = new ThreadTest1(2);

    Thread thread1 = new Thread(test1);
    Thread thread2 = new Thread(test2);

    // now run the threads
    test1.start();
    thread2.start();
  }
}
```

When you extend `Thread`, you are creating the equivalent of a one-shot thread. That is, once you have called `start()` and the thread completes execution, you cannot restart the thread from the beginning. On the other hand, classes which implement the Runnable interface can be restarted as many times as you need just by calling `start()` as required.

Apart from these differences there is the usual Java design decision about extending classes compared to implementing interfaces. Do you restrict yourself to a particular derived class structure with `Thread` or do you just add in the threading capabilities at the level that is needed by implementing the Runnable interface? As always, the final choice should depend on your particular needs for the project.

Threading Implementations

Although we try to maintain a platform-independent view of the world when it comes to programming in Java, it always pays to be aware of what the underlying implementations are.

Let's start with a situation of having three threads running, all with the same priority. All three should share equal amounts of the CPU. All of them will contain a really heavy calculation routine which is very CPU-intensive. Run this on a Win32 machine and then run the same code on a Unix machine, for example a Solaris box, both of which use an x86-compatible CPU.

What you should notice is that there is very different behavior between the two. On the Win32 machine you should notice that each thread gets an equal amount of CPU time and all threads will exit at pretty much the same time. In contrast, on the Solaris machine, you will notice that one thread will run to conclusion before the next one starts. Why is this so?

The differences are fundamental to scheduling—dealing with multiple pieces of code running at once. There are two ways of dealing with the problem of code competing for CPU resources. The first is to just let one code piece run until it stops because it needs something else such as a file from disk, then run the next one waiting. The second alternative is to share the time equally between all the code; this is known as time slicing.

If you are using Sun's JDK on a Win32 machine, then the thread handling is implemented by using the native thread implementation provided by the OS kernel, which is time-sliced. Each thread of the same priority is given equal access to the CPU, regardless of how intensive the usage is or whether it stops running while waiting for other input.

The Solaris implementation uses its own threading implementation, called Green Threads, which is handled entirely within the VM itself. There is no time slicing involved here. Once a thread starts to run, it stays running until it either voluntarily gives up or it needs to stop while waiting for I/O. The other major problem with this is that, when running on a multiple CPU machine, the threads will not distribute across the CPUs; everything will remain on the single CPU.

This problem is being rectified with later patch versions of JDK 1.1.4 and with Java 2. Sun has available a native thread implementation of the Solaris Java implementation. However, remember that these differences are due only to the Sun implementation of the JVM; other providers of Java on each platform may well do something different. You need to read the documentation that comes with your individual installed Java implementation.

Controlling Threads

With ordinary threads there are lots of things you can do. These will allow you to manage incoming network connections quickly and efficiently. Once your software starts to grow, you may desire more control over what individual threads are doing. For example, you may want to know whether certain threads are still running and, if they aren't, remove the references to them.

Thread State

Having created a thread, you will at some time want to manage it. This may be as simple as checking if it is still running, pausing it, or even stopping its execution. Before we look at this, you need to know what sort of conditions that a thread can exist in.

Figure 4-4 illustrates the various states in which a thread can exist and how they can transition. Upon creating a new thread instance and before calling the start() method, you will find it in the *new* state. The thread exists, but no code is running yet. Once you call start(), the thread becomes *runnable*; however, it may not yet have started running. If your new thread has a lower priority than another already executing thread, it won't be started even though it is eligible to run. At some time later when your thread is actually running, it may have to stop for some reason, say to wait for some network I/O to occur. At this point it changes to the *not runnable* state. It will stay in this state until the blocking action has finished (more input on the socket connection) and becomes runnable again. When the VM thread handler can fit in the thread, it will continue to execute again. If the thread ends by exiting the run() method, or it is deliberately killed from outside, then it goes

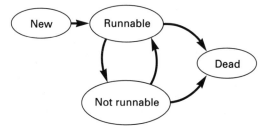

Figure 4-4
The states of a thread
during execution.

to the *dead* state. Once dead, a thread cannot return to a running state unless it is restarted with `start()`.

Thread Control Methods

There are some basic things that you would like to be able to do with a thread—start it, stop it, pause it, check if it is running, or have it wait on input from another running thread. All of these commands are available in the Thread class.

isAlive()

```
public final boolean isAlive();
```

The first option is to check if a thread is running. The `isAlive()` method returns a boolean indicating the status of the thread. An alive thread is one that is in either runnable or not runnable state and the method returns true.

`isAlive()` can be used for many things. One of its chief uses is in thread management. As you will see later, one thing that is commonly done is keeping a list of all the current threads that have been started. Every so often the controlling thread runs through this list and checks the threads' status. Any dead threads are then removed for the garbage collector to deal with, after any results that are needed have been extracted.

suspend() and resume()

```
public final void suspend();
public final void resume();
```

If your program needs to stop threads running, then you can always request that a thread be suspended by calling the suspend() method. This immediately halts that thread instance, putting it in the not runnable state. All the other threads are able to continue running. To continue with the processing, you need only call resume() on the thread and it will pick up where it left off (depending on the priority of the other currently running threads).

NOTE: The resume and suspend methods have been deprecated for Java 2. The reason is that if you suspend a thread that has locked a system resource, no other thread can access this resource until the suspended thread resumes. If the thread that would resume the target thread attempts to lock this system resource monitor prior to calling resume, deadlock results.

Sleep

```
public static void sleep(long milliseconds);
public static void sleep(long milliseconds, int nanoseconds);
```

If completely killing the thread from executing is not what you had in mind, then you might want to just make it stop for a certain period of time. The sleep method is used to suspend the execution of the thread for a certain period of time before resuming. At this time the thread is in the not runnable state.

You will notice that the sleep methods are static, which means they can be called at any time, by any code. This is a very handy thing, as it allows you to control timing of any code that you like. Say you were implementing an FTP or Telnet server in Java. After three login attempts for a given connection, you decide that the user should be made to wait for some period of time. This is a fairly common sort of reaction to login failures to stop automated guessing of passwords. The wait could simply be a sleep for so many seconds before continuing, for example:

```
int i = 1;
while(i < MAX_NUMBER_ATTEMPTS) {
  // get the user's login name and password

  // if correct then exit from the loop
```

```
// otherwise if this is the third, sixth, ninth .. attempt sleep
// for a while
if((i % 3) == 0) {
  try {
    Thread.sleep(SLEEP_TIME);
  }
  catch(InterruptedException e) {
    // just continue on, ignoring it
  }
}
i++;
}
```

Interrupting

```
public void interrupt();
public boolean isInterrupted();
public static boolean interrupted();
```

One problem that you might run into is that the thread is blocked, waiting for some I/O. In the example outline in the previous section the call to `sleep()` might throw an InterruptedException. This exception is thrown when the `interrupt()` method is called on the thread instance.

The effect of calling interrupt is to break the thread code out of whatever stalemate position it might be in. One reason you might want to do this is if you want to implement a timeout while waiting for a response from an already established network connection. This would require two threads, one for the network connection and then one for the monitoring code that would call the interrupt method.

You can always check on the state of the thread if it has been interrupted by calling either `isInterrupted()` or `interrupted()`. The static version refers to the currently executing thread—that is, the thread instance returned by `Thread.currentThread()`;

With Java 2 deprecating the stop and suspend/resume methods, the interrupted methods now greatly increase in importance. To force the exit of a thread you now will have some loop condition and internal calls that would catch the `InterrruptedException` and exit nicely. For example:

```
public void run {
  // open a socket connection
  boolean keep_running = true;

  while(keep_running) {
    try {
```

```
      // read something from the socket or block waiting
    }
    catch(InterruptedException ie) {
      keep_running = false;
      continue;
    }
  }

  // clean up and close the socket connection.
}
```

Sometimes `InterruptedException` is not directly thrown by the code, and this may cause the compiler to complain. To overcome this problem and ensure that you exit only in the appropriate circumstances, you should catch `Exception` and then in the catch block make a call to `isInterruped()` to break out of the handler code. For example:

```
while(keep_running) {
  try {
  // read something from the socket or block waiting
  }
  catch(Exception e) {
   if(isInterrupted())
     keep_running = false;
   continue;
  }
}
```

Yielding Earlier in the chapter I talked about the differences in the implementations of the threading policies in the Java VM. What happens if you do have some code that is affected by these differences in implementations? The easiest way to ensure that all threads running at the same priority get the same access to the CPU is to hint to the VM itself that a thread is prepared to give up time. This is done by calling the `yield()` method.

Yield is the indicator to the VM that now would be a good time to let another thread run. If another thread of the same priority is waiting, then it should be run now instead of the currently running thread, like so:

```
public void run() {
  while(true) {
```

```
        // doing something here
    
      Thread.yield();
  }
}
```

With careful use of yield, you can replicate the time-sliced nature of some thread implementations even on machines that do not have this capability. It is always a wise investment to use yield, regardless of whether you need it or not, as it ensures that the principles of a multi-threaded application survive even with one process hogging the CPU and that close to consistent behavior is maintained across different VM implementations.

Waiting for a Thread to End

```
public final void join();
public final void join(long milliseconds);
public final void join(long milliseconds, int nanoseconds);
```

A not so commonly seen method that will be useful to you is the ability to stop execution of one piece of code, while waiting for another thread to complete. This is the join() method. Join waits either for the specified timeout or forever, depending on the arguments supplied, for the thread instance to end before allowing the code to continue executing.

You might use this, for example, to have the thread do some work like fetching some information (say from a database) while the other code continues to do some initialization (say of a Java frame to display the returned database information).

```
public void displayData() {
  Thread db_fetch = new DBFetch(.....);
  db_fetch.start();

  // continue building the Frame contents
  Frame db_window = new Frame();
  ...
  // now wait for the database fetch to return
  db_fetch.join();

  // update data in the window
  db_data = db_fetch.getData();
  ...
```

```
// finally set the window visible
db_window.setVisible(true);
}
```

Setting Priorities

```
public final void setPriority(int newPriority);
public final int getPriority();
```

One more thing that you would like to be able to do is change the priority of your thread. The priority value is a relative indicator on a per-platform basis. For this reason it is appropriate to use the defined constants MIN_PRIORITY, MAX_PRIORITY, and NORM_PRIORITY for the minimum, maximum, and default priority values that can be assigned to threads. Unless you have a lot of different threads running, there is probably not that much need to vary from these values. The minimum priority is usually used by system-level functions like the garbage collector.

Java defines that there are 10 different priority levels to run at. However, in the real world, operating systems don't necessarily support that many different levels. The mapping of Java levels to OS levels is different on a per-implementation basis, so it is usually wise to stay with just the default values ±1.

Grouping Threads

When it comes to dealing with network connections, the number of threads in use can quickly become very large on a high-volume server. Dealing with every thread on an individual basis can be a complex and bug-ridden affair. Java allows you to group threads together with the ThreadGroup class. Applying actions to the group means that all the threads in that group will be dealt with.

ThreadGroups can be arranged in a hierarchical fashion allowing you to group together common threads and also common groups of threads. Each Thread instance can only belong to a single ThreadGroup, and once set that cannot be changed. If you do not specify a ThreadGroup, then a default one for the whole application is used. For example, your server has a number of TCP ports that it is dealing with. You could create a series of ThreadGroups like that shown in Figure 4-5.

You will notice in the figure that there are also a couple of extra threads and ThreadGroups in there. These are what Java uses to main-

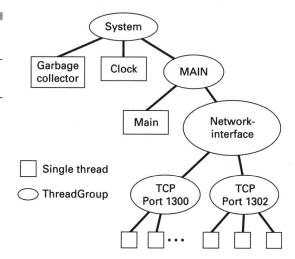

Figure 4-5
ThreadGroup arrangements in a fictitious Java network server.

tain its own internal organization within the application. The System thread at the top of the diagram is the thread that runs the garbage collector, system clock, and any other external functions. Below the System thread is the application that we are currently running when you type `java <application>` on the command line. The main method starts as one thread and then the rest of the application gets its own Thread-Group to operate any additional threads that it creates. Finally, within the application's own ThreadGroup we programmatically create our own two new ones, one for each port.

Now, with a single line of code, we can disable or enable activity on either port. With an AWT GUI associated with it, you would be able to control the port functionality simply from a single button click. No messy loops or other code is necessary.

Should it be necessary for your application, the ThreadGroup class also contains methods to navigate the ThreadGroup tree hierarchy. This allows you to wander around the tree and get the list of all the currently running threads (subject to security checks by the SecurityManager).

Controlling Resource Access

Earlier in the chapter I talked about resource contention in a general fashion. Now we look at the Java version of this. In your travels through the various Java APIs you have probably noticed that some methods are declared to be `synchronized`, while others are not (have a look at `java.util.Vector` for a good example).

Per-Method Control   Synchronize is Java's way of labeling to the VM that this piece of code is only allowed to be run once at any given time. In our counter example, it is possible that both threads could call either the increment (or decrement) method at the same time. This could cause serious problems, as the count value would not be updated correctly.

By placing the keyword `synchronized` in the method declaration it prevents multiple pieces of code executing that method in that instance of the class simultaneously. Code that is capable of having multiple simultaneous calls is called reentrant and is a tricky proposition to write. Synchronize can be used in more ways than one.

Inline Control   Sometimes you don't need to protect the whole method, just parts where the data structures have values changed. If the values change only as a result of some condition, then it can be a waste stopping multiple access to the method if the critical section of the code is executed only sometimes. To overcome this problem, Java allows you to wrap just a line or more of code in a synchronized block rather than the whole method.

Synchronized blocks of code are most useful when you are dealing with custom data structures. Your server might keep a track of bank transactions where the importance of keeping correct track of a client's balance is critical. You've written a new web front end where clients can do their banking from a web page. The first part is always the authentication; if that is OK, a client can continue with the transaction. There is no need to actually lock the record until after the authentication is successful.

```
public void removeMoney(AuthenicationInfo auth, float dollars)
   throws TransactionFailedException {

   // first authenticate the user
   try {
     authenticate(auth);
   }
   catch(AuthenticationFailedException e) {
      // oops, user gave incorrect authentication info
      throw e;
   }
   // They are who they say they are so continue
   UserAccount acc = getUserAccount(auth);
```

```
    // lock access to the particular account record
    synchronize(acc) {
      acc.removeMoney(dollars);
    }
    // all finished
  }
```

All that is required to lock a particular object is a reference to it. Then place the keyword synchronize and some parentheses around it and now you can guarantee that your code will have exclusive access to that object. If another piece of code has claimed access to the object, then your code will wait until that lock has been released before acquiring it for itself and continuing to execute.

Static Method Control   When dealing with normal methods that have been synchronized, the results are fairly obvious. However, static methods do not have a particular Object reference to deal with, so what happens when you declare a static method to be synchronized?

The language specification states that synchronized static methods have only a single per-class monitor. So if you have two static methods in your class labeled as synchronized, only one of them can be executing at any given time.

Combining Threads with Networking

By now you should have a fairly good idea of how to combine networking with threading. In this section I'll just go back over the basic code outlines because we'll be looking at the in-depth implementation issues in the next couple of chapters.

We've pretty much established that with each net TCP socket connection you will need to create a new thread to handle it. For ease of maintenance you will also want to create a ThreadGroup for each port number that your server is listening to. To accommodate all of these requirements, you will need to create a class that does the processing of the incoming data:

```
    // The java packages needed
    import java.net.*;
```

```
public class TCPProcessor extends Thread {
  private Socket = null;

  // constructor does minimal work
  public TCPProcessor(Socket socket, ThreadGroup group) {
    super(group, "TCPProcessor thread");

    // copy the reference to the socket
    this.socket = socket;
  }

  // The run method for the thread
  public void run() {

    // get the incoming stream from the socket
    while(true) {
    // read the next lot of data available from the input stream
    // process that data (potentially in another method)
    // give up control to any other thread running
    Thread.yield();
    }
  }
}
```

Given the above outline for the processing code, it now makes it easy for the listening code to be written. We can now take the code sample from the first section of this chapter and make a few minor changes to it to add the threading capability.

```
// create the parent ThreadGroup and the listener socket
ThreadGroup port_3000_group = new ThreadGroup("Port 3000 Group");
ServerSocket listener = new ServerSocket(3000);

while(true) {
  // wait for a new connection
  Socket incoming = listener.accept();

  // create a new processing class instance and run it
  TCPProcessor handler = new TCPProcessor(incoming,
port_3000_group);

  handler.start();

  // give up control to any other thread running.
  Thread.yield();
}
```

That pretty much covers building a TCP server at the most basic level. The rest of the implementation is dependent on what sort of features you would like in your server. Obviously you will have to write your protocol handling code for the run method in the TCPProcessor class. There is a lot more that you may want to add to the basic socket code as well.

Dealing with UDP sockets is a different story. Whereas TCP connections can last for very long periods of time, a UDP connection contains a single piece of information. For a high traffic server you will need to adopt a tactic similar to the TCP server with threads for the incoming data. However, if you end up creating one thread for each incoming connection you will very quickly find yourself with a couple of thousand threads running. The VM will be spending more time changing between threads than actually executing them. It is a design choice that you need to be very careful of.

Summary

The topics presented in this chapter don't completely cover all of the threading issues. There are far better texts on this topic both for general concurrent programming issues and for Java-specific resources. What I have aimed to show you are the relevant parts of threading for dealing with networking issues, which is this book's main concern. For example, thread pooling is one method of dealing with large numbers of socket connections that reuses existing threads, thus saving on expensive thread setup overheads.

In the next couple of chapters you get to put all of what you have learned so far in the book into practice. The next chapter deals with TCP to show you how to write clients and servers. Chapter 6 deals with UDP and multicasting issues.

Writing TCP Communications

Having absorbed an awful lot of theory in the previous chapters, you are now ready to put this all into practice. By the end of this chapter, I expect that you should be feeling confident enough about writing TCP-based programs for either client or server. Server issues are a much bigger concern for a programmer, as there is so much more that you need to be careful of.

Servers, by their very nature, need to be robust. It is all right if an individual client falls over every now and again, but if a mission-critical server hiccups, then the consequences are much more far reaching. Building a server of any kind means making sure that it catches any and every error that it could encounter. When it comes to networking, that can be quite a range.

The Project

To illustrate the points in this chapter, we're going to construct a small custom application. This application will be a banking system. The server will have two bank accounts in it—both yours. There will be a client that allows you to make transactions to move money around the accounts, add it, and delete it. The client will be standalone running from the command line and have a very simple interface written in Java 1.1 AWT.

Networking Protocols

The protocol will be a simple text string that labels what the transaction is—deposit, withdrawal, or transfer—and indicates the amount of money involved. Since there are two bank accounts, you will need to select which account you are operating on as well as which operates as another command. This is such a simple exercise, we won't include user authentication as part of the transaction. The protocol will also return a message after each request to indicate the success or other outcome of the transaction.

Also part of the communications will be the bank balance. Everyone wants to know how much is in the bank! Because we have two accounts, the message from the bank to the client must indicate what account the balance is for. The reason for this is that your balance may change on only one account when you do a transaction, so you only need to update that account value. Note also that an update will not always be in direct response to the client sending a command. When the balance changes due to an interest calculation it will also send out a balance update message.

Code Outline

There are two parts of this project: the server and the client. We'll start by constructing the client first, as that will illustrate a lot of the basic networking points. Following that we'll build the server.

The code for these two parts will be contained in two separate packages, `rwjn.chapter5.client` and `rwjn.chapter5.server`. There will be two start-up files that don't belong to any package, one each for the client and the server. The server package will also contain the list of the current valid keywords to be used in the protocol.

The Server

Finally, the server will also approximate a real bank—you'll get interest credited on your account. The current account balance for each account will be sent back to the user automatically for update on the screen. The bank is owned and operated by Scrooge McDuck, who is also its only customer. Interest is calculated every 5 seconds!

The server will illustrate many of the threading concepts that you've learned in the previous chapter. Also, we are going to illustrate some of the concepts required to make it reasonably bulletproof from a networking perspective. There is nothing worse than having a server crash on you every time it gets just slightly erroneous input. Anyone can write a basic server, but a good server must be able to withstand almost anything thrown at it.

Writing a Client

The first, and probably easiest, decision you have to make concerns the protocol you are writing a client for. For this chapter we are dealing only with TCP clients. If it is for an already established server then the job is easy. If you need to write both the server and the client, then you are probably better off jumping to the server, writing that, and then coming back to the client.

Once you have made the choice of what protocol you are writing for, you will need to find out a few more pieces of information, starting with the address or name of the server that you are contacting. This could well be dynamically set if you are writing an applet or writing from some sort of configuration file. You will also need the port number on that server that you will be connecting to.

With these two pieces of information, you can now start to get a basic client going. For our basic server the port number will be 8000 and the address is the localhost (127.0.0.1) so that you can see both client and server running on the one machine, although you should be able to change this from within the application.

Design Outline

The outline of the client is very simple. There is the network interface and the user interface. These two entities will remain separated because that allows you to put in whatever user interface (UI) you like while maintaining the fixed network interface.

The class that represents the network interface to the bank is called BankClient. The methods it has are just the basic transactions that can take place between the user and the bank server. All of the network handling code is wrapped within the one class.

At the other end with the user interface, we could build whatever we like. It could be command-line driven or from a GUI front end. I chose the latter. Before we look at the various parts, look at Figure 5-1, which is a screen dump of the application.

The user interface presents all of the transactions to the user as simply as possible. There is a dollar amount and then a small toolbar with the three buttons representing the three transaction types. The connect dialog is popped up by a menu item under the Bank menu (which also contains the Exit item). A press on any of the buttons in the toolbar makes the appropriate request of the BankClient interface after collecting whatever is needed.

Codewise, the outside view of the user interface is through the Main-Window class. This represents all of the user interface code. In its constructor it assembles all the parts together to create what you see on

Figure 5-1
The McDuck Bank
client GUI.

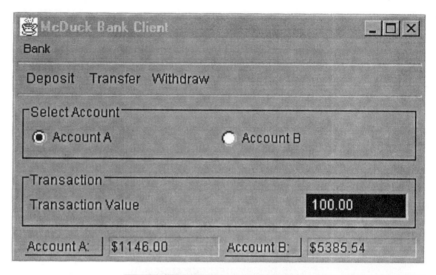

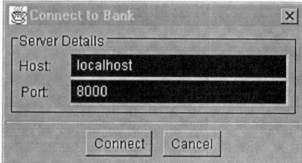

screen. Most of the UI components are contained in a series of package-access-only classes. These provide a very simple, easy-to-maintain view to the code to build the UI.

Finally, there is a separate class that contains the main method to start everything up. It makes an instance of the BankClient, and then creates the user interface, passing in a reference to the network interface in the process.

The Bank Network Interface

The most important part of the application is the interface to the network. In this one class it takes the requests of the user and turns them into the networked communication to the bank. At the same time it has to deal with the messages coming back from the bank. As noted previously, these messages are asynchronous, not necessarily in response to a request to the bank. This suggests that a process of send request/listen for response will not work. Why?

To listen for asynchronous responses means that we need to have a separate listener for them, implying that a thread needs to be running all the time. That thread will be sitting on the socket, waiting to grab the next thing that comes down the connection. If you also then had a write followed by a read in the code where you send a request, you cannot tell which of the two reads will end up getting the response. The worst case is if the thread grabs the read and leaves the request reader hanging, resulting in the rest of the program hanging.

By now you should be starting to get a bit of a picture of the code that needs to be written. There is a thread that listens for incoming traffic, a number of methods that send outgoing traffic, and a couple of maintenance methods for doing things like establishing and tearing down the connection.

The Keywords Class   To be sure that both sides are using the same commands, I've decided to construct a class of constants that represent each of the commands. This is all part of the data hiding, as it allows the author to change the commands as needed without having to recompile both the server and client each time something changes.

The protocol is defined by what the server can accept, so the Keywords class will be kept in the server package. This is the only class that is used by both the client and server. All that this class contains is a collection of `public static` variables for each command. (See Figure 5-2.)

Code Design   Earlier it was stated that I want to keep all the code in the one class. At the same time it was also said that we are going to need a separate thread to deal with the information coming back from the server. This implies that our network interface class needs to be a thread.

For a very basic system, it would not matter whether the class extended Thread or implemented the Runnable interface. What we need to consider is the effects that the encapsulation and user interface might play on the choice. The BankClient code is created as a separate entity from the user interface and then passed to the UI code. This implies

Figure 5-2
The Keywords class.

```
package rwjn.chapter5.server;
// Imports
// none
/**
 * McDuck Bank Client
 * <P>
 * The network command keywords
 * <P>
 * @author <A HREF = "mailto:justin@vlc.com.au">Justin Couch</A>
 * @version 1.0
 */
public final class Keywords
{
    /** Select an account to manage */
    public static final String SELECT = "select";

    /** Deposit money into an account */
    public static final String DEPOSIT = "deposit";

    /** Transfer money from one account to another */
    public static final String TRANSFER = "transfer";

    /** withdraw money */
    public static final String WITHDRAW = "withdraw";

    /** account balance information */
    public static final String BALANCE = "balance";

    /** An error occurred */
    public static final String ERROR = "error:";

    /** Exit from the network connection */
    public static final String EXIT = "exit";
}
```

that the UI code cannot just sit and create new instances of the thread, which is what is required if the code were to extend Thread.

Why is this important? We are not going to initiate the connection to the server when we first create an instance of the class. Instead, we are having a separate connect/disconnect method that allows us to control when and where we connect. Until we have a network connection to the server, we cannot set up any listening to incoming data. Until we have incoming data, there is nothing to have a thread for. There is this nice little chain reaction which implies that the BankClient code is going to need to be starting its own threads in response to connect and disconnect requests. Implementing Runnable means that we can create the new threads entirely within the client code, maintaining the single class requirement.

Returning Information from the Server   One last thing that we need to consider in the design: How do we get the returned information back from the server out to the user interface? One method to do it is to hard-code a particular class into the client interface. Obviously, this is not a particularly nice solution, as it locks us into one user interface.

Figure 5-3
The listener interface
for the account bal-
ances.

```
package rwjn.chapter=.client;

// Imports
// none

/**
 * McDuck Bank Client
 * <P>
 * The listener interfaces to changes in the bank account balances.
 * The listener is notified each time the bank has updated the
 * balance on each account. This could be called at any time in
 * response to a transaction or just an interest calculation.
 * <P>
 * @author <A HREF = "mailto:justin@vlc.com.au">Justin Couch</A2>
 * @version 1.0
 */
interface AccountBalanceListener
{
    /**
     * Notify the listener of the new balance in account A
     * @param balance The new balance to be displayed
     */
    public void accountAChanged(float balance);

    /**
     * Notify the listener of the new balance in account B
     * @param balance The new balance to be displayed
     */
    public void accountBChanged(float balance);
}
```

The best answer is to use the features that Java has given us—interfaces. We create an interface that represents the Callback class for information coming from the server. Any piece of UI code can then implement that interface and our BankClient doesn't know the difference. Just register an implementation of the listener with the BankClient code and the rest is taken care of.

We could implement the listener in any way so long as it contained information about which account changed and the balance. Since we know we are dealing with only two accounts, I've taken the easy way out and just used two methods, one for each account (as shown in Figure 5-3).

Putting It All Together   With all the above information, piecing together the client code should be very easy. First, we need to connect to a nominated server and port number. If the server is already connected, we'll disconnect it before moving on. As we go through the process of creating the network connection and associated handlers, there is the possibility something will fail. If at any time we have something go wrong then we simply exit the method and set a flag to stop errors later on. We need a socket connection:

```java
void connect(String host, int port)
{
  disconnect();

  // start a new connection.
  try
  {
    bank_connection = new Socket(host, port);
  }
  catch(UnknownHostException e2)
  {
    System.err.println("Error finding server");
    System.err.println(e2);
    return;
  }
  catch(IOException e3)
  {
    System.err.println("Error accessing server");
    System.err.println(e3);
    return;
  }
  ...
```

A socket connection is no good unless we have some way of reading and writing data to it. The next step is to get the I/O streams and turn them into something usable. In this application we are reading and writing text, which means a stream that has text capabilities built in would be the one to use. For output the PrintWriter is the logical choice, as it is designed for text and has simple commands to write out the data. For input we'll need to use the BufferedReader. This makes sure that all of the input has arrived before allowing the caller to access what was sent. It also has the corresponding read methods for the write methods used in the PrintWriter.

```
// Get the IO streams for it
try
{
  InputStream in = bank_connection.getInputStream();

  bank_input = new BufferedReader(new InputStreamReader(in));
  bank_output =
     new PrintWriter(bank_connection.getOutputStream(), true);
}
catch(IOException e4)
{
  System.err.println("Error getting I/O from socket");
  System.err.println(e4);
  return;
}
```

NOTE: *The socket only returns an InputStream while the Buffered Reader constructor requires a Reader. To make the conversion, we need to use the InputStreamReader to wrap the stream returned from the socket.*

When constructing the PrintWriter, make sure that you use the constructor that allows you to set the automatic flush. If the autoflush is not set, you must explicitly call it every time that you write something to the output. With it set to true, each time you call the `println()` method of the PrintWriter, it automatically sends the data. Without flushing, you can write as much as you like, but the output is never sent from the client to the server until `flush()` is called. This can be a little annoying when you are trying to debug your server code and find that you aren't getting anything at the server and wondering what is going on.

Once the server connection is established and the streams are connected up, the code can start listening for information feeding back from the server. With interest being calculated at the rate it is, you should be getting a new balance report coming down the line very quickly. To make sure you catch this, you will need to establish the thread running with the code listening to incoming data. At the same time, set the internal flag that says the server connection is now available.

```
// Make a thread out of it
input_thread = new Thread(this);
input_thread.start();

// if we've made it this far, things must be OK
service_available = true;
}
```

The run() method is used to do our listening. It is very simple—it waits for the next message to come from the server, sends that off to a processing method, then yields to any other threads running.

```
public void run()
{
  String input_string = null;

  while(true) {
    try {
      input_string = bank_input.readLine();
    }
    catch(IOException e) {
      // ignore it and continue on
    }

    if((input_string ! = null) && (input_string.length() ! = 0))
      processString(input_string);
    Thread.yield();
  }
}
```

The readLine() method is used because individual commands are issued one line at a time. Each is terminated by a new line (courtesy of using the println() method on the sending end), so the readLine method complements that very well. I always like to throw in a quick sanity check to make sure that the input string is not null or zero length before trying to parse it.

Parsing is a fairly standard routine. First, put it into a String Tokenizer, then check whether the first word is either the balance keyword or an error state. If it is the balance, then take the next two words and convert the first to the account and the second to the balance. If at any time something goes wrong, such as badly formatted numbers, then the whole lot is dropped. The information is being updated so rapidly that there is no point in trying to recover from bad data. Much better to cut your losses and just discard erroneous input.

NOTE: *This may not always be possible. Some protocols, such as HTTP, always return some message, even if it is an error code. What you do in each circumstance is defined by the protocol you are implementing. In our case, we have made the arbitrary decision to ignore erroneous input.*

```
private void processString(String str)
{
  StringTokenizer strtok = new StringTokenizer(str);
  String token;

  try {
    token = strtok.nextToken();
  }
  catch(NoSuchElementException e) {
    // Que?? How did this happen?
    return;
  }
  if(token.equals(Keywords.BALANCE)) {
    int account;
    float balance;
    String balance_str;

    try {
      token = strtok.nextToken();
      balance_str = strtok.nextToken();
    }
    catch(NoSuchElementException e1) {
      // Well, can't do much about it. Just exit
      return;
    }

    // get the account number and balance
    try {
      account = Integer.parseInt(token);
```

```
        balance = Float.valueOf(balance_str).floatValue();
    }
    catch(NumberFormatException e2) {
      // exit as well
      return;
    }

    // send this to the listener
    if(listener ! = null) {
    if(account == 0)
        listener.accountAChanged(balance);
      else
        listener.accountBChanged(balance);
    }
  }
  else
    // An error on the server end has occurred. Print it out.
    System.err.println(str);
}
```

The last thing that we need to do is send the requests to the server.
After checking that the server is available and the value to be sent is
correct, you just need to write the value down the output stream. For
example, the deposit method looks like this:

```
void deposit(float amount) {
  if(!service_available)
    return;

  if(amount > = 0)
    bank_output.println(Keywords.DEPOSIT + " " + amount);
}
```

That's it. The server interface is now done. With this, you can build
whatever user interface you like onto it. There is an example UI that
I've included with the code on the CD that you can use.

Writing the Server

With the client written, the next part is the server. The server is almost
the opposite of the client codewise, and there is no need for a user interface. Not only must the server deal with transaction requests from a

number of clients, but it also must calculate the interest and make sure that everyone knows what the new balance is.

Server Design Outline

The server requires three parts: a network interface, the accounts that are being manipulated, and the code that handles an individual client connection. Figure 5-4 illustrates the basic class outline of what is needed to implement the server.

Network Interface   First there is the network interface. This does the same job that the `BankClient` class did for the client end of the code. It handles all the new connections coming into the server. For each new connection, it creates an instance of a class to handle the commands coming in and then returns to the listening. As you have seen in examples in previous chapters, the code to listen for new connections is very simple and is taken care of in a few lines.

Account Management   The second part is the accounts themselves. These look after the balance and any transactions that nominate that particular account. The problem that we have to deal with is the interest calculations. There are two choices—either each account must look after its own interest calculation, or an external class must do it for them.

With the first option, less code needs to be written and everything is self-contained. Consider what would happen if this were a real bank with hundreds of thousands of accounts. Suddenly you are dealing with

Figure 5-4

The class usage diagram of the server design.

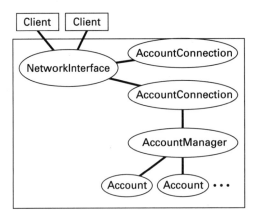

hundreds of thousands of individual threads. Interest calculation becomes a performance nightmare as all these threads come active at once every few seconds. If you tried to spread them out, then you loose consistency with the real world where everyone's interest is calculated at the same time.

Using a thread running such that every time the interest needs to be calculated will alleviate this problem. But where do we calculate the interest? Should the thread request each account for its balance, calculate the interest, and deposit the money back in? Or should it just tell each account to calculate its interest "now"? Again, the second option is better. What happens if a deposit comes in halfway through the calculation of interest? (Remember the problems with the counter example in Chapter 4. This is another example of exactly the same sort of problem of multiple threads all accessing the same resource.) In the first case, you will need to implement some sort of locking mechanism that can be called from outside the class. In the second, the class takes care of all those details and hides if from the user.

Another benefit of having each account calculate its own interest is that you can set different interest rates on a per-account level. This again makes it more realistic, as you won't find a bank anywhere with only a single account type.

Transfers are handled by using a withdraw and a deposit. In real life the transfer might be between banks, not just a couple of accounts on the same bank. It also cuts down on the amount of intelligence required by the individual accounts. To the outside world, the account manager still implements a separate transfer method.

Parsing Requests   The final part is the listener to the incoming information. This class takes the commands, parses them, and then makes the appropriate request of the account manager.

Each request is straightforward to parse. First there is the command keyword. If the keyword is not the one to exit the connection, then a number follows it. The number is either a dollar amount for the transaction or the account number in the case of a select command.

In a real life server, each connection must be self-sufficient. It must know what account it is dealing with all the time because the account manager does not want to be bothered by maintaining a list of connections and their open accounts. Every time a request is made from the connection interface to the account manager it will include the "account number." Therefore our select statement will not make direct requests of the account manager. Instead it will set an internal flag for each connection so that it knows what it is dealing with.

Like the client end, if the parser receives invalid input, it just drops the entire command. The response time is quick enough that the user will notice something has not happened and attempt to redo the command. Invalid responses might be a wrong keyword or the number in an invalid format. The server needs to be even more robust, so any time there is even a chance of something going wrong, you should be catching exceptions and dealing nicely with it (such as printing out an error message to `System.err`).

Once the server has received the exit command, it needs to make sure that it closes itself down properly. In this example, we are not doing any external management of the thread. Once the run method has begun, that is the only thing keeping that instance of the account connection valid. Exiting requires that we be nice and close down all the resources used by that connection. This applies not only to the socket, but also to the streams associated with that socket. Exiting the socket means that the account connection is dead, exiting the run method, and ensuring the death of that thread.

Sending Information Back to the Client Sending the information back is probably the trickiest part of the entire exercise. There are a couple of competing problems. First, we could have multiple client connections to the server. Second, we are trying to keep the networking side separate from the account management as much as possible. If we were to pass the output stream to the account management, this would break a lot of our rules.

To find a solution, we need to look at other places within Java where this problem occurs—the GUI toolkit AWT. The solution is to register a listener, just as we did in the client code for the balance information. This time the rules are a little different. There could be many socket connections to the one server and all of them could want the data at the same time, so we need to register and hold all the listeners.

One way to implement this solution is to build something similar to the AWT multicaster used to send AWT events. Another solution is to custom-build your own handling code with linked lists, arrays, or other data structure. The solution that I prefer is based on creating a derived class of Java's Vector class. This gives me all the management for adding and removing things, while on top of that I have access to the underlying array that allows me to build fast routines to distribute the events. You will see this later on. All our network interfaces need to do now is implement the listener interface and turn this into something suitable for sending back along the network connection.

Implementing the Server

The method of implementation will start with the Account class, continue with the listener and manager classes, the account manager, and the account network connection, and conclude with the network interface code.

The Account   Accounts are not as straightforward as you would imagine. Sure you have a balance and an interest rate, but what if one client wants to withdraw money while another is depositing?

If you were reading the previous chapter, you would know that you can declare methods to be synchronized, which will stop multiple simultaneous accesses to the one method. In the case above where one is withdrawing and another is depositing, it complicates things a bit more. What is needed is a lock on the actual account balance itself.

Locking the account balance itself is another idea that looks fine in theory, but practically, it won't work. In the Account class, the balance is simply a float. It is a primitive type. You cannot associate a lock with a primitive type, since the Java specification says that monitors can be associated only with objects. Probably your next thought is to put the float into a `Float` object, as this now gives you an object that you can associate a monitor with. Once you have created one of these primitive class representations, you cannot change the value. If the original value of the primitive type changes, you need to create a new instance of the primitive class representation. What happens with the following lines of code?

```
Float balance_obj = new Float(balance);

...

void deposit(float value) {
  synchronized(balance_obj) {
    balance + =  balance;
    balance_obj = new Float(balance);
  }
```

The result is that you'll generate an exception in the line where you try to create the new float instance with the updated data. The problem is that there is a lock on variable pointing to the locked object, which results in the exception. Also, as soon as this happens, anything else that has been waiting for that monitor no longer points to the same instance as the newly created one. If you had three or more pieces of code waiting on the original monitor release, you are going to be in a lot of trouble. Any code that comes along at some time after this will attempt to lock the newly created `balance_obj` rather than the old one, and things get themselves into a right old mess.

What is really needed is a constant object reference that is not going to change. The solution lies in the Object class itself. All we need to do is create a single object instance right at the time the account is created, and every access to the balance variable must first be surrounded by synchronizing on the object instance first.

Now our account methods would all resemble the deposit method:

```
float deposit(float amount) {
float bal;

synchronized(lock) {
  balance + = amount;
  bal = balance;
}
  return bal;
}
```

The return is used to pass information back to the manager about the balance as a result of this transaction. A separate local variable is needed because we can't do a return inside the synchronize statement and expect a sensible result (we could, but the state of the monitor is unknown and could cause problems). The safest way is to make a local copy before releasing the monitor and then returning that value.

Balance Listening   When writing the client and the listener that we had there, I made an arbitrary decision that we would never see more than two accounts. On the server end, although I could make the same decision, it would mess up a few other nice pieces of code. This time the balance listener interface will have only a single method, and that will contain both the account number and the balance.

```
/**
 * McDuck Bank Server
 * <P>
 * The interface to be implemented by any class that is interested in
 * knowing about changes to the bank balances in the server end.
 * <P>
 * This interface is usually used by any networking interface code
 * that can then send data back to the client that it is dealing
 * with.
 * <P>
 * @author <A HREF = "mailto:justin@vlc.com.au"<Justin Couch</A>
 * @version 1.0
 */
interface BalanceListener
{
    /**
     * An update has occurred on the nominated bank account and here
     * is the new balance.
     * @param account The account number
     * @param balance The new balance
     */
    void updateBalance(int account, float balance);
}
```

As I mentioned in the code design section previously, the manager of the listeners is based on a derived class of `java.util.Vector`. To provide the most flexibility, the three constructors of Vector will need to be replicated in the derived class. Each of these constructors simply calls its corresponding superclass constructor.

Basing the management code on Vector means that all we now need to provide is one extra method. This method takes the account number and balance to be broadcast and sends it to all the registered listeners. The vector has the array of elements that it contains and the number of them as `protected` variables in the array. This saves us a lot of time, as we don't need to fool about getting hold of Enumerations and such things. A quick for loop and its all done with:

```
synchronized void sendBalanceUpdate(int account, float balance) {
    int i;

    // for each element in the vector send an event
    for(i = 0; i < elementCount; i++) {
        try {
```

```
    ((BalanceListener)elementData[i]).updateBalance(account,
                                              balance);
  }
  catch(Exception e) {
    System.err.print("An error occured while trying to send ");
    System.err.println("a balance update listener");
    System.err.println(e);
    e.printStackTrace();
  }
}
}
```

Note that, when sending out the update, we make sure that we've bulletproofed the code. An error in one listener should not be allowed to stop any other listener from receiving the information. As a service to the code writer for debugging, any error is reported to the standard error output and a stack trace is dumped of what happened.

Account Management   With the account class and the listener classes completed, the next item to look at is the management of all these. The AccountManager class pools together the two classes and forms them into a single interface for whatever communications interface might be used. Requests are made to the account manager and the changes in balances are reflected back through the registered BalanceListeners.

At start-up, the account manager creates two instances of the Account class. One is started with $500 and the other with $2000. To illustrate that they may be independent, they are given different interest rates as well.

As stated a number of times already, the interest is calculated separately, and by this class. To do this while handling normal user input means that the class needs to run as a separate thread. Again we chose to implement the Runnable interface rather than extending Thread, as it allows further room for expansion at a later date. All the thread management is contained within the class (although this could be done just as well by extending Thread) and leaves room if we want to make the AccountManager into a subclass of another class. Subclassing could be used for having different managers for the same bank.

The run method needs to calculate the interest at a given period. I haven't hard-coded this, as you may want to change it to observe different effects.

```
public void run() {
  float balance_a;
  float balance_b;

  while(true) {
    // sleep for a while
    try {
      Thread.sleep(INTEREST_SLEEP_PERIOD);
    }
    catch(InterruptedException e1) {
      // well, they get their interest early
    }

    // calculate the interest
    balance_a = account_a.calculateInterest();
    balance_b = account_b.calculateInterest();

    // send the output
    listeners.sendBalanceUpdate(0, balance_a);
    listeners.sendBalanceUpdate(1, balance_b);
  }
}
```

For this simple application, you will note that the above code always sleeps for a fixed period of time. The problem with that is execution of the other code takes a small, but noticeable, time. Over a long period of time each execution of the loop will take maybe 5.001 seconds (assuming we are sleeping for 5 seconds), and the result is a slowly drifting calculation. If we looked at the time when the interest is supposed to be calculated and when it really is, you will find that it might be out by a second or two.

In mission-critical applications this time drift is a definite no-no. What you need to do is work out the execution time just as you wake up and just after finishing processing, and subtract that from the sleep period before sleeping. The times can be found by calling `System.current TimeMillis()` which returns the current time in milliseconds. The difference between two calls to this is the execution time of the code.

Performing transactions on the account all follow the same pattern. You make a call to the nominated account with the amount, record the returned balance, and then send that to the listeners. Again, the deposit method will illustrate the point:

```
synchronized void deposit(int account, float amount) {
  float balance;
```

```
if(account == 0)
  balance = account_a.deposit(amount);
else
  balance = account_b.deposit(amount);

listeners.sendBalanceUpdate(account, balance);
}
```

In this case the method has been declared synchronized, as there will only be one instance of the account manager for any individual account instance. At the same time it allows multiple clients to pursue transactions on the separate accounts simultaneously if need be. It is acceptable if two clients try to access the one account, because the account itself deals with the multiple access problem, as you've seen already.

Parsing Client Commands Next on the agenda of classes is the `AccountConnection` class. This is the class that deals with an individual client making requests of the server. At the time the class is instantiated, there is already a valid socket connection. The account connection class must then take care of the rest of the details of the setup and listening.

The socket that has been passed to the constructor is exactly the same as the one used in the client. To prevent problems the server will use exactly the same type of streams that the client does, so there is no need to repeat all the setup code. In fact, you've already seen a lot of the code before in the client.

At start-up, the constructor simply takes a copy of the references to the socket and account manager and starts the thread running. The idea of this is that creating the streams can be a rather time-consuming task. We want to be able to return to the code listening for new connections as quickly as possible.

Creating the streams for the socket takes place at the start of the run method. If at any time it fails, then it exits immediately. As in the client, a thread needs to be created for the listening of the incoming data. If the run method does not make it to the line where it starts the infinite loop for reading incoming data, there is no problem with an early exit. The rest of the server is not keeping a reference to the newly created class instance, so it immediately becomes a target for the garbage collector because the thread is now declared to be dead.

Once the thread is running, you need to be reading command by command from the incoming stream. Again, this looks almost identical to the client code. After checking that the string is not null, the client code sends it off to the processString() method.

Within processString, the first task to find out what the first word of the command is. If the word is the exit command, there is no need to do any further processing. The method exits with a true condition returned. This true condition tells the loop that there is nothing further to be done on this connection and it should start shutting the connection down. At this point it breaks from the loop and closes all the streams and sockets. Also remember that it must remove itself as a listener from the Account-Manager, otherwise the code will never be cleaned up.

NOTE: *The clean-up code is kept entirely within the run method—all the socket killing and streams. The reason for this is that you should never rely on the finalize method being called to do your cleanup for you. In a short run application, the garbage collector may never even run. The result is that you exit leaving open socket connections at the operating system level. Every operating system has a finite number of resources. Leaving open socket connections means that these resources will potentially remain allocated until the next time the machine is shut down. If you are developing code, starting and stopping the server frequently, this could be a bad thing, as you'll quickly consume all the resources, leading youself to all sorts of strange, non-Java-related errors. Always make sure that you explicitly clean up all the networking resources you use.*

If the first word is not the exit command, then processString grabs the next token and attempts to convert it into a floating point number. This number may be either the account to select or the amount of the transaction. If it cannot find a number or parses it badly, then it just ignores the error and sends an error condition back to the client while exiting with a false condition.

Once the incoming code has passed through all the hoops, a small if-else ladder is used to do string compares on the command. Any unrecognized command sends an error back to the client. Those that are recognized then call the appropriate method of the account manager. As a result the processString method looks like this:

```
private boolean processCommand(String command) {
  if(command.equals(Keywords.EXIT))
    return true;
  // The other commands need to be stripped of the command and
value
  StringTokenizer strtok = new StringTokenizer(command);
  String cmd;
  float amount;

  //The command string
  try {
    cmd = strtok.nextToken();
  }
  catch(NoSuchElementException e1) {
    System.err.println("Invalid input");
    bank_output.println(Keywords.ERROR + " invalid command");
    return false;
  }

  // The number of dollars that this represents
  try {
    amount = Float.valueOf(strtok.nextToken()).floatValue();
  }
  catch(NoSuchElementException e1) {
    System.err.println("Invalid input");
    bank_output.println(Keywords.ERROR + " invalid command");
    return false;
  }

  // And then act according to the command
  if(cmd.equals(Keywords.SELECT)) {
    current_account = (int)amount;
  }
  else if(cmd.equals(Keywords.DEPOSIT)) {
    account_manager.deposit(current_account, amount);
  }
  else if(cmd.equals(Keywords.TRANSFER)) {
    account_manager.transfer(current_account, amount);
  }
  else if(cmd.equals(Keywords.WITHDRAW)) {
    account_manager.withdraw(current_account, amount);
  }
  else
    bank_output.println(Keywords.ERROR + " invalid command");
  return false;
}
```

One more point needs to be raised. When you are closing the socket and streams, you need to catch IOExceptions for all of them. If you placed them all into one try/catch block you may run into some problems. For example, if the code was implemented like this:

```
try {
  client_connection.close();
  in.close();
  client_input.close();
  bank_output.close();
}
catch(IOException e) {}
```

what would happen if the client_connection close request generated the exception? It would immediately jump to the catch block and the other close requests would never be called. To ensure that they are called, you will need to make sure that each line is in its own separate try/catch block.

The Network Interface   The first point of contact for any new connection request to the server is the NetworkInterface class and almost completes the code that needs to be written. The sole job of this class is to accept new connections and spawn a new AccountConnection for each.

In the previous chapter it was shown how to start a new server socket connection. That is pretty much the entire contents of this class. The constructor takes a reference to the account manager and the port number. After copying these it starts the thread running. There is no reason for choosing either Thread or Runnable as the basis for the thread, so I stuck with Runnable because that is what has been used elsewhere.

Once the server thread is running, a ServerSocket needs to be established for listening to connection requests. This connects to the nominated port number and patiently waits for a new connection. When a connection is found, it passes that Socket reference to the new AccountConnection object created to handle it. Once that is done, it yields and waits for the next connection. The run method consists of the following code:

```
public void run() {
  Socket incoming_socket;
```

```
ServerSocket server;
AccountConnection account;

// setup the server socket
try {
  server = new ServerSocket(port);
}
catch(IOException e0) {
  System.err.println("Error creating server socket");
  System.err.println(e0);
  return;
}

while(true) {

  // pick up a new connection
  try {
    incoming_socket = server.accept();
    account = new AccountConnection(incoming_socket,
                                    account_manager);
  }
  catch(IOException e1) {
    System.err.println("Error accepting socket");
    System.err.println(e1);
    continue;
  }

  // let someone else have a go.
  Thread.yield();
  }
}
```

Starting the Server Now that the server code is all written, all that remains to be done is to start it up. You will have noticed that the constructor to the `AccountConnection` class requires an instance of the `AccountManager`. The only way to get that is to pass it in through the constructor for the `NetworkInterface`. Although the `NetworkInterface` code could have created a new `AccountManager` as part of its constructor, I wanted to keep the two parts of the application independent. You will see why this is important in the next chapter.

To add just a little splash to the application, the code will take a single argument—the port number. If your machine is already using the default port (8000) for another application, you would like to be able to specify a different one. The code within the `main` method looks at the number of arguments. If there are any more than one, it prints out a

Unix-style usage message. If argument cannot be converted to an integer then the code defaults to 8000 and continues.

Once through this, the code creates an instance of the AccountManager and an instance of the NetworkInterface:

```
// Imports
import rwjn.chapter5.server.AccountManager;
import rwjn.chapter5.server.NetworkServer;

/**
 * McDuck Bank Server
 * <P>
 * The startup code for the McDuck Bank Server code.
 * <P>
 * @author <A HREF = "mailto:justin@vlc.com.au">Justin Couch</A>
 * @version 1.0
 */
public class Server {
  public static void main(String[] args) {
    int port_number = 8000;

    if(args.length > 0) {
      if(args.length > 1) {
        System.out.println("Usage: java Server [port]");
        return;
      }
      try {
        port_number = Integer.parseInt(args[0]);
      }
      catch(NumberFormatException e) {
        System.out.println("Usage: java Server [port]");
        return;
      }
    }
    // start the account handler
    AccountManager acc_mgr = new AccountManager();

    // start the network server
    new NetworkServer(port_number, acc_mgr);
  }
}
```

SECURITY: *If the default port suggested in the user interface dialog is used and the client and server are running on the same machine, nothing further needs to be done. However, if they are running on separate*

machines, you will need to add an appropriate `java.net.SocketPer mission` *to your policy files on both the client and server machines in order to specify the machine and port number. For example, the client machine would need to have the following added:*

```
permission java.netSocketPermission "server.machine","connect";
```

To start the server all you need to type is `java Server <port number>`. You won't see anything on the command line because the server is generally silent unless an error occurs.

Summary

Now you've seen how to build a basic server and client for networking. At the same time, we've covered a lot of ground illustrating various points to Java threading as it can be used in networking. The user interface part of the client has been deliberately low key, since the networking is the important part to demonstrate. I could fill another chapter just on the UI design. If you would like to test the code, it is all included on the accompanying CD.

In the next chapter we are going to take this basic project and modify it, using first UDP communications and then multicast communications. The idea is to illustrate the differences in the basic coding techniques between the various network connections. The best way to do that is to implement the same thing in the three methods.

Writing UDP and Multicast Communications

In the previous chapter a server and client were built that communicated using TCP sockets. TCP is not the only way to communicate between two machines over a network. The User Datagram Protocol (UDP) and multicasting are just as valid alternatives. The choice of which to use is very dependent on what the application requires.

So that you may make a better judgment, this chapter is devoted to modifying the code presented in the previous chapter to work first with UDP communications, and then with multicast-based communications. The idea is that showing the same functionality implemented in each of the three strategies will guide you to understanding the strengths and weaknesses of each approach. This sort of knowledge will then help you make the right choice later on when you have to deal with nontrivial applications (unlike this one).

The UDP Client

In Chapter 2, "Internet Networking Concepts," the differences between TCP and UDP network connections were explained. The biggest difference, in terms of impact on our code, is that the connection is a one-way connection. Each end sends data out and the other end has to implement a full server-style reception for the incoming data. If the client wants to hear data from the server, then it too must set up identical code to listen for incoming information.

What difference is this going to make to our code? To the GUI code: absolutely none. There is still the `BankClient` interface with the identical method calls. All we will be doing is changing the underneath code a little.

Now that we don't have a stream that we can just write text to, is there any point in using a text-based approach? Well, for this example we'll change to using a pure binary format to illustrate the differences. This will also give you some experience in writing a binary parser for the network communications.

The User Datagram Protocol

The text-based protocol of the TCP connection contained only two items of information: the command string and a number. Turning this into a binary form means just making the equivalent commands as a series of bytes.

For the return message from the server to the client, it is not so easy. The return message in the TCP version consists of a command word and then either balance information or a string representing an error message. The byte version of this is a little trickier to implement.

Client to Server   While we could just represent each command as an integer and then the number following as a float, the technique is the same. To introduce a little variety, we'll make the command a single byte and the following number a plain float. The result is a message structure that looks like that illustrated in Figure 6-1. As you can see from the diagram, the protocol is very simplistic. There is no error checking involved.

So, that was a good start. What was the one thing that we forgot? UDP is a connectionless service, which means each packet is a standalone item. There is no standing connection to send information back to the client. That means the server can no longer be responsible for selecting which account is served. It becomes the responsibility of the client and also the protocol to tell the server which account to make the transaction on.

To accommodate this problem, the protocol will also need to support the account number as well. We'll slip this in between the command byte and the amount. The adjusted protocol is now given by Figure 6-2.

Of course, now that we don't have a select message to send to the server, we can remove that from the Keywords class. Removing one thing has lead to another problem: letting the server know that the client exists in the first place. Consider a person who connects to the

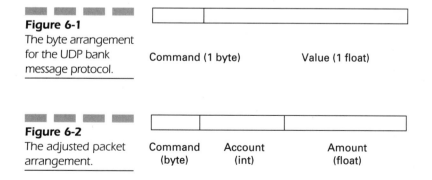

Figure 6-1
The byte arrangement for the UDP bank message protocol.

Command (1 byte)   Value (1 float)

Figure 6-2
The adjusted packet arrangement.

Command   Account   Amount
  (byte)   (int)   (float)

bank, but does not perform any transactions. With the UDP client there is no such thing as a "connection." That is, the bank end does not know anything about the client until it receives a packet from it. So if the user just "connects" with the bank without any transactions it will never receive any balance data.

Overcoming this problem requires that there be some sort of notification to the bank that the client exists. Where we dropped out the select command, we've replaced it with a register command. This should be sent as soon as the user hits the connect button on the dialog and is used to inform the bank that the client wants to know about balance information. The result is that the server should note down the IP address of the client and send it the information until that address is removed (through the exit command, as in the TCP implementation).

Server to Client   The return journey from the server to client requires that it have a separate protocol. In the forward journey the message was always the same. In the reverse it isn't. If it is a balance, then the protocol must include the account number and the balance. If it is an error condition, then we need to either include an error code or just a string message.

For illustrative points, we'll use a string message, as it will illustrate how to pass string information in an otherwise binary message. The result of these two decisions is that the server-to-client protocol now depends on the value of the first byte. If the byte indicates a balance, then the interpretation is given in Figure 6-3a; otherwise Figure 6-3b indicates what to do.

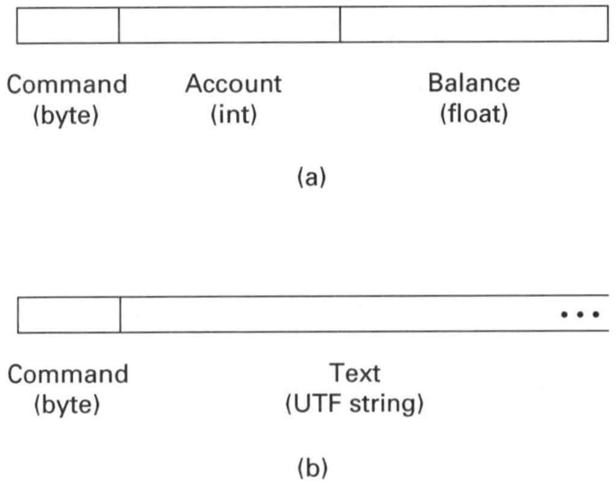

Figure 6-3
The protocols for the server-to-client communications for (a) a balance update and (b) an error condition.

Command (byte)   Account (int)   Balance (float)
(a)

Command (byte)   Text (UTF string)
(b)

Keywords   We will need to convert the Keywords class to reflect the change from strings to binary. This allows us to change the protocol handling with minimal code changes. This is one of the reasons I decided to use a dedicated class rather than a series of static final values embedded in the client and server code. Also, we'll change the select command to a register command, as noted in "Client to Server," above.

Changes to the General Code Structure

In the previous chapter, the BankClient code was a single class. Now that we are implementing a different version of the networking interface, yet with the same API, it would be nice if we didn't have to change the rest of the code. The main problem is that all the UI code belongs in the `rwjn.chapter5.client` package and the classes are all relative to that package.

There are two approaches to solving this problem: use either an abstract class or an interface to define the basic API. In this case I've decided to go for an abstract class, as the `BalanceListener` code does not need to change between the different implementations. To accommodate these changes, I renamed the `BankClient` class to `TCPBankClient` and made it implement the `BankClient` interface. The BankClient abstract is just a copy of the original BankClient with all the executable code taken out for most of the methods, which are then just declared abstract. Note also that if we had originally extended Thread with this class, it would have made our life a little more difficult in making these basic changes. It would have forced every network interface implementation into being threaded, even if we may not have wanted it to be.

At the start-up end of the client, I renamed both the `Server` and `Client` classes to indicate that they were `TCPServer` and `TCPClient`. The constructor for the BankClient now just makes an instance of `TCP BankClient`. This change has been made to the code that appears on the CD so that you won't see the original code as presented in the previous chapter.

The UDP BankClient

Writing for UDP communications is a different technique. First, you are sending discrete communications. There is no real concept equivalent of the TCP establishing a connection. The receiving of data is done by a different socket than the one that is sending it, and as a result there is much less to do for setting up streams for communications. On the downside, this now means that you need to do a lot more work each time that you want to send data across the network.

Because each command needs to do an almost identical action, we'll create a new private method that just takes the command and the value and does all the network-specific communications.

SECURITY: *Like all network code, the UDP socket code is subject to security checks. If the default port suggested in the user interface dialog is used and the client and server are running on the same machine, nothing further needs to be done. However, if the client and server are running on separate machines, you will need to add an appropriate* `java.net.SocketPermission` *to the policy files on both the client and server machines in order to specify the machine and port number.*

Connecting to the Host While UDP sockets do not have a permanent connection, you still need to set up a socket for UDP. In the case of UDP, all communications are provided with the `DatagramSocket` class. The difference between a reading or writing UDP socket is purely in the constructor that is called when creating a new instance.

For the connect method, it is necessary to establish an outgoing socket. To do this we need to use the default constructor. While you might be tempted to use the constructor that takes an integer and `InetAddress`, it should not be used for this application. `InetAddress` represents the local address on the machine that you are running the address on. This would be used only if your machine had two or more IP addresses associated with it.

NOTE: *An explanation of how the InetAddress class works and multiple IP addresses is covered in Chapter 3, "The* `java.net` *Package."*

You will still need to fetch an address though. Each packet you send out must contain the destination address. The most efficient way of doing this is to fetch the address once and then reuse it every time you create a new packet to send. Fetching the `InetAddress` is done by calling the static `getHostByName()` method of the `InetAddress` class.

As in the TCP version, we want first to go through and clean up any previously allocated connection with a call to the `disconnect()` method. Also like the TCP version, if at any stage we run into problems, we bail out immediately, printing out an error message as we go. Figure 6-4 shows the completed code for the connect method.

As you can see from the above code example, we also create the incoming socket at the same time. This is to ensure that we have communications both ways before we even start the thread listening for updates from the server. The basic philosophy is this: If you cannot send instructions out, then you shouldn't be allowed to listen to information coming from the server (the server won't know where to send it to anyway).

Also of note is the incoming port number. It is not the same as the server's receiving port. We could pick any reasonable port number for our listening socket; it does not need to be the same as the server on the other end. To make it easy to remember (as we'll need to code this on the server side too) the base port of the server plus one will be used.

NOTE: *You may have also noticed that our sending socket does not contain a port number at all. When data is being sent from a machine, a random, uncontested, port number is picked by the operating system and used to send the outgoing information from. Typically the outgoing port exists above 32 K (highest-order bit set).*

Sending Data   With an established socket, the next task is to write the code that will send the instructions out. In the `connect()` method, the output streams were created for you already.

Before writing any data to the output stream, you will need to make sure that it is set to the beginning. The code makes a lot of the reuse of data to avoid having to allocate new objects all the time. The `Byte ArrayOutputStream` that is the basis of the output needs to be reset each time it gets used. If you don't reset it, then your new information gets appended to the end of the previously written data. The result is that you wonder why you keep getting the same request at the server end each time that a command is sent.

Having reset the stream, you then use the appropriate method to write the type of data that you want. A `DataOutputStream` is used in

Figure 6-4
The connect method
of the UDP bank
client.

```java
public void connect(String host, int port) {
  disconnect();

  // Get the address of the connection
  try {
    server_address = InetAddress.getByName(host);
  }
  catch(UnknownHostException e2) {
          System.err.println("Error finding server");
          System.err.println(e2);
          return;
  }

  // Create the UDP outgoing socket
  try {
    bank_connection = new DatagramSocket();
  }
  catch(SocketException e3) {
          System.err.println("Error creating outgoing UDP
socket");
          System.err.println(e3);
          return;
  }

  // Create the UDP outgoing socket
  try {
    incoming_connection = new DatagramSocket(port + 1);
  }
  catch(SocketException e4) {
          System.err.println("Error creating incoming UDP
socket");
          System.err.println(e4);
          return;
  }

  server_port = port;

  // create the output streams for the outgoing data.
  bank_byte_output = new ByteArrayOutputStream()
  bank_data_output = new DataOutputStream(bank_byte_output);

  // Now make a thread out of it
  input_thread = new Thread(this);
  input_thread.start();
```

Figure 6-4
(*Continued*)

```
    // if we've made it this far, things must be OK
    service_available = true;

    // just make sure that the client has registered for listening
    sendCommand(Keywords.REGISTER, 0);
}
```

this case because it contains all the methods needed to write the basic primitive types with minimal effort. Organizing the correct byte order in the packet is just a case of calling the methods with the data in the order that they appear in the diagram.

With the data safely written to the output stream, we just need to convert this to something to send on the network. For UDP communications this takes the form of the `DatagramPacket`. The **Datagram Packet** represents the information that is to be sent over the network including all the information like destination address and port number.

NOTE: *In the TCP example the stream was the network output, while in the UDP case the stream is a middle ground to put things in the right order before creating the output.*

Finally, with the newly created packet, use the `send()` method of the UDP socket to send the data to the host. Figure 6-5 shows the three major parts described above.

Methods that now wish to send a message to the server just need to call this method with the appropriate arguments. There is not that much difference between the TCP code and UDP code in this respect. Our favorite example, the deposit method, now looks like this:

```
public void deposit(float amount) {
  if(!service_available)
    return;

  if(amount >= 0)
    sendCommand(Keywords.DEPOSIT, amount);
}
```

Receiving Server Information   Having already created the incoming listening socket with the `connect()` method, we now need to cap-

Figure 6-5
The private method
sendCommand() to
send commands to
the bank.

```
private void sendCommand(byte command, float value) {
  DatagramPacket packet;
  // Write the data to the output stream
  try {
    bank_byte_output.reset();
    bank_data_output.writeByte(command);
    bank_data_output.writeInt(selected_account);
    bank_data_output.writeFloat(value);
  }
  catch(IOException e1) {
    System.err.println("Error writing an ouput packet");
    System.err.println(e1);
    return;
  }

  // Construct a packet to send
  packet = new DatagramPacket(bank_byte_output.toByteArray(),
                              bank_byte_output.size(),
                              server_address,
                              server_port);
  // Send the packet
  try {
    bank_connection.send(packet);
  }
  catch(IOException e2) {
    System.err.println("Error sending bank request");
    System.err.println(e2);
  }
}
```

ture and process incoming information. Once again the code is contained
in the run() method for executing as a thread.

This time, listening for new data is completely different from TCP.
You will remember that a TCP socket creates a special ServerSocket
that has an accept() method. The accept() method passes back a
completed Socket instance to deal with. For UDP connections, it is just
a case of using a different constructor and then listening with the
receive() method of the DatagramSocket. This receive method must
be passed a completed DatagramPacket before data can received.
When a new UDP packet has arrived, the send method fills in the contents of the DatagramPacket (which is just an array of bytes) and then

returns to the caller (your code). What you now have is a filled array of bytes to deal with.

As in the TCP implementation, we also call a separate method (processInput()) to do the parsing of the incoming data. In this method, we strip data from the byte array and turn it into something meaningful. The first step in doing this is to turn it into a stream to be read. This is a two-step process, first to a ByteArrayInputStream and then to a DataInputStream. The second stream is needed and chosen because it is the other half of the Input/Output stream used on the server end. We know with confidence that what was written in can be read back out easily.

NOTE: There is a standard defined byte ordering for writing primitives such as floats and ints to network. The specification of how bits and bytes are written to the network is termed Network Byte Order *and is defined in Appendix B of RFC 791, Internet Protocol. This allows programs written in any other language to communicate with one written in Java. Java uses network byte ordering on all streams, regardless of whether they write to a socket or to a local file on disk.*

With the streams now established, we can begin to read the data out. First, the command must be read. Depending on the command we can do one of two things: read an account number and balance or read a string. The first case is relatively trivial; you have already done something similar except that you were writing, not reading. As always, if we encounter any errors during the process, an error message is printed and the whole command is dropped.

Dealing with the text message of an error broadcast by the server is easier than you might think. This is in part due to some nice design by the Java API developers. Strings in Java are stored in UTF format when written to a stream. The UTF format as a string includes in the first two bytes the length of the following UTF-encoded string. To read a string from the input stream into a Java string requires just one call to read UTF() of the DataInputStream. After this you just use the string as you would any normal string.

The resulting code for the processInput() method is presented in Figure 6-6. Notice that at the end we make sure to clean up the streams and any other resources that we have created during the execution of the method.

Figure 6-6
The `processInput` method used to deal with data coming back from the server.

```java
private void processInput(byte[] input_data) {
  ByteArrayInputStream byte_input =
              new ByteArrayInputStream(input_data);
  DataInputStream in = new DataInputStream(byte_input);

  byte command;

  try {
    command = in.readByte();
  }
  catch(IOException e1) {
    System.err.println("Error reading data from input");
    System.err.println(e1);
    return;
  }

  // if it is an error
  if(command == Keywords.BALANCE) {
    int   account;
    float balance;

    try {
      account = in.readInt();
      balance = in.readFloat();
    }
    catch(IOException e2) {
      System.err.println("Error reading data from input");
      System.err.println(e2);
      return;
    }
    // send this to the listener
    if(listener != null) {
      if(account == 0)
        listener.accountAChanged(balance);
      else
        listener.accountBChanged(balance);
    }
  }
  else {
    String message = null;

    try {
      message = in.readUTF();
    }
```

Figure 6-6
(Continued)

```
catch(IOException e3) .{
  System.err.println("Error reading data from input");
  System.err.println(e3);
  return;
}

// Now print this to the err output
System.err.println("Server returned Error: " + message);
}
// Finally close the streams up.
try {
  in.close();
  byte_input.close();
}
catch(IOException e4) {
  // can't do much about this so just ignore it
}

try {
  byte_input.close();
}
catch(IOException e4) {
  // can't do much about this one either so just ignore it too.
}
}
```

The UDP Server

The server should be much simpler now that you have covered all the basic techniques with the client. There is nothing much new left to learn when you implement the server.

After dealing with the basics of just reading and writing the packets, the more interesting problem comes in dealing with the connectionless nature of the communications. This poses more than one problem for the code writer. First, there is no long-established connection for sending server information back to the client. On top of that, you don't really know when there might be a client that is interested in knowing details or when one is no longer interested. This all requires extra code to be added to the server if you wish to replicate the TCP functionality.

Receiving New Data Connections

So far you have already covered the code that reads the data in from the server. This was a single client dealing with data from the server. At the server end, things are a little different. You might have potentially thousands of clients all banging on your server at once. You cannot go off and parse each new packet before returning to the server. However, each packet as a separate thread is going to cause all sorts of problems when you have hundreds of packets arriving all the time. There are various techniques used to deal with this, such as threads with buffers of commands, with a new thread being created for every *X* number of commands or thread reuse through the technique of thread pooling.

For a small-scale server like this, the single thread per packet implementation is quite acceptable. It is very rare that you would have to deal with more than two or three incoming packets at a time. Increasing it to 20 or 30 clients might be a whole new story. For the moment, and for simplicity, we'll just continue with the model that was already established for the TCP server—a thread for each new "connection."

NOTE: *Each transaction now produces a new packet at the server level that needs to be dealt with. For each client there may be a number of transactions performed, but the server has no idea of continuous connections.*

Returning the Call

If the server has no idea about what connections exist and what clients are there, how does it know where to send the outgoing communications for balance updates? One solution is to pass on balance updates only in response to an incoming request. Another is to just broadcast them on the local LAN and hope that someone is listening. The final option is to keep track of who may have a connection and has not yet canceled it.

Of these solutions, only the last really makes sense. In the first case, a client that is connected, but has not yet sent a transaction request, will not get regular balance updates from interest calculations. The second suggestion ignores the fact that the user may well be on some other network not directly connected to the server. The last solution still has a few holes in it, but is workable.

NOTE: *Another possible solution is to add a new command that queries the server for the current balance. Then the client could send the periodic requests to the server. This is not considered since it involves changing the client code, too much for our simple exercises, to add another thread for the timing of balance requests.*

What needs to be done is to keep a table of the clients that have sent a request to be registered. A client remains in this table until the server receives an exit command. In the meantime, every time that the balance changes for an account, all the registered clients are sent the balance information.

One nice feature of the code setup is that the only time information is sent back to the server is when there is an error or when the balance needs to be updated. If we ignore the error part for the moment, the balance has always been sent asynchronously from the actual request that drove it. That is, the code that implemented the BalanceListener interface was responsible for sending information back to the client.

Hopefully you are starting to see the picture coming through now of what needs to be done. We have a new class that registers as a balance listener and takes the connection management issues into consideration at the same time. This class needs to be able to add and remove destinations very easily.

Before choosing a method of dealing with this implementation, we need to know how to deal with determining what the client is. The only way to identify a client is by its IP address or some other unique identifier. The unique identifier concept is a bit out of the scope of this simple project, so we'll base the identification on the originating IP address. The IP address is provided as an `InetAddress` instance from the `getAddress()` method of the `DatagramPacket` that is received. All we need to do is add and remove the client IP addresses from the manager and let it take care of the rest. Each client has a unique IP address (you can't run two clients on the one machine), so this sounds like an ideal job for a Hashtable.

Figure 6-7 shows the outline of the class. There are a few things to note here. First, the class is a subclass of the hashtable. This allows us to make use of a number of the functions very quickly and transparently to the user without harming our own code. For example, we've added an add method that does a quick check for a preexisting client of that same IP address before committing to the addition. Also, we have built in a

Figure 6-7
The complete
ConnectionManager
class.

```java
package rwjn.chapter6.server;

// Standard imports
import java.io.*;
import java.net.*;
import java.util.*;

// Application specific imports
import rwjn.chapter5.server.AccountManager;
import rwjn.chapter5.server.BalanceListener;

/**
 * McDuck Bank Server
 * <P>
 * The network connection manager for the UDP server. Needed so that
 * it can handle the connectionless protocols for updates on balance
 * <P>
 * @author <A HREF="mailto:justin@vlc.com.au">Justin Couch</A>
 * @version 1.0
 */
public class ConnectionManager extends Hashtable
  implements BalanceListener
{
  // The port number of the listening clients
  private int client_port = 8001;

  // The outgoing socket connection
  private DatagramSocket socket = null;

  // The I/O streams for banking
  private ByteArrayOutputStream bank_byte_output = null;
  private DataOutputStream bank_data_output = null;

  // The most recent copy of the connection manager established
  private static ConnectionManager local_copy = null;
  /**
   * Create a default sized vector
   */
  public ConnectionManager() {
    super();

    createSocket();

    local_copy = this;
  }
```

Figure 6-7
(*Continued*)

```
/**
 * Create a vector with the given intial capacity
 * @param initialCapacity The initial number of available space
 */
public ConnectionManager(int initialCapacity) {
  super(initialCapacity);

  createSocket();

  local_copy=this;
}
/**
 * Create a vector with the given initial capacity and increment for
 * when it gets full
 * @param initialCapacity The initial number of available space
 * @param capacityIncrement The amount to increment the vector size
 */
public ConnectionManager(int initialCapacity, float factor) {
  super(initialCapacity, factor);

  createSocket();

  local_copy=this;
}
/**
 * create the socket needed to talk to the clients
 */
 private void createSocket() {
   // Create the UDP outgoing socket
   try {
     socket=new DatagramSocket();
   }
   catch(SocketException e3) {
           System.err.println("Error creating outgoing UDP socket");
           System.err.println(e3);
   }

   // create the output streams for the outgoing data.
   bank_byte_output=new ByteArrayOutputStream();
   bank_data_output=new DataOutputStream(bank_byte_output);
}
/**
 * Set the port number of the client. Invariably, this should be
the
 * port number of the server plus one.
 * @param port The port number to listen to.
```

Figure 6-7
(Continued)

```
  */
  void setPort(int port) {
    client_port=port;
  }
/**
 * Get a reference to the currently installed connection manager
 * @return The last created instance of the connection manager
 */
static ConnectionManager getConnectionManager() {
  return local_copy;
}
/**
 * Add the nominated address to the list of desinations to receive
 * notice of changes
 * @param address The new address to be stored
 */
void add(InetAddress address) {
  // firstly check the hashtable to see if this address is
  // already there
  if(contains(address))
    return;
  // is ok so put the address in there.
  put(address, address);
}
/**
 * send a balance update for the nominated account number
 * @param account The account number
 * @param balance The new balance
 */
public synchronized void updateBalance(int account,
                                       float balance) {
if(socket == null)
  return;
// construct the packet to be sent.
int i;
DatagramPacket packet;

// Write the data to the output stream
try {
  bank_byte_output.reset();
  bank_data_output.writeByte(Keywords.BALANCE);
  bank_data_output.writeInt(account);
  bank_data_output.writeFloat(balance);
}
catch(IOException e1) {
  System.err.println("Error writing an ouput packet");
```

Figure 6-7
(*Continued*)

```
    System.err.println(e1);
    return;
}

// Construct a packet to send
packet = new DatagramPacket(bank_byte_output.toByteArray(),
                            bank_byte_output.size(),
                            null,
                            client_port);

// for each element send the packet, making sure
// to set the address each time.
Enumeration e = elements();

while(e.hasMoreElements()) {
  packet.setAddress((InetAddress)e.nextElement());

  // Send the packet
  try {
    socket.send(packet);
  }
  catch(IOException e2) {
    System.err.println("Error sending bank request");
    System.err.println(e2);
    }
  }
}
```

couple of methods to set the server port number independently of the constructors. This could have been included as part of the constructor parameters, but I wanted to keep the confusion down as we are almost directly mapping to the underlying hashtable constructors. It does not make any difference which way you go, it is purely a matter of personal programming style.

An important little note that you may have missed while skimming through the code is the static `getConnectionManager()` method. There is a good reason for this. The method returns a reference to the last allocated copy of the connection manager. Why is this necessary? The basic reasoning is that for most of the packets received, there is no need to reference the connection manager. Indeed only when a register and exit command are received is it needed at all. Although the code could pass in a reference for every packet, it is a waste since the code will need to take an internal copy as well, and yet may never even need it. A static method like that enables the code to simply grab the current reference and perform method calls without the extra baggage.

Packet Parsing

Once the packet has arrived at the server it needs to be processed. Like the TCP interface, it directly calls the same AccountManager code (which has not changed from that in Chapter 5). The only difference is in how it extracts what the command and values are.

The first thing to do after setting up the streams is extract the command from the packet, which is shown in Figure 6-8. If the command is to exit or register then a call to the connection manager is made. If not,

Figure 6-8
The processing of command packets at the server in the AccountConnection class.

```
public void run() {
   byte[] input_data = (byte[])source_packet.getData().clone();
   ByteArrayInputStream byte_input =
         new ByteArrayInputStream(input_data);
   DataInputStream in = new DataInputStream(byte_input);

   byte command;

   try {
      command = in.readByte();
   }
   catch(IOException e1) {
      System.err.println("Error reading data from input");
      System.err.println(e1);
      return;
   }
   if(command == Keywords.EXIT) {
      // remove this from the data handler
      InetAddress destination=source.getAddress();

      ConnectionManager.getConnectionManager().remove(
                                       destination);
   }
   else if(command == Keywords.REGISTER) {
      // register this client
```

Figure 6-8
(Continued)

```java
      InetAddress destination=source.getAddress();

      ConnectionManager.getConnectionManager().add(destination);
    }
    else {
      intaccount;
      float amount;

      // read the rest of the message
      try {
        account = in.readInt();
        amount = in.readFloat();
      }
      catch(IOException e1) {
        System.err.println("Error reading data from input");
        System.err.println(e1);
        return;
      }
      // now process it
      if(command == Keywords.DEPOSIT) {
        account_manager.deposit(account, amount);
      }
      else if(command == Keywords.WITHDRAW) {
        account_manager.withdraw(account, amount);
      }
      else if(command == Keywords.TRANSFER) {
        account_manager.transfer(account, amount);
      }
    }

    // clean up the streams
    try {
      in.close();
    }
    catch(IOException e2) {
      // no point doing anything
    }
    try {
      byte_input.close();
    }
    catch(IOException e3) {
      // no point doing anything
    }
  }
```

then the account and amount are also read from the packet and the appropriate call is then made to the account manager. Having done this, then the streams can be closed and everything tidied up; the processing for this packet is complete and the instance of the class is done.

A very important note is what happens with the byte array that forms the source of the data stream. You might have noticed in the client code in the `UDPBankClient` class that—after constructing the byte array, passing that to the constructor of the packet, and receiving a new packet—I never extract that byte array from the packet before passing it to the `processInput()` method (Figure 6-6). That suggests that the byte array is never actually copied internally in the `DatagramPacket`. If this is the case, then as soon as you have the next packet come in, it will overwrite the data in that byte array. You must be very careful about this in a high-volume server. In this example, you may have never even noticed a problem, but it will have crept up sometime in the future.

Avoiding the problem is easy. Simply make sure that you clone the contents of the array as soon as possible before returning control back to the receive method of the socket. Cloning the array makes sure that the data is safe in your processing code and will not be overwritten. Note what the first line of the run method is. Practically speaking, that probably should be done even earlier—in the constructor—to make sure that we really do have a clean copy. (It is possible that the run method might be delayed for a long period of time and the packet contents corrupted.)

Running the Code

The start of the server is no different from the previous chapter. We've even kept the class name the same. All we had to do was change the import line at the top and rename the class name to `UDPServer`, do a quick recompile, and it is all done. Starting it at the command line is the same as before.

Starting the client should be no different either. In effect, the user should not notice any difference between the two implementations. One thing to notice is that the UDP server updates are marginally quicker. There are a couple of reasons why this may be the case. First, the UDP packet has almost no overheads associated with it. At the low-level OS code, there is very little error checking done or acknowledgments of a correctly received packet to be sent. Second, the difference between string and binary processing would make UDP quicker as well. There is no string parsing to be done, and this should help the speed by a large amount. However, in small packet sizes like this, it probably doesn't make any noticeable difference.

The Multicast Client

By now you should be starting to get the hang of what is happening in the server. The final variation that we will deal with is basing the protocols on multicasting connections. Multicast, you will remember, is a broadcast protocol. Users who are interested in listening can attach themselves to that broadcast and listen in without needing to register with the server.

When it comes to sending out requests from the client, there is no need to broadcast it to the entire world because only one server will ever be dealing with your requests (can you imagine the mess of having multiple servers for the one bank account all acting independently?). Our design for the multicast version of the client/server pair will be a lot less radical than the previous change. The broadcast from the server will be done with multicasting, while the messages to the server will remain UDP.

Design Changes

With the change to multicast from the server to the client, there is not that much need for design changes in terms of the structure of the code. The server just generally broadcasts the information, which means that there is no need to either register or exit from its internal records. The client just needs to attach itself to the appropriate multicast stream.

As you may remember from Chapter 3, "The `java.net` Package," the Java implementation of the multicast socket is a derived class from DatagramSocket. That is, you still use DatagramPackets to send and receive data. This has a real bonus for our code: Once the socket is set up, there is almost no code changes needed from the UDP code for constructing and interpreting packets!

For file names, the classes that have changed for this variation are prefixed with MCast. They are still kept as part of the `rwjn.chapter6` package hierarchy.

SECURITY: *Multicasting is subject to security checks for all situations. (You cannot use* `localhost` *as a valid multicast group.) In order for the code to run, you will need to add the following permission to your policy file:*

```
permission java.netSocketPermission "230.0.0.1", "accept,connect"
```

The notation 230.0.0.1 should be replaced by the IP address of the multi-cast group that you are joining.

Code Changes

The first place to start is where we make the socket—the connect method. After creating the outgoing UDP socket, we need to replace the incoming `DatagramSocket` with a `MulticastSocket`. This is attached to the same port that the original UDP version was: the outgoing port number plus one.

The one difference between the UDP and multicast versions of the socket is that the multicast version must also join a group. This group is like the destination address, but since multicast is a broadcast protocol there is no "destination" or server. All users, so long as they are part of the group, can broadcast information. The group is defined as being a class D IP address (see Chapter 2, "Internet Networking Concepts"). Like the UDP example earlier, the Java representation of this is retrieved by using the `getByName()` call of the InetAddress class. In a concession to reality, we've hard-coded as a constant the group that we will be joining. Ideally this should be part of the connect dialog box with an extra field, but we will not allow the user to change it for this example. The address that will be used is 230.0.0.1.

Figure 6-9 shows the modifications that are made to the connect method to accommodate the changes for multicast. Only the changes, not the whole method, are shown.

If we join the group at the connection, then, during the disconnect, we must also leave the group.

```
try {
  incoming_connection.leaveGroup(mcast_group);
}
catch(IOException e) {
  // ignore it
}
```

Figure 6-9
Modifications to the
connect method to
accommodate
changes for
multicast.

```
public void connect(String host, int port) {
  disconnect();

  // Get the address of the connection
  try {
    server_address = InetAddress.getByName(host);
    mcast_group = InetAddress.getByName(MCAST_GROUP);
  }
  catch(UnknownHostException e2) {
    System.err.println("Error finding server or multicast
group");
    System.err.println(e2);
    return;
  }

  // Create the UDP outgoing socket
  ...
  // Create the multicast incoming socket
  try {
    incoming_connection=new MulticastSocket(port+1);
    incoming_connection.joinGroup(mcast_group);
  }
  catch(IOException e4) {
    System.err.println("Error creating incoming UDP socket");
    System.err.println(e4);
    return;
  }
  // complete the rest of the setup
  ...
}
```

Receiving data from a multicast connection requires no change in the code at all. Data is sent in the form of DatagramPackets, which is the same as the UDP code. The message format is identical, so the processing code does not need to change either. This means our client code is now finished.

The Multicast Server

While the client required only minimal changes, there are a few more that need to be done for the server end. At the client, you only need to read the incoming data, while at the server you need to broadcast it.

With the server just generally broadcasting the information, there is no need for the connection manager that was introduced for the UDP implementation to keep track of interested clients. So basically all that needs to change is a new BalanceListener implementation on the server side, and the listening code of the BankClient interface on the client end. The client sending code remains the same.

Now that the server is just broadcasting all the time, there is no need for the register command from the client. In the same vein, there is no need for the exit command either. Our account connection handler will just ignore any messages like this that it may receive.

Design Changes

The previous few paragraphs have mainly outlined the changes in the design that need to be made. The new class that we have created is called Broadcaster. The role of the class is to implement the balance listener for the account changes and broadcast those changes on a multi-cast group. Unlike the connection manager that was needed for the UDP implementation, once started, it can act independently and no other class needs to interact with it.

Reducing the number of commands needed by the client means that we can remove some code from the parser. However, reducing the number of commands is all that we need to do. The AccountConnection class listens for incoming information, not the outgoing, so there is nothing that really needs to change.

Of course, with a new server interface to the outside world, we are going to need a new NetworkServer class (now named Mcast NetworkServer) to handle the changes. Again, there is nothing really special that needs to be done here except remove references to the old ConnectionManager and insert the Broadcaster instead.

Code Changes

Starting with the AccountConnection class (now named MCast AccountConnection), we remove the references to the Connection Manager. To do this we go to the parseInput() method and combine the two if statements that check for the command type into a single one that checks the command for not being an exit or register command. If it passes this test, then allow the parsing to continue.

```
if(!((command == Keywords.EXIT) || (command == Keywords.REGISTER))) {
  int    account;
  float amount;

  // read the rest of the message

...etc
```

The `Broadcaster` class is completely new. An instance of this is used to act as the listener for account balance information and also to broadcast to the world the information. The constructor takes the port number that is to be used as the broadcast channel and builds the socket and streams needed to make it ready to go. In the same way that the client end joined a hard-coded group, so does the server. Figure 6-10 shows the constructor of the `Broadcaster` class.

Figure 6-10

The constructor of the `Broadcaster` class.

```
public Broadcaster(int port) {
  client_port = port;
  // Get the address in InetAddress form
  try {
    group=InetAddress.getByName(MCAST_GROUP);
  }
  catch(UnknownHostException e1) {
    // I hope not!
    System.err.println("Error getting multicast group");
    System.err.println(e1);
    return;
  }

  // Create the multicast socket
  try {
    socket = new MulticastSocket(port);
    socket.joinGroup(group);
  }
  catch(IOException e2) {
    System.err.println("Error creating outgoing multicast
socket");
    System.err.println(e2);
  }
  // create the output stream for the outgoing data.
  bank_byte_output = new ByteArrayOutputStream();
  bank_data_output = new DataOutputStream(bank_byte_output);
}
```

Sending data is taken care of by the `balanceUpdate()` method that is required by implementing the listener. Multicast sockets, being derived from DatagramSocket, use the same DatagramPacket class to send information. We can take the code straight from the `balance Update()` method of the `ConnectionManager` class and use it. The only modification needed is to take out the loop through the elements, since we only ever have one destination to send to—the multicast group.

```
public synchronized void updateBalance(int account, float balance) {
  if(socket == null)
    return;

  // construct the packet to be sent.
  int i;
  DatagramPacket packet;

  // Write the data to the output stream
  try {
    bank_byte_output.reset();
    bank_data_output.writeByte(Keywords.BALANCE);
    bank_data_output.writeInt(account);
    bank_data_output.writeFloat(balance);
  }
  catch(IOException e1) {
    System.err.println("Error writing an ouput packet");
    System.err.println(e1);
    return;
  }

  // Construct a packet to send
  packet = new DatagramPacket(bank_byte_output.toByteArray(),
                              bank_byte_output.size(),
                              group,// see constructor
                              client_port);

  // Send the packet
  try {
    socket.send(packet);
  }
  catch(IOException e2) {
    System.err.println("Error sending bank request");
    System.err.println(e2);
  }
}
```

Finally, to complete the code, we copy the `UDPServer` `class`, rename it `McastServer` and change the creation of `NetworkServer` to `MCast` `NetworkServer`. This will complete the exercise.

After compiling all the above code you should now be able to run the client and server as you have for the other examples. Connect to the server and you should soon start to see balance updates. Starting multiple clients on the one machine will work this time too, allowing you to see the broadcast in action.

Summary

With the code complete from this chapter, you can now see how the different networking connection types can affect your code. Hopefully you will now have a much better understanding of the different approaches needed to handle each of the network connection types.

Now that the basics are complete, the rest of the book will head into the areas of applied networking. We take the basic concepts that you have learnt here and apply them to a variety of areas by building higher-level APIs on top. The first area that you will need to know about are some areas that were new to Java 1.1—object serialization and Remote Method Invocation, otherwise known as RMI.

Object
Serialization

When Sun announced Java 1.1, a number of new features were added to the core of the Java environment. One of the more interesting, and fundamental, changes was the ability to write an entire object instance to a stream, then read it back out and completely rebuild an exact replica of that instance on another machine. This capability is called *object serialization.*

Object serialization is built into the core of the language and the Java virtual machine. Serialization is one of the special classes of interfaces like `Cloneable` and `Runnable` that are used by VM to deliver special capabilities to a class instance. Whenever an object is marked as serializable, the full capabilities are given without the need to write a single line extra of code, although the option does exist if needed.

What Is Object Serialization?

At the most basic level, object serialization is the ability to write an object instance to a stream and then reconstruct that stream into the exact replica object instance, potentially on another machine. Or, more simply, it is turning an object into a bunch of bytes then turning those bytes back into an object.

Serialization of objects is not really a new concept, created just for Java. While the technique has existed in other languages like C/C++, it has not been so easy to use or complete as Java's implementation. Much of this capability is because the implementation is done at such a low level, in not just the language but the virtual machine environment.

Goals of Serialization

Sun defines the goals of object serialization as:

- Have a simple yet extensible mechanism.
- Maintain the Java object type and safety properties in the serialized form.
- Be extensible to support marshaling and unmarshaling as needed for remote objects.
- Be extensible to support persistence of Java objects.
- Require per-class implementation only for customization.
- Allow the object to define its external format.

As you can see, object serialization is a lot more about just being able to write out any series of bits and then read them back in to reconstruct the object. Java provides two methods of doing this: The `Serializable` interface, which does everything for you, and the `Externalizable` interface where you must roll your own.

Writing your own serialization code means that you can customize the serialization process as much as you like. In doing this, the serialization can be made to write out only the important information that is needed to restore it later on. Say your class kept a bunch of references to other classes—you might not want to keep those, so you just don't write them out. The default implementation will write out not only your object, but also all the objects it references, plus any they reference and so on. You could well be writing out a lot of useless information that takes up valuable time and disk space.

Serialization Classes

Already in this chapter, two of the classes (or more correctly, interfaces) needed to perform object serialization have been mentioned. The `Serializable` and `Externalizable` interfaces are used to mark an object as capable of serialization. While this might be useful, you still need to use other classes to do the job of turning that class into that bunch of bytes.

As already mentioned, implementing the `Serializable` interface allows the class to be serialized with no extra work on the part of the programmer. In contrast, the `Externalizable` interface forces the programmer to write the code to implement serialization in a customized form. If your class does not implement these, then when any code attempts to serialize your object it will throw a `NotSerializableException`. The classes, interfaces, and exceptions are all defined in the `java.io` package.

With your classes appropriately nominated as being serializable, then you need somewhere and somehow to write them. The somewhere is defined by what you want to do. For example, you might want to serialize a class to send it over a network connection to another machine, or you might want to write a persistent database, so the destination might be a file or JDBC connection. The somehow is implemented in two classes: `ObjectOutputStream` and `ObjectInputStream`. These classes are responsible for the respective jobs of writing out and reading in a serialized object or objects.

Object streams follow the norms of all the other Java streams; they present all the methods needed to write their particular speciality out to an underlying class. That could be anything that can handle an array of bytes (we've already mentioned sockets and files as two examples). For serialization, Object streams make calls to the `writeObject` and `readObject` methods of the given class. With this, they then expect that the class will be able to deal with its own requirements.

On top of the ability just to read and write a class, the object streams add extra capabilities to make annotations or even replace objects within the stream. The idea of the stream is just that—it is a stream of data that can be interpreted as required. That stream is more than likely to contain more than a single instance of a class. It may contain hundreds or even thousands, particularly for network connections.

How Object Serialization Works

Object serialization, as has been said before, is just the process of taking an object and turning it into a stream of bytes that can be read and turned into an exact replica of the object at the other end of the stream. The problem now is: How do you know what order to interpret the stream in?

Reading and Writing Basic Types   If you are using just the default serialization provided in the `Serializable` interface, then you don't have much direct control. Underneath all the covers, the writeObject method reads each of your internal variables and then calls the appropriate `write <Type>` method of the object stream. The object streams are derived from the DataInput/Output streams, which give you methods for each of the Java primitive types.

When Java goes about writing an object to the stream, the first thing it does is write a small header that consists of a number of things, the most important for your understanding being the object type and version information. The structure is much more complex, and well beyond the scope of this book.

NOTE: *The full specification of the protocol used to write out streams is provided with the Java documentation in the document titled "Object Serialization Stream Protocol."*

After writing the header, then the rest of the object can be written. The code will go through each variable that can be written within the class and call the write method for that type. The methods used to write the data are the same ones that we used in the previous chapter to write binary information to the DatagramPacket. For the default write, this can be in whatever order the VM is allowed by the specification.

Reading objects, and turning them into a class again, is just the opposite process. All of the write methods are accompanied by read methods for the incoming data. You also have more control on the read end if you do not wish to read some of the data. Because you have all the normal stream access methods, and you know the order in which you wrote information (assuming you have implemented your own write), you can skip unwanted data.

Dealing with Derived Classes   One common problem that you may be faced with is serializable classes that are derived from other classes that are not explicitly marked for it. What happens depends on which of the serialization classes you implement.

If you implement the `Serializable` interface, Java will take care of all the subclassing problems for you as best it can. Serializable classes will build an instance of each class down the hierarchy as needed by your class.

One major restriction to doing this is the construction of the classes themselves. As mentioned elsewhere in this chapter, serialization does not recreate the exact instance of the class. What it creates is an identical copy. However, to create this copy in the first place, the local VM is required to create a new instance of the class. Creating a new instance of the class requires calling a constructor. It cannot be any old constructor; it must be the default no-argument constructor. The constructor must also be public. So, for every class that you expect to be serializable, you must provide an implementation of the default no-arg constructor. Also note, you cannot rely on using a default constructor provided by Java if you don't have any constructors—you must always explicitly implement a default (empty if need be) public constructor for serialization to work.

However, if your class implements the `Externalizable` interface, you don't need to worry about any of these issues. Externalizable classes do not automatically generate serialization information for the superclasses. Therefore, you will need to explicitly deal with this yourself.

Multiple References to a Class Instance   Another very common situation that you will come across is dealing with multiple references to a given class instance. Serialization takes care of this very simply.

As the stream is being written out, the serialization mechanism keeps track of every instance of each class. As it encounters a new instance, it assigns it a new unique identifier which is written to the stream as part of the header. Whenever it encounters that same object reference again within the life of that stream, it will now write out only the identifier. On the other end of the stream, the reader will take note of this identifier and perform the reverse process of substituting in the correct object reference.

Versioning Issues

A couple of paragraphs ago, it was mentioned that version information is included in the header. Whenever you write something out and then read it back some time later (or on another machine), there is a very real possibility that the versions of information will have changed. The serialization system must be able to deal with this.

Java defines two types of changes—compatible and incompatible. Incompatible changes are defined as those which Java cannot guarantee that the two class versions will be interoperable. Java does try to be as nice as possible, but there are cases where it cannot. For example, a field that no longer exists in the newer version or a change in the class hierarchy can cause major problems from which the serialization process may throw an exception (particularly with the `readObject()` method of the `ObjectInputStream`).

One important issue to note is that versioning issues are dependent on the method you use to do your serialization. Classes that implement the `Externalizable` interface are entirely responsible for version control. Only classes implementing `Serializable` have automatic version control enabled.

Incompatible Changes   In defining compatible and incompatible changes, the responsibility rests on the newer version of the class to ensure correct functionality. At the same time, in an apparent contradiction, the reader of the stream is the one that is responsible for making whatever adjustments are needed to complete the just-created class instance.

A field is deleted only if it exists in an early version of the class, and not in a later. If the reader is the new version of the class, it silently ignores the value of the deleted field. However, if the reader is the elder version then it must supply a default value for that now deleted field. Close reading reveals that there is really no contradiction between the two goals.

The Java documentation defines the incompatible changes (those which cannot guarantee interoperability) as being the following:

- Deleting fields—if a field is deleted in a class, the stream written will not contain its value.

- When the stream is read by an earlier class, the value of the field will be set to the default value because no value is available in the stream. However, this default value may adversely impair the ability of the earlier version to fulfill its contract.

- Moving classes up or down the hierarchy—this cannot be allowed since the data in the stream appears in the wrong sequence.

- Changing a nonstatic field to static or a nontransient field to transient—this is equivalent to deleting a field from the class. This version of the class will not write that data to the stream, so it will not be available to be read by earlier versions of the class. As in deleting a field, the field of the earlier version will be initialized to the default value, which can cause the class to fail in unexpected ways.

- Changing the declared type of a primitive field—each version of the class writes the data with its declared type. Earlier versions of the class attempting to read the field will fail because the type of the data in the stream does not match the type of the field.

- Changing the `writeObject` or `readObject` method so that it no longer writes or reads the default field data or changing it so that it attempts to write it or read it when the previous version did not. The default field data must consistently either appear or not appear in the stream.

- Changing a class from serializable to externalizable or vice versa is an incompatible change since the stream will contain data that is incompatible with the implementation in the available class.

- Removing either `Serializable` or `Externalizable` is an incompatible change since when written, the class will no longer supply the fields needed by older versions of the class.

Compatible Changes   Compatible changes are almost any other change that can be made. In the interests of symmetry, the Java definitions of compatible changes (as specified by Sun) are:

- Adding fields—When the class being reconstituted has a field that does not occur in the stream, that field in the object will be initialized to the default value for its type. If class-specific initialization is needed, the class may provide a `readObject` method that can initialize the field to nondefault values.

- Adding classes—The stream will contain the type hierarchy of each object in the stream. Comparing this hierarchy in the stream with the current class can detect additional classes. Since there is no information in the stream from which to initialize the object, the class's fields will be initialized to the default values.

- Removing classes—Comparing the class hierarchy in the stream with that of the current class can detect that a class has been deleted. In this case, the fields and objects corresponding to that class are read from the stream. Primitive fields are discarded, but the objects referenced by the deleted class are created, since they may be referred to later in the stream. They will be garbage-collected when the stream is garbage-collected or reset.

- Adding `writeObject`/`readObject` methods—If the version reading the stream has these methods then `readObject` is expected, as usual, to read the required data written to the stream by the default serialization. It should call `defaultReadObject` first before reading any optional data. The `writeObject` method is expected as usual to call `defaultWriteObject` to write the required data and then may write optional data.

- Removing `writeObject`/`readObject` methods—If the class reading the stream does not have these methods, the required data will be read by default serialization, and the optional data will be discarded.

- Adding `java.io.Serializable`—This is equivalent to adding types. There will be no values in the stream for this class so its fields will be initialized to default values. The support for subclassing nonserializable classes requires that the class's supertype have a no-arg constructor and that the class itself will be initialized to default values. In the case that the no-arg constructor is not available, the `NotSerializableException` is thrown.

- Removing `java.io.Serializable` so that it is no longer `Serializable`—This is equivalent to removing the class, and it can be dealt with by reading and discarding data for the class.

- Changing the access to a field—The access modifiers public, package, protected, and private have no effect on the ability of serialization to assign values to the fields.

- Changing a field from static to nonstatic or transient to nontransient—This is equivalent to adding a field to the class. The new field will be written to the stream but earlier classes will ignore the value, since serialization will not assign values to static or transient fields.

Controlling Versioning with Serialver Once you have started to experiment with serialization, you can quickly run into versioning issues and incompatibilities between class implementation. One way to keep track of this is to use some of the tools provided with the JDK. Earlier it was mentioned that each class instance has a unique identifier within the stream. On the larger scale, so does each version of the class. This version information is included as part of the object stream to make sure that the VM knows how to deal with a class as it is read in.

By default, Java will create a hashcode for your class based on the sequence of bytes that are written out that are used to define the class (that is, the signature of variable names and types, and the class name). Therefore, every time that you make a change, the hashcode will be different. For greater control over versioning, you can provide your own version ID. The version ID, which is usually known as SUID, must be declared exactly as follows:

```
static final long serialVersionUID = 3487495895819393L;
```

The actual number used in the SUID can be found by using the serialver program. This comes with the standard JDK and can be used to determine if a class is serializable and, if so, what its SUID should be set to. Serialver has two modes: a command-line option where you give it a fully qualified classname (see Figure 7-1) or the -show option used as a basic GUI program (see Figure 7-2).

Figure 7-1
The serialver command-line option.

```
c:\>serialver java.lang.String
java.lang.String:            static final long serialVersionUID = -
6849794470754667710L;
```

Figure 7-2
The serialver program
-show option.

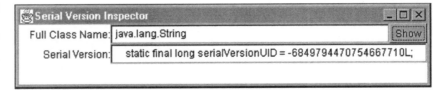

The output of serialver can then be used to set the `serial VersionUID` value in your class. Each time you make a major modification to the class, such as adding or deleting variables or methods, then you should rerun serialver and update the SUID. Java says that you must declare the SUID in every version of the class that you write after the initial serializable version.

NOTE: *In practice, serialization continues to work regardless, although you do suffer a performance penalty because the reader must generate a new SUID each time the classes are read in rather than rely on the preset value.*

Security Concerns

Serialization means writing a class out as bytes, and then reading it back in. That period in between, while the data is in a byte format, leaves it open for attack. At this point in time, there is no protection provided by the Java environment. A malicious person could intercept the data and modify the contents without your knowing.

While the main problem of security of the bytes in transit is out of the reach of Java, there are a number of precautions that you as a programmer can take to avoid as many problems as possible.

First, make sure that you don't write out any information that uses operating-specific resources. This could include `File` descriptors, sockets, thread references, and others. The simplest solution to this is to mark any variable using these types as being `transient`. All transient variables are ignored when written out and are set to default values when the object is reconstructed. It is important to remember that the object after being read from the scene is *not* the same as the one written in. It is an identical copy, but not the same instance. The == comparison would return false. In fact, the specifications state that:

The serialization package cannot be used to recreate the same object, and no object is ever overwritten by a deserialize operation. All that can be done with the serialization package is to create new objects, initialized in a particular fashion.

A second alternative is to provide your own custom serialization either by implementing Externalizable, or by overriding the read Object() and writeObject() methods. In this way, only the class itself knows what data are really being written and what is not. There is no way for any other class to determine what is being written and read. At the same time, it allows you to write your own checking code so that you can implement validity checking.

If you are really paranoid about security, then there is the option of encrypting the entire stream. There are a number of different packages available on the Internet as freeware that build encrypted streams for you. Using these classes provides a completely transparent extra layer of security due to the stream abstraction ideas.

Finally, if you are extremely paranoid, and encryption is not enough for you, just don't allow the objects to be serialized. Make sure they don't implement Serializable or Externalizable anywhere within the class hierarchy and declare the top-level class as final (so that nobody can build a derived class from your class and then serialize the lot). Alternatively, just write the writeObject and readObject methods so that they immediately throw a NotSerializableException, and make them final too.

SECURITY: *The security policy arrangements for serialization vary depending on the underlying stream source. For example, a socket would require a* java.net.SocketPermission *entry while a file would require a* java.io.FilePermission *entry.*

Understanding Streaming

Before we get too heavily into serialization, it pays to take a look at some of the underlying principles. One of the core pieces to any networking code is the Java streams concept. You may have come across the concept and term *stream* in other languages. C++ makes heavy use of the term for anything dealing with I/O. Java also associates it with I/O but on a completely different level.

Java makes the distinction between the actual process of doing the I/O actions, and the facilities needed to make that action occur. The result is the ultimate in flexible code. I can write some code to output binary data. The first implementation sends it to a file, and then later, if I change only a couple of lines of code, the entire lot now works with a socket connection. In other languages this is usually not the case.

Providing Core Services

At the bottom end of Java are the core services. These are I/O services that must interact with the operating system in order to achieve their goal (byte arrays are the one exception). Sockets, files, and pipes between applications are all dependent on the services of the underlying operating system.

The core services are just one step above the OS-dependent implementations. They are always based on the Input/OutputStream classes (or Reader/Writer classes for unicode text support). Unfortunately, the way that stream access is granted to each type is different. For a socket, you directly ask for the streams with `getInputStream` and `getOutput Stream`, while for files you pass the `FileOutputStream` an instance of the file that you want to use or just give it the filename in the constructor.

Commonality between all these access methods belongs in the basic functionality of providing the lowest level access to the data. That is, each just provides an array of bytes that must then be read and interpreted or written out. The core services do not attempt to make any meaning out of the array of bytes, as that is left to the higher levels of abstraction.

Providing core services means that you need to provide the basic requirements for any user. Streams represent a series of bytes presented in the same order that they were created. Missing so much as one byte from that stream can mean an awfully big mess. The problem with streams is that they are just that—a stream of information that starts, and cannot be reversed. Once information starts to come in, the consumer must deal with every single byte. Those bytes must all be read and dealt with—even if it is just to discard them because they are not needed.

NOTE: Streams that support marking may be rewound to the last point that the stream was marked. All data prior to that mark is discarded. You can check to see if a stream supports marking by calling `markSupported()`.

From Bytes to Values

For most applications, a stream of just bytes is not particularly useful; they need to be turned into something. While the core services provide a stream of bytes, another layer of classes is needed to interpret those bytes into usable values by your application.

During the course of the first few chapters of the book you have already come across numerous examples of the pairing of low-level services and a higher-level writer. In Chapter 5, "Writing TCP Communications," you saw the use of a socket input stream with a PrintWriter. The socket provided the low-level byte handling while the PrintWriter took the job of taking your Java Strings and writing that into the byte array. At the other end of the network connection, a PrintReader then did the job of converting those bytes back into Java Strings.

Why do we need two levels of handling for stream communications? Perhaps the best reason is for flexibility of the code. A user can change the underlying output device with very minimal changes to the code and make no changes to the business end of writing/reading the protocols. Another reason is that it removes the petty details of byte ordering and interpretation that is required to ensure consistent interpretation. The higher-level classes are customized for different purposes. A PrintWriter is designed for text, while a DataOutputStream is for primitive types. More relevant to this chapter is the ObjectOutputStream, which is designed for writing out the contents of a particular object instance.

Writing a Serialized Object

Our first step in writing an object to a stream is to make sure it implements one of the two interfaces, `Serializable` or `Externalizable`. The choice of which to use depends on your application. I have found most of the time that it is more convenient to use the standard serialization provided with the `Serializable` interface than having to deal with versioning and other complexities that are present in the alternative.

Setting Up for Serialization

Before an object can be serialized, we must first have a stream to serialize the object to. With the basic stream constructed, we also need the high-level stream to deal with writing the object instance out. This is provided by the ObjectOutputStream and uses the low-level stream that has been created.

For example, if you wanted to send a serialized object to a TCP network connection, you would need the following code:

```
// Create the socket
Socket socket = null;
try {
  socket = new Socket("somehost.com", 1234);
}
catch(UnknownHostException e1) {
  return;
}
catch(IOException e2) {
  return;
}
// Get the output stream
OutputStream os = null;
try {
  os = socket.getOutputStream();
}
catch(IOException e3) {
  return;
}
// Make this into an Object stream
ObjectOutputStream output = null;
try {
  output = new ObjectOutputStream(os);
}
catch(IOException e4) {
}
```

I've left out the nice exception handling. There could be a lot of code reduction by putting everything into a single try/catch block, but I wanted to point out what exceptions were generated for each part of the code.

Basic Object Writing

With the stream setup complete, you can now start to write your objects to it. The simplest method is just to call the `writeObject` method with the object that you would like to write as the parameter. If you have

Figure 7-3
Writing out an array
of objects.

```
for(int i = 0; i < array.length; i++)
  try {
    output.writeObject(array[i]);
  }
catch(IOException e5) {
  // ignore and continue ??
}
```

multiple objects to write, such as an array, you just call writeObject multiple times, as shown in Figure 7-3.

The good part about just writing entire objects like this is that if the object passed in contains references to other objects (say as a linked list), then those referenced objects will be written out automatically. In the linked list example, your code would only need to write out the first object, and the rest of the list would be written automatically for you.

Besides just writing the objects themselves, you might like to do some fancier things like including extra information with the stream. This extra information might help you decide which of the objects to retrieve out of the stream and which to discard. The stream includes methods for writing out all of the basic primitives and strings. You can use these methods outside the basic classes to add your own information.

Say we also wanted to include the index number of the array before each class in the stream as well. The resulting code snippet is shown in Figure 7-4.

After all the objects and extra information have been written, you must call the flush() method on the stream. This ensures that the data, which is usually buffered within the top-level stream, is sent to

Figure 7-4
Including extra infor-
mation with the
object stream.

```
for(int i = 0; i < array.length; i++)
  try {
    output.writeInt(i);
    output.writeObject(array[i]);
  }
  catch(IOException e5) {
    // ignore and continue ??
  }
```

the destination. You may remember this problem coming up in the TCP example back in Chapter 5. If the client did not call flush on the socket's stream, then the server never saw the information. The same principle applies here—regardless of whether the core service provider is a socket or file or any other stream.

Building a Customized Serialization

If you aren't happy with the standard object-writing routines, you can always provide your own. These may allow you to implement a more efficient serialization, or you may only want to write certain pieces of data to the stream, not the whole object. The methods to implement depend on which of the two serialization interfaces you choose to implement.

`Serializable` **Interface** If you implement the `Serializable` interface, then you will need to provide implementations of the `write Object` and `readObject` methods. These methods are required to exactly implement the following signatures:

```
private void readObject(java.io.ObjectInputStream stream)
    throws IOException, ClassNotFoundException;

private void writeObject(java.io.ObjectOutputStream stream)
    throws IOException;
```

The `writeObject` method has the ObjectOutputStream that the object should write its information to. The stream is already constructed so you can start to write information directly to it. The same methods that you use to annotate extra information outside the class can also be used to write the contents of the object.

The `writeOutput` method can be used to selectively write contents of the class. However, you also might want to consider using it to privately control what data gets used internally when the object is reconstructed. For example, the first thing that might get written to the stream is a flag indicating some condition. Then, your code uses this flag to decide whether to set an internal variable, or leaves it as a default value.

A twist on this option is using the flag to override something that has already been written. Say your flag indicated whether some condition would be held internally, or whether it should be set back to a default. There is only one variable that is affected by this flag and it is marked with `private` access. The external writer of the class cannot do anything, as the variable is marked private, therefore only code internal to that object is able to change the value of this condition variable. It would be really annoying to have to write the code that individually writes every single field to the stream.

What you really want to do is use the default write of the object and change something only if needed. Luckily you can. The `default WriteObject()` of the ObjectOutputStream can be called only internally to the class. This dumps the entire contents of the class to the stream using the default write protocol. You can then use the other variables written to the stream to control your actions. For example:

```
public class SerialTest
  implements Serializable
{
  private boolean some_flag=false;

  private void writeObject(ObjectOutputStream stream)
    throws IOException
  {
    try {
      stream.writeBoolean(some_flag_condition);
      stream.defaultWriteObject();
    }
    catch(IOException e) {
    }
  }
}
```

At the other end, the reading code can read in the flag, then read the default object information and set the value of the private flag according to some set of rules.

`Externalizable` Interface　Sometimes your code needs more control over exactly what gets written to the stream. If this is the case then the `Externalizable` interface is probably more along the lines of what you want. Corresponding to the `write/readObject` methods are `write External` and `readExternal` methods of the interface.

```
public interface Externalizable extends Serializable {
        public void writeExternal(ObjectOutput out)
                throws IOException;
        public void readExternal(ObjectInput in)
```

```
                    throws IOException, java.lang.ClassNotFoundException;
}
```

If changing between the two interfaces was as simple as renaming a couple of methods, there would be no gain. Externalizable adds one extra requirement: The super classes are not automatically written to the stream. You are required to look after any information that may be needed within your own methods. Also, there is now no default writing of an object (note that the argument is now `ObjectOutput` rather than `ObjectOutputStream`). Your code is required to look after all the formatting details. The superinterface `DataOutput` of `ObjectOutput` provides primitive level support but does not include a `writeObject()` method.

Superclasses that contain a collection of private variables may cause you some problems. If your class is not the original implementation of the `Externalizable` interface then you should just be able to call the superclass implementation and let that handle it. Otherwise, you must write out whatever you have access to. As you can see, this can be a bit restrictive in what you have access to, so the `Externalizable` interface is usually better used in a very shallow hierarchy.

One major thing to look out for if you are worried about security is that these methods are declared public. All users can call these methods with their own stream and dump the contents of your class.

Advanced Customization

If you feel that the level of customization presented so far is still not enough for you, then you might find the next section useful. In the advanced customization stakes, you can selectively place objects in the stream, add extra class information, partially flush the output and reset the stream.

Replacing Objects   Earlier in the chapter an example was given of adding extra information to the object stream for setting flags. A fairly simple example was given of just replacing a variable. The `replace Object` method allows you to go one step further by selectively replacing objects in the stream on the fly.

Replacing objects cannot be done from within a class itself; it can be performed only by a subclass of the ObjectOutputStream. First, the stream must be trusted to be allowed to do this. There is no way for you to set this trust programatically. You can check whether you are allowed to do this by first calling `enableReplaceObject()`. If your implementation is considered to be a security risk, it will generate a `Security Exception`. Since the `enableReplaceObject` method is declared protected, this means that you will be able to check for this in the constructor or some other method only within your derived class.

After you have passed the security check, every time that you have an object to write, the `replaceObject` method is called. At this time, you have the option to just pass the object back through the return value, or replace it with another object. If you replace it with another object, then either the two must be compatible, so that reading one out with a standard stream on the other end works, or the reader stream must deal with the reverse substitution. It is legal to return null as the object to be substituted in, but the usual precautions must be taken to prevent `NullPointerExceptions` for any class that references this object.

`ReplaceObject` is called only once for each reference. Remember that if an object has multiple references to it, then only one instance is written and a pointer is kept to that reference in the stream for each subsequent write. The `replaceObject` method follows the same rule— it is called only the first time that the reference is encountered. Also, if multiple references are made to the object at different levels of the class hierarchy for the original object, then the replaced object must be compatible, otherwise `ClassCastExceptions` will be generated. If you are not watching for these exceptions in your code, then this is bound to stop the sending of the outgoing stream.

SECURITY: *Replacing objects in the stream requires two permissions to be enabled in addition to any others you may need. First you need to allow subclassing of `ObjectInputStream` and `ObjectOutputStream`. To allow the complete replacement of objects on the stream, you will need to explicitly allow these with permissions. This can be accomplished by adding the following to your policy file:*

```
permission java.io.SerializablePermission
"enableSubclassImplementation"
permission java.ioSerializablePermission "enableSubstitution";
```

Per-Class Information   Occasionally, you may need to add extra information to the stream about a particular class. The `annotateClass` method is different from the techniques used previously in that it is only called once per class, not once per instance of that class. After the class descriptor has been written to the stream, your class is given its opportunity to add information to that when the VM calls the `annotate` `Class` method. As always, you must remember to implement the corresponding read method (`resolveClass`) so that your stream information does not become corrupt by reading incorrectly. One small catch is that arrays are not considered to be a class for this method.

Managing the Stream   The last way to customize your code handling is the management of the stream itself. First, you may wish to clear the stream. In the previous chapter, you may remember that every time we wanted to write a new DatagramPacket, we just cleared the existing stream of any data by calling `reset()`. Reset in this context performs a similar function. It clears the underlying stream of all information and resets as though it was just newly constructed. The effect of this is dependent on the underlying core service that previous objects were written to.

Output streams, like files and byte arrays, would be completely erased of their contents (the stream marker would be set back to the beginning of the array or file). Any new information written would overwrite the previously written information. If the output was a socket, then two things could happen. Information that has already been received at the other end is untouchable—you cannot erase it. Objects that have been read before the `flush()` method has been called are erased like files and byte arrays.

An unusual method provided by the ObjectOutputStream is the `drain()` method. When called, this method flushes the data from the ObjectOutputStream into the underlying stream, but does not call the `flush()` method on that stream. This may be handy if you have constructed a number of object output streams that feed into the single underlying stream. How would you end up in this situation? Well, with the `Externalizable` interface you might decide to create your own instance of the ObjectOutputStream. At the end of the `writeExternal` method, you wish to close that stream so you first call drain and then close the stream. This leaves the underlying management of the underlying stream to the caller.

Reading a Serialized Object

Having gone through the process of writing out the objects, the process of reading them back in is almost the exact reverse process. Wherever you see the word *write*, replace that with the word *read* and you are almost done. If only life was that simple!

Basic Object Reading

Whatever you do on the writing end, should be matched with the identical reverse process on the reading end. Deciding to use the default serialization with the writing of objects will require that you use the default reading process as well.

In basic programs, it is pretty much that simple. Having implemented the `Serializable` interface, the reading is also taken care of by the VM. In Figure 7-3 we wrote out an array of classes. To read in that same array, the example in Figure 7-5 would be used.

How do we determine the number of objects to be read? Well, this is a great example of needing to write extra information to the object stream. The example in Figure 7-4 might have been more useful if we had first written out an integer which was the number of elements in the array to read rather than the index number before each object that was written. We could then have read that in as the first thing in Figure 7-5 and used that to construct an array of the correct length. As the example stands, we are reading in the blind and would need to catch one of the stream exceptions to determine when we had run out of objects.

Customized Reading

Unlike writing of objects, reading of objects is much more likely to be a customized implementation. In a way, this is similar to cloning. While

Figure 7-5
Reading in object written out in Figure 7-3.

```
SomeClass[] array = new SomeClass[length];

for(int i = 0; i < array.length; i++)
  try {
    array[i] = (SomeClass)input.readObject();
  }
  catch(IOException e5) {
    // ignore and continue ??
  }
```

the basic clone is OK, invariably you end up providing your own implementation of the clone method. The same goes for object reading. Why is this? Well, to start with, you may want to set to default values some items that have been declared transient—a vector of listeners or a file reference, for example.

To start you on the way, you will need to implement either the read Object method for the Serializable interface or readExternal method for the Externalizable interface. These are the starting points for you to read in object information. From here, you can go in one of two directions.

Serializable Objects If you have implemented the Serializable interface, you can now read the object directly in, or you can build a customized read which only fills in the bits that you need. The most common approach is somewhere in between.

At the time the readObject method has been called, an instance of your class has already been created. That is, readObject is reading information pertinent to that particular instance of that class. However, at the point of entry to the readObject method, no information has been assigned to the internal variables; you have a virgin instance of that class.

NOTE;   *If you have multiple references to an object instance, the* read Object *method is only called the first time that another object makes reference to that instance. This is in keeping with the instance identifiers mentioned in the "Multiple References to a Class Instance" section previously in this chapter.*

If you had a default serialization of the object (you didn't implement the writeObject method, for instance) you will want to read the entire object of the class and then replace some key pieces of information. As you have no idea of the order in which variables and the subclasses were written out, you will need to rely on the stream to do that for you. Luckily, the ObjectInputStream gives you the defaultReadObject method, which reads in the entire class definition. It is recommended in the specifications that this be the first thing that is done in your read Object method.

This takes care of the basic initialization of all the variables, other object references, and subclasses. This method is available only inside the `readObject` method; if you attempt to call it outside of this method it will throw a `NotActiveException`.

Having called the `defaultReadObject` method, you are now free to make whatever other adjustments are needed. For example, you might want to create new vectors of some information, open up some file for more information, or do any number of other things.

Externalizable Objects   As mentioned previously, externalizable objects do not provide anything for you. If your class is some distance up the class hierarchy and is the first to implement the `Externalizable` interface, you could be in for a very interesting time.

If you know what has been written out with the `writeExternal` method, implementing a `readExternal` should not be a problem. You just read things in the same order that they were written out.

There are a couple of points to remember with externalizable objects: First, if your class has overridden the `readExternal` method of a base class, `super.readExternal()` should always be called first; then you deal with your own specific code. Second, `readExternal` is public, which means other objects could potentially gain access to your internal class information—be very careful about what you provide, as this is a potential security hazard. Last, make sure that you read things in exactly the order that you wrote them out and watch out for versioning problems!

Applications of Serialization

The ability to write out whole classes and data structures in one hit is not particularly exciting by itself. Having the ability to write these to any arbitrary destination is. One immediate use for serialization is a binary file format for writing out data between runs of an application. Now, instead of having to write your own save and load routines, you can just write the entire classes to file and read them back in with little more effort than opening and then closing the file streams themselves.

Persistence

A variation on this theme is persistence of data. Because you are able to write out the entire class file and all its associated data links, persistence not only of the data itself, but also structure, is now guaranteed. In other languages, the storage of the data structure is easy, but recreating the links between items (say a linked list) requires much more effort from the programmer in reading the data back in.

Most modern databases now include the ability to store binary data. Combining this with serialization is a powerful tool for creating persistent data stores for large applications. A typical binary stream from a serialized set of classes may be 50 Kbytes in size, but the data linking information and other attributes stored alongside the data in those classes are worth the object size. The database is used as a storage mechanism for data, and the application can then retrieve this at will, and in any order. An example of this I have seen is a database that stores messages in the database, and the associated class is used to provide security through encryption and access keys.

Message Handling

Perhaps the biggest current user of serialization is Java itself. RMI bases most of its functionality on serialization to pass classes to and return them from the remote objects.

In order not to limit what RMI can do, calls to the remote objects need to look just like any other method call. This includes the ability to pass objects in as parameters and return them in the normal fashion. To achieve this, RMI sets up a socket connection and then serializes the object instances over that link to the methods on the other end. To both ends of the party, they appear to have the objects themselves to work with.

NOTE: *Passing of parameters with RMI is different from normal Java methods where objects are passed by reference. Instead, a remote object actually receives them as a pass by value—an entire copy of the object is made and passed in, not a reference to the original object itself.*

You can always build your own system along similar lines. Instead of using all the setup costs involved in RMI, you can create a simple socket connection, serialize the data into that socket stream, and reconstruct it at the other end. This is most useful if you want to provide some sort of data encapsulation. For example, you might want to pass a set of geographic coordinates, but you don't know what sort of format the application on the other end requires. (At last count there were about 60 different coordinate systems for mapping the Earth!) You simply build a geographic class with the appropriate `get` methods, and let the receiver ask for the information in the form that it wants.

Developing Applications

Almost every useful application requires the ability to store some sort of data to disk and then read it back in at a later date. With the advent of serialization this is extremely quick and easy to do. Simply serialize your data classes to disk, and then read them back again to open them.

In developing an application, serialization can be a bit of a nightmare to handle. In the rapidly changing code you are developing, versioning issues become a real problem. If you are keeping the code developed in-house then for the beginning, some other form of binary file format might be a better choice. The choice of implementing `Externalizable` or `Serializable` really depends on what your needs are, and what is happening with the code. I generally work with the following rules:

I tend to favor extending the `Externalizable` interface if I have a very shallow class hierarchy or early in the development life cycle with rapidly changing code (e.g., prototyping). The `Externalizable` interface is always extended by the lowest class in that hierarchy with all the derived classes overriding the `readExternal/writeExternal` methods. `Externalizable` is very close to being a basic custom binary file format, with the extra advantages of serialization. The values written out are only the ones that matter, and hence Externalizable classes are very efficient in disk space.

However, if you are late in the code development life cycle when you choose to use Serialization, or the class hierarchy is particularly deep, then I would recommend using the `Serializable` interface. However, you will pay a performance penalty with this, as there is much more data to be read and written each time. Watch out for structures like Hashtables and vectors that extend `Serializable` and will automatically write out their contents.

Summary

Now that you've been given a basic run-through of Serialization, it is time to use it for some practical purposes. During the chapter we discussed briefly how Serialization is used as the core of RMI. In the next chapter we'll look at using RMI and how Serialization forms a part of that.

Learn to use Serialization and all of the tricks involved in it. Like cloning of objects, it can be both extremely simple and annoyingly complex at the same time. Many times you will be trying to debug something that has been written to disk and read back only to find that something has been serialized that you didn't want to. Watch out for the event listener structures; I guarantee these will be one of the largest sources of bugs in Serialization code!

Remote Method Invocation

Along with serialization, Java 1.1 added another new feature—the ability to use objects that exist on another machine as though they were just part of the local application. This can lead to some incredibly powerful applications programming concepts.

Remote Object Concepts

Creating, managing, and interacting with remote object instances is not a new idea. There have been many attempts to create standards based on this over many years. The most notable to date has been Component Object Request Broker Architecture, or just CORBA for short. Microsoft also has its own proprietary standard called DCOM (Distributed Component Object Model).

Sun invented its own architecture called Remote Method Invocation, or RMI. As you will see shortly, it has many similarities to the other architectures. What is this remote object concept all about anyway?

RMI versus Sockets, URLs, and JDBC

Remote objects are a way of abstracting the client/server approach so that the programmer needs to know only what functionality and what data need to be passed to the server, without having to know how to get it there and back.

At the very lowest level, any communication between two machines requires the use of the network. Invariably, that involves the use of a socket connection. Over that connection data must flow. How to interpret that data is the responsibility of the application at each end.

In the very early days of computing, the person writing the application also had to write all of the code to deal with the communications between machines, right down to the reading of pieces of information from the wire and dealing with error checking. As time progressed, coders started to move up the food chain. The University of California, Berkeley, released an abstract way of dealing with network connections called sockets, which has become the backbone of IP communications today over the Internet. Shortly thereafter, a bunch of protocols for things like email, file transfer, and other activities were agreed upon. Libraries were written to abstract these details away yet again. Programmers wanting to do their own thing could still write their own protocols, but the basic processes were covered. During the late 1980s and early 1990s, people started looking at the idea of creating yet another abstract layer—this time completely hiding the idea of the network connection and dealing only with entities on either end. It still required the use of socket connections; however, what was sent over those connections and how they were established was completely hidden from the programmer. In effect, this was the start of the remote object trends for networking applications.

An application must decide where to place itself relative to that network connection. Sockets are the lowest level and have been dealt with already in this book. How does RMI sit relative to the other networking parts of Java such as JDBC and ContentHandlers?

RMI sits at about the same level as JDBC. That is, it provides a similar level of abstraction above the networking protocols. ContentHandlers are used to interpret data coming from a URL-based socket connection, so that makes them lower on the list compared to both JDBC and RMI.

RMI and CORBA

One of the often repeated questions is "How does RMI relate to CORBA?" They are basically two different solutions, with different assumptions, to the same problem.

CORBA provides object abstraction and management capabilities at a language-neutral level. You might write your client code in C++ while the server has its object code written in Smalltalk. CORBA has defined a language-independent way of describing the services provided by a standard called Interface Definition Language (IDL). When a client requests an object from a server, the capabilities are returned and defined using IDL. The communications then take place purely on the basis of this definition. This definition can be mapped to any language. For example, there are IDL libraries available for Java, PERL, Visual Basic, C/C++, and almost any other language you can think of.

The Java designers decided that CORBA was initially too heavy for the capabilities they required. Specifically, they wanted something that was suitable to the Java philosophy. Also, there is a key element missing from CORBA—there was no way to pass object instances as part of method parameters. You are limited to primitive types or arrays of them.

Today, RMI objects and CORBA objects are incompatible. You cannot access one with the other technology. Sun has committed to implementing a version of RMI using CORBA. It is likely that this will produce a version of RMI with reduced capabilities, considering the difficulties mentioned previously. To overcome this, Sun has also committed itself to work with the Object Management Group (the group responsible for the CORBA standard) on filling in the holes between the two.

NOTE: *IDL and CORBA are part of the JDK 1.2 core classes. Check the org.omg.CORBA packages provided as part of the core implementation.*

Setting Up for RMI

Setting up objects for use as remote instances takes a little more work than just writing a normal Java class. There are a number of steps to go through before your application will become ready to use.

Files Needed for RMI

Building an RMI-based system requires at a minimum three files. First you will need an interface that defines what methods are going to be used. Next you will need an implementation of that interface—the server code. Finally you will need something that uses the server code—the client.

The reason for needing an interface is that both the client and the server must know at compile time what requests will be made of the server. The interface also provides a level of abstraction so that the server code implementation can be changed without disturbing the client.

We'll get to the implementation details of these files shortly, but first we need to know a bit more about the tools required to implement our RMI code.

RMIC—The RMI Compiler

Another compiler? Sort of. During the coding of your classes, you will still need to use the normal javac compiler. In your Java class files, you

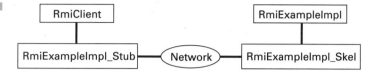

Figure 8-1
The flow of control
from the client to the
server and back.

are writing what you want to access, but there is still no way of defining how to access them—apart from saying that you want RMI to do it.

RMIC provides the glue between your code and the networking code. It takes your serverside implementation of the code and produces two extra files—a skeleton and a stub. In these files are hidden all the low-level networking code. The stub is located on the client and the skeleton is located on the server. The stub provides a proxy that generates the actual calls to the skeleton, which then forwards the requests onto the real implementation instance on the server. The process is illustrated in Figure 8-1.

Running RMIC   Running RMIC is similar to running javac. You provide it with the name of the class that you want to make a remote object and perhaps an optional directory, and it does the rest for you. Say you have a class RmiExampleImpl that lives in the package rwjn.chapter8. You would use the following command line:

```
rmic rwjn.chapter8.RmiExampleImpl
```

which would produce the following two files:

```
RmiExampleImpl_Skel.class
RmiExampleImpl_Stub.class
```

both of which belong to the rwjn.chapter8 package. If these belonged to an applet, then you would have them both existing in the same directory on the server. For an application, you will need to create the right directories to correspond to the packages used by the server code.

Changing Code   RMIC takes a signature of the code that you have developed. Changes in the source for RMIC mean that you will need to realign the two again under the following circumstances:

■ If you recompile your server implementation code, you will need to rerun RMIC over it before it will work correctly again. If you change the interface, then both the server and client code will need to be compiled again and hence RMIC will also need to be run.

■ Just changing the client code itself does not require you to rerun RMIC.

RMI Registry

Having the server code and client code almost completes the package. The final part is something that listens for RMI connections and deals with the issues of loading the correct class instances and connection and termination of clients. The RMI registry is responsible for doing this.

Normally the registry is run from the command line during code development. The reason for this is that it takes the current class image and serves that to clients. If you change the server code implementation, the changes will not be picked up by the client. You need to stop the registry and restart it with the new code. Once your code has been deployed to a real server, it is usually run as a demon process.

The application is called `rmiregistry` and takes one optional argument—the port number for listening to requests. On Unix machines, the process can be backgrounded with

```
rmiregistry &
```

while on Microsoft-sourced operating systems you will need to make use of the start command such as

```
start /B rmiregistry <port_number>
```

■■ ■■ ■■ ■■ ■■ ■■ ■■ ■■ ■■ ■■ ■■ ■■ ■■ ■■ ■■ ■■ ■■ ■■ ■■

SECURITY: *The RMI registry is a Java program just like many of the other facilities. As such, it is subject to the same security restrictions as your other applications. As our code dynamically creates the registry and makes use of many other RMI capabilities, you will need to enable the following permissions for the code in this chapter to run:*

```
permission java.net.SocketPermission "localhost:1024-",
"accept,connect,listen";
```

Depending on the JDK implementation, this may still throw security

errors. Instead of localhost, you may need to explicitly place the name of your machine in the permission statement. RMI does not appear to treat localhost and your machine name as being equivalent.

The RMI Packages

You will be seeing a lot more of the various classes within RMI shortly, but it pays to be aware of the various packages, and what they can provide you the programmer. RMI consists of four packages: `java.rmi`, `java.rmi.dgc`, `java.rmi.registry`, and `java.rmi.server`.

`java.rmi` is the basic class for all the RMI capabilities that you will be using as a client. It consists of the interface that all RMI-capable objects need to implement, classes for object management, and its own security manager. Of course, there is also the large collection of exceptions for the wide variety of networked exceptions that could occur in such an environment.

`java.rmi.dgc` contains classes for dealing with the remote garbage collection (distributed garbage collection, or dgc). It is very rare for a programmer to need the capabilities provided in this package, so it won't be covered in this book.

`java.rmi.registry` contains the basic interface classes for dealing with the registry. The registry is used for containing reference information and lookup capabilties for the remote objects.

`java.rmi.server` holds the classes used on the server side of a remote connection. In RMI terms, a server is any machine that offers an object for remote access. As you will see later, this concept is quite different from the traditional client/server approach. RMI also introduces the idea of customizable socket handling capabilities. This concept is not dealt with until the next chapter, but note that the basic capabilities allow you to substitute in any socket for the underlying connection. This gives you the ability to add in transparent secure network connections, and is quite different to the socket factory for the `java.net.SocketFactory` class.

RMI Server

In contrast to our discussions of the other implementations, this time we will treat the server code first. The first thing that you need to do when writing an RMI solution is to decide on what methods you are going to want for the communications. This decision forms the basis of your interface.

Once again we'll visit our bank client-server system. This time the interface between the two will be using RMI. The capabilities won't change, just the way of accessing them will.

Building the Remote Interface

There are a few simple rules that you need to follow when defining the Remote interface. The interface determines exactly what services the remote object is going to give us. For our bank that means we'll need four methods, one each for deposit, transfer, withdrawal, and selection of an account.

Rules for Remote Interfaces The first rule for writing remote objects is that the interface must be declared as public so that the client code can access it from anywhere. (Remember, the client code may not exist in the same package as the server code and the interface.)

Second, your interface must extend the `java.rmi.Remote` interface. This identifies the object as a remote object. Any methods specified as an extended interface of the Remote interface are available to a remote client. Any others in an implementing class will not. Of course you can have many remote interfaces extended by the one class.

Third, any method that is declared in this interface must throw `java.rmi.RemoteException`. The exception is used to catch any error that may occur because of networking problems or other issues.

Finally, any object reference that is passed as a parameter or as a return value must also extend `java.rmi.Remote` so that it can be marked as a remote object. These objects don't need to go through the same extending of the remote interface like this basic one; they just need to extend the remote interface.

Sending Information to the Server With the preceding rules about the interface design in mind, our first cut at the remote interface would look something like Figure 8-2. In the previous chapters, the communication has always been directly through a network connection.

An interesting aspect of now using a remote object reference is that

Figure 8-2

The `RemoteBank` interface for interacting with the server via RMI.

```java
package rwjn.chapter8.server;
// Standard imports
import java.rmi.*;

// Application specific imports
// none

/**
 * McDuck Bank Server
 * <P>
 * Remote interface definition for communications between the server
 * and the client.
 * <P>
 * @author @vlc.com.au">Justin Couch
 * @version 1.0
 */
public interface RemoteBank extends Remote
{
  /**
   * Select an account for use
   * @param account The ID of the account to use.
   * @exception RemoteException if there is a problem with the
   remote transaction.
   */
  public void select(int account)
    throws RemoteException;
  /**
   * Deposit money in the selected account
   * @param amount The amount of money to deposit
   * @exception RemoteException if there is a problem with the
   remote transaction.
   */
  public void deposit(float amount)
    throws RemoteException;

  /**
   * Withdraw money from the selected account
   * @param amount The amount of money to withdraw
   * @exception RemoteException if there is a problem with the
   remote transaction.
   */
  public void withdraw(float amount)
    throws RemoteException;
  /**
```

Figure 8-2
(*Continued*)

```
    * Transfer money from the selected account to the other account
    * @param amount The amount of money to deposit
    * @exception RemoteException if there is a problem with the
  remote transaction.
    */
  public void transfer(float amount)
    throws RemoteException;
}
```

error conditions no longer form part of the design. It is impossible for the application to mess up the message that is sent. A call to the deposit method on the client results in a direct call to the deposit method on the server, with the exact value specified. There is no chance of an error being made. As a result, we don't need to replicate the error conditions of the previous socket-based clients with similar constructs (either return values or exceptions).

Getting Information Back to the Client   One of the features of our little client/server system so far has been the asynchronous feed of information back from the server to the client. You will notice that the interface defined in the previous section has not defined any way of getting this information back.

We have a number of options, such as using a socket to return the balance information, all of which have been demonstrated before in this book. To the client code, the remote object looks just like any other local object. Java has already set a number of design precedents for us to follow. Java 1.1 introduced the event listener concept for the return of asynchronous information. Why not use the same concept with remote objects? All we need to do is to register our listener interface with the server and it will communicate information back to us.

A previous section laid out the rules regarding remote objects and their design. Since our client class that implements the balance listener is a remote object to the server, our rules specify that it must extend the remote interface. We have only one piece of information to relay back to the client—the balance of the account. Following the design of the previous chapters, we need to include the account number and its balance in the returned information. This naturally leads to the interface given in Figure 8-3.

Figure 8-3
The remote listener
for balance
information.

```
package rwjn.chapter8.server;
// Standard imports
import java.rmi.*;

// Application specific imports
// none

/**
 * McDuck Bank Server
 * <P>
 * Remote interface definition for sending balance information
from
 * the server back to the clients
 * <P>
 * @author <A HREF="mailto:justin@vlc.com.au">Justin Couch</A>
 * @version 1.0
 */
public interface RemoteBalanceListener extends Remote
{
   /**
    * Update the balance information for the nominated account to
    * the following values
    * @param acc The account to update
    * @param value The new balance value
    */
   public void updateBalance(int acc, float value);
}
```

Of course, adding a listener requires that the RemoteBank interface in Figure 8-2 now include two more methods—one to add and one to remove the listeners.

```
public void addBalanceListener(RemoteBalanceListener l)
    throws RemoteException;

public void removeBalanceListener(RemoteBalanceListener l)
    throws RemoteException;
```

Implementing the Server

Now that the remote interface has been completed, finishing the rest of the server is a seemingly trivial task. Just extend the RemoteBank interface and provide an implementation of those methods that talk with the account manager. In reality, it is not that simple. RMI places a number of restrictions on us.

One Object and One Object Only To register an object with the RMI registry as a remote object you must use the Naming class. You bind an object to a particular URL. If you examine the bind and rebind methods of the `java.rmi.Naming` class you will find that it takes a string (its URL) and a `RemoteObject` instance. That is, you bind only one instance of an object to a name. The clients, when they request a remote object, all get a reference to the one object instance. This is completely unlike a network connection where you can start a new thread for each client and each has its own state. As far as the object instance sitting on the server is concerned, it has no idea how many clients are connected to it; all it gets are method calls. This makes dealing with individual client states more difficult to achieve.

There are three ways of dealing with the problem. The most obvious is to include some sort of client ID information parameter in every method. The server side code then goes away and looks up that particular client's current state, then processes the request based on this information. The second way of dealing with this is a variation of the first. If your code has extended the `UnicastRemoteObject` class, then you can ask for the name of the current calling client with `getClientHost()`. This string can be used to perform the lookup of per-client information.

Alternatively, we could create multiple instances of the remote object and give each a separate name. The responsibility then falls on the client end to make sure that it is talking to the correct object instance for what has been selected.

NOTE: *Although it may be possible to have multiple client objects on the side, the RMI specification only provides for a single point-to-point communication between a single object—referenced by URL—and all clients with the* UnicastRemoteObject. *See "Advanced RMI" section below for more information on alternative approaches.*

For illustrative purposes, we will take this second approach to our server. Naturally, we are going to need to make some more changes to our `RemoteBank` interface from Figure 8-2. There is no need for the select method any more. Selection of which account to use is done at the client end after retrieving references to both remote accounts. The client then makes the call to the individual account to make a transaction.

Dealing with the account balance listeners is also an interesting problem. We could modify the listeners so that they are individual for each account, thus requiring you to register as a listener with each remote object instance. Another approach is to create a second remote object that handles only listener information. The final approach is to make the method implementations on the server end static, and therefore you will only need to register with any class only once.

Considering the solution that we've taken to have multiple objects available through RMI, the most sensible solution to the problem is to create a second remote object type that deals just with the management of the remote listeners.

Having come to the above decisions, we now have the two remote interfaces defined in Figure 8-4.

Implementing the Remote Interfaces With the interfaces now defined, we need to make real implementations of them. With the RemoteBankInterface interface, I created a RemoteAccount class. Earlier in the chapter you were presented with a set of rules that relate to the interfaces themselves. The actual implementation of those interfaces is also subject to a set of rules.

If you examine the bind and rebind calls again you will notice that the second parameter must be a subclass of RemoteObject. RemoteObject is the glue that goes between the skeletons generated by RMIC and your methods in the interface. It is RMI's way of ensuring that you have the correct communications methods by extending `java.lang.Object` to provide the capabilities of remote objects.

Your implementation of the class must extend `RemoteObject` in order to provide remote capabilities. At what level you then extend that depends on what you require in terms of services. Java 1.1 really provides only one option—the `UnicastRemoteObject` and although Java 2 also has Activatable objects, these objects aren't usable by our system. Both of our classes for providing remote capabilities to the client extend this class. For example the RemoteAccount class is declared as follows:

```
import java.rmi.server.UnicastRemoteObject;

public class RemoteAccount extends UnicastRemoteObject
  implements RemoteBankInterface
```

Figure 8-4
The final two remote
object definitions. (a)
For the listeners; (b)
for an account.

```
package rwjn.chapter8.server;
// Standard imports
import java.rmi.*;

// Application specific imports
// none

/**
 * McDuck Bank Server
 * <P>
 * Remote interface definition for communications between the server
 * and the client.
 * <P>
 * @author <A HREF="mailto:justin@vlc.com.au">Justin Couch</A>
 * @version 1.0
 */
public interface RemoteFeedbackManager extends Remote
{
  /**
   * Add a listener for feedback of the balance information from the
   * client.
   * @param l The listener to add
   * @exception RemoteException if there is a problem with the
remote transaction.
   */
  public void addBalanceListener(RemoteBalanceListener l)
    throws RemoteException;

  /**
   * Remove a listener for feedback of the balance information from
   * the client.
   * @param l The listener to remove
   * @exception RemoteException if there is a problem with the
remote transaction.
   */
  public void removeBalanceListener(RemoteBalanceListener l)
    throws RemoteException;
}
```

(a)

Figure 8-4
(*Continued*)

```
package rwjn.chapter8.server;

// Standard imports
import java.rmi.*;

// Application specific imports
// none

/**
 * McDuck Bank Server
 * <P>
 * Remote interface definition for communications between the server
 * and the client.
 * <P>
 * @author <A HREF="mailto:justin@vlc.com.au">Justin Couch</A>
 * @version 1.0
 */
public interface RemoteBankInterface extends Remote
{
  /**
   * Deposit money in the selected account
   * @param amount The amount of money to deposit
   * @exception RemoteException if there is a problem with the
remote
   *     transaction.
   */
  public void deposit(float amount)
    throws RemoteException;

  /**
   * Withdraw money from the selected account
   * @param amount The amount of money to withdraw
   * @exception RemoteException if there is a problem with the
remote transaction.
   */
  public void withdraw(float amount)
    throws RemoteException;

  /**
   * Transfer money from the selected account to the other account
   * @param amount The amount of money to deposit
   * @exception RemoteException if there is a problem with the
remote
   *     transaction.
   */
  public void transfer(float amount)
    throws RemoteException;
}
```

(*b*)

165

A result of extending `UnicastRemoteObject` is that its constructor throws a `RemoteException` if it cannot make the contact. In most instances, I simply make sure that the derived class constructors pass on the exception to the invoking class; this way, it can stop attempting any following actions such as binding, if our class cannot fulfill its duty as a remote object.

Internally, the two classes can then do as they please in dealing with the account manager class. One point that you should note is that the constructor of the object should never be responsible for registering itself with the RMI registry. As this example application illustrates, there might well be two or more instances of the same object registered with the registry. Attempting to accomplish this in the object constructor ends up with only one instance being registered, because binding a new instance to an already bound URL results in the old URL one being removed.

Registering the Objects   With the properly constructed class instances, all we need to do to complete the start-up code is register them with the RMI registry. As has been pointed out a few times already, this is done through the Naming class.

In order to be consistent with the code structure of the other servers, I've created a separate NetworkServer class. Unlike the other code so far, this class does almost nothing except perform the initial startup of the remote objects. Once these objects have been bound, it performs no useful task.

At the top of the class I have defined strings that represent the three URLs—one for each object instance that we are exporting. To make the code flexible, the URLs are created dynamically from the local host IP address that is retrieved through the InetAddress class. Three complete URLs are constructed, and these URLs used as the basis of the bind call.

One important aspect of any program, even test ones like this system, is security. Before we even start playing with objects, we want to make sure that the system is set up correctly. RMI provides its own custom security manager that I always recommend using. It limits what can be done on an application to only those things needed by RMI to function correctly. However, the needs of individual applications may vary so you may need to implement another security manager, or run with the default.

Figure 8-5
Binding Objects to
remote URLs.

```
RemoteAccount account_a;
RemoteAccount account_b;
FeedbackManager balance_manager;

// bind them to the registry
try {
  account_a = new RemoteAccount(0, mgr);
  account_b = new RemoteAccount(1, mgr);

  balance_manager = new FeedbackManager();

  Naming.rebind(base_url + ACCOUNT_A_URL, account_a);
  Naming.rebind(base_url + ACCOUNT_B_URL, account_b);
  Naming.rebind(base_url + FEEDBACK_URL, balance_manager);
  System.out.println("Remote objects bind complete");
}
catch(RemoteException re) {
  System.out.println("rmiregistry has not been started " + re);
}
catch(MalformedURLException mue) {
  System.out.println("Incorrect RMI URL format " + mue);
}
```

With all the preamble complete, we can now get on with the job of registering our classes. The code in Figure 8-5 is taken from the NetworkServer constructor to illustrate the final steps needed to get our remote objects running.

NOTE: *I always like to put a* `println` *in to say that the bind operation has been successful. Just one of those little assurances that everything is working OK, particularly when the server has much more complex start-up routines than this.*

Completing the Server Setup Once all the code compiles correctly, there are only a few short steps left to complete. First, we need to generate the stubs and skeletons of the remote objects using RMIC. In the top-level code directory, simply type the following command at the prompt:

```
rmic -d . rwjn.chapter8.server.RemoteAccount \
  rwjn.chapter8.server.FeedbackManager
```

This generates the stub and skeleton classes, and makes sure that they are located in the correct directory without your having to manually move them.

To run the server and make sure that everything is OK, just start the RMI registry as shown previously, and then use Java or jre to start the server class:

```
c:\>start rmiregistry
c:\>java RMIServer
```

The next thing that you should see come up on the command line is the message that says the bind operation is OK. That's it; we now have a complete functioning RMI server waiting for a client.

Starting Your Own Registry   Unless you are intending to start many different Java processes that all use RMI, the idea of separately starting up the RMIRegistry from the command line can quickly become a pain. Because there would normally be only one RMI application server instance running per server, the RMI APIs include a programmatic way of starting the registry. The `java.rmi.registry` package contains everything you need to get started.

The registry package does not contain much—only the `Locate Registry` class is really of interest in everyday programming situations. In this class you can find out if a registry is already running on a machine (variations of the `getRegistry()` method) or start a new one (`createRegistry()`).

To maintain consistency with the other servers, the code to create the registry is located in the RMIServer class. After reading in the command-line arguments, the registry is created. (I assume that there is not one already running on the machine.)

```
import java.rmi.registry.*;
import java.rmi.RemoteException;
import rwjn.chapter5.server.AccountManager;
import rwjn.chapter8.server.NetworkServer;

public class RMIServer
{
  public static void main(String[] args)
```

```
{
  ...
  // start the RMI registry
  try
  {

    LocateRegistry.createRegistry(Registry.REGISTRY_PORT);
  }
  catch(RemoteException re)
  {
    System.out.println("Error creating registry");
    System.out.println(re);
    return;
  }

  // start the account handler
  AccountManager acc_mgr = new AccountManager();

  // start the network server
  new NetworkServer(port_number, acc_mgr);
  }
}
```

And that is all there is to starting a new registry. Note that there is no real need to keep the reference to the registry object returned from the `createRegistry()` call. This may be needed if you wish to bind objects on a remote registry or other similar operations.

Design Discussions

Before we start looking at the client side code, there are a couple of areas that need some further discussion. The solution presented so far is not what you are likely to implement in a real solution. Most of the design was developed with teaching points in mind. So, in a real server, what sort of decisions would you be looking at?

Single or Many Remote Objects   In the design presented, to get around the multiple account problem and only a single object instance for any one RMI URL, we made two instances and shared them out as separate objects. Most systems will be designed to have many clients acting on the one server.

Sharing out multiple objects all with separate URLs has a number of drawbacks. Obviously, the most noticeable one is the lack of scalability for large systems. In our test client we knew that we were operating with only two accounts. Real banks would have thousands or millions of accounts. Having a separate remote object instance for every possible account is completely out of the question. In a traditional socket-based approach, there would be no problem with this, as each client would consume an incoming socket only when it needed to connect. For its million accounts, a bank might have only a couple of thousand simultaneous clients, each of which might be accessing a couple of different accounts. Have you noticed the difference yet?

Socket-based systems are completely oriented around how many clients are supported. Once a connection is established, many different services can be controlled through a single connection. However, remote objects are those services themselves, and they have little or no knowledge of how many clients are requesting them. Scalability in a remote object server is defined by how many different services are offered, while in a socket system it is defined by the number of clients. Designing an object server uses a completely different set of rules to gauge what code should be placed on the server and what on the client.

Listener Design Close inspection of the listener structure on the server reveals that quite a bit of optimization could have been done. The `RemoteBalanceListener` could have just extended `Balance Listener` and clients could have registered immediately into the account manager, eliminating the need for the extra remote object. A couple of extra lines of checking code in the account manager to make sure we don't add the same listener twice and we could have cut out a couple of extra classes.

Ideally, the registration process should have been carried out through the class that you are changing information in—the RemoteBankInterface. The design just didn't lend itself to that approach.

RMI Bank Client

(On with the client code.) Like the other clients that we've implemented, the code that does the real talking with the server will extend the BankClient interface that we designed back in Chapter 5, "Writing TCP Communications." We noted previously that there will need to be a slight change in the implementation of that interface. Previously we have passed the select calls directly through to the server. Now we need to keep them locally and use that information to decide which of the two remote objects to call. With a little bit of thought, this can be easier than you think.

Connecting to the Server

Our first port of call is the `connect()` method, as this establishes the connections for us. Making a connection to a remote object is not a particularly painful task. Unlike socket connections, there is no need to get both the network connection and the I/O streams to write to that connection. We simply ask the remote server for the reference to the appropriate object, which is defined by a URL string.

RMI URLs Accessing a particular remote object is handled through a URL. The URL is specific to RMI. In its general form an RMI URL looks like this:

```
rmi://<server>:<port>/<object name>
```

Anything after the object name will result in a `MalformedURL Exception` being generated. Like other URLs, the port number is completely optional. If it is not specified, then it defaults to the RMI default of 1099. The object name that is specified is the one that we used to bind in the server code. For each object name, there is only one object instance. All clients that request a given URL will be returned a reference to the same object instance on the server.

If no machine name is specified, then the URL will default to the local machine.

Asking for a Remote Object Trying to make requests of a remote object is no good unless we have a reference to that object in the first place. To get that reference we once again make a visit to the Naming class. This time it is the `lookup()` method that is of interest to us.

Lookup takes only a single parameter—the URL of the remote object that we are interested in. It returns a reference to the RemoteObject. With this reference you then cast it to the particular object type that you need to deal with. Figure 8-6 shows the code that is used in the RMIBankClient implementation.

Figure 8-5
Binding objects to
remote URLs.

```java
public void connect(String host, int port)
{
  disconnect();


  try {
    String base_url = "rmi://" + host;

    if(port != 1099)
      base_url += ":" + port;

    account_a =
        (RemoteBankInterface)Naming.lookup(base_url +
                                      ACCOUNT_A_URL);
    account_b =
        (RemoteBankInterface)Naming.lookup(base_url +
                                      ACCOUNT_B_URL);

    feedback_manager =
          (RemoteFeedbackManager)Naming.lookup(base_url +
                                        FEEDBACK_URL);

    // everything is OK so register ourselves as a listener.
    current_account = account_a;

    feedback_manager.addBalanceListener(this);
  }
  catch(NotBoundException nbe) {
      System.out.println("The named object is not " +
                          "currently bound");
      System.out.println(nbe.getMessage());
  }
  catch(MalformedURLException mue) {
    System.out.println("Badly formed URL: \n " + mue);
  }
  catch(RemoteException re) {
    System.out.println("Unable to grab a remote object\n " +
                          re);
  }
}
```

Notice that once we are assured that the remote object references are valid, we then register ourselves as a listener with the remote object. This completes the round-trip circuit for the information, as the balance will now be returned.

Figure 8-6
The RMIBankClient implementation for fetching a remote object reference.

```
public void deposit(float amount) {
  try {
    current_account.deposit(amount);
  }
  catch(RemoteException re) {
    System.out.println("Error depositing money " + re);
  }
}
```

Using a Remote Object   Making method calls to a remote object is identical to what you would now do for any other object. You can call any method that was declared in the remote interface. Since those method calls also throw an exception—which just happens to be a remote object exception—you need to catch that with every method call you make, just like a local object. Figure 8-7 demonstrates the deposit method.

Disconnecting from the Remote Object   When the user decides to leave the bank connection, the disconnect method is called. Remote objects act like normal objects—there is a garbage collector that runs to collect remote references. Also, the network connection is implicit in the remote references; there is no way of explicitly closing a remote object connection.

When we wish to leave, one thing that we don't want anymore is balance updates. Removing these is easy—just make a call to the feedback manager asking it to remove the listener for this client. With that done, no more updates are received, but we still have references to the remote objects. Just as with local objects, we simply set the references to null to remove them, letting the distributed garbage collector look after them some time later.

Cannot Export Object RMIBankClient?   If you were to take the BankClient connect method exactly as you saw it in Figure 8-6 and then attempt to run it, you would quickly find that RMI starts throwing errors at you. No doubt you would see something along the lines of the following error message:

```
Unable to grab a remote object
  java.rmi.MarshalException: Error marshaling arguments; nested
  exception is:
```

```
java.rmi.StubNotFoundException: Remote object not
exported: rwjn.chapter8.client.RMIBankClient
```

What does this really mean? Well, if you want to have a remote object of any description, it first must be made available to the RMI system. It is fine labeling an object as capable of remote access, but unless you actually register the object with the remote object handling system, it cannot offer references to that object to other applications. In the server, you extended the UnicastRemoteObject that took care of all of this for you. Simply by creating an instance of the class and binding it to the server, you ensured that it was automatically exported for others to access.

This time, we have a client object that is offering itself back to the server so that the server may make remote object references to it as well. Where? The offending line of code causing the exception is

```
balance_manager.addBalanceListener(this);
```

What has happened is that you have offered the bank client as a remote object without telling RMI that you wanted to do this.

Luckily fixing the problem is very simple. java.rmi.server. UnicastRemoteObject includes a static method exportObject() which takes care of all the export process for you. So all we need to do is make sure that just before our offending line of code we insert a new line:

```
UnicastRemoteObject.exportObject(this);
```

This takes care of that exception and now things are right to function correctly.

Advanced RMI

In general practice, the steps you've taken so far with RMI coding will be sufficient to complete most tasks. Occasionally, you need to know a little more. Perhaps the most annoying restriction that I have encountered is that of the UnicastRemoteObject. This has only a single remote instance. At times, you wish you had individual object instances for each client. To do this requires your knowing a lot more about the internals of RMI.

The Roles of Stubs and Skeletons

One of the least understood parts of RMI is what these separate stubs and skeletons are needed for. To many they appear to be an item that just gets created by RMIC and is deployed on the server with the rest of the RMI server. To understand their role in life requires a bit of reexamination of some earlier issues, in particular parameter passing of an object to remote objects.

Method parameters that convey primitive types are fairly easy to deal with. Just take the value, turn it into a bunch of bytes and then reconstitute them at the other end. Dealing with object references is a little trickier. We want the objects to behave just like a local one—changing a value on the server should be reflected on the client without any further effort on the part of the programmer. Somehow, all of those objects must operate over the network transparently. Unless there were an extreme redesign of the way Java works, this would be impossible to implement just by using the current language features. Therefore, a few restrictions were placed on the programmer, while the Java design team hid the rest of the issues from us.

The solution that they came up with was to make sure that every object that was to work over the network contained a couple of properties defined through the use of interfaces, and then hide the rest in the tools. What these tools do is make the networked communications part of the transactions transparent. There is still the onus on the programmer to name all the classes that are needed to work through remote connections.

Parameter Passing Passing of parameters in a normal Java program is done by passing the value of primitive types and passing a reference to every object regardless of type. Remote objects need to operate by the same rules if they are to achieve the goal of behaving in exactly the same way. Reaching this goal required some minor restrictions on the code, as noted previously.

In order to pass an object over a network connection, there is really only one solution: Turn it into a byte stream and then reconstruct it on the other end. If you remember from Chapter 7, "Object Serialization," serialization, this means that the object on the other end is not the same as the original one—an exact copy maybe, but not the same. Hiding this problem requires that some extra work be done on the underlying protocol; all object references need to communicate by some sort of message passing rather than just copying the entire object and sending that to the server (or back to the client). This is the role of the stub and skeleton.

When you pass an object reference to a remote object, the real object is not actually passed. Instead, the stub and skeleton step in to fill that role and provide the appearance of proper object references.

Parameters and Serialization   Object passing would be fine if all objects were implicitly capable of being transported over the network. But Java wasn't designed that way to start with. The overheads of making every single object implement the remote interface, all of the exception handling, and so forth would be enormous. So the Java designers came up with a compromise.

Any Java object that is labeled as a remote object will use the stubs and skeletons for communications. If the object doesn't implement `java.rmi.Remote` but is serializable in some form or another, then RMI will serialize that object and pass a copy to the remote object. Finally, if the object does not implement any of these, then an exception is thrown. The best part of this is that most of the Java core objects already implement serialization, so you only really need to look after your own code in order for remote objects to work in some form or another.

NOTE: *Although the core Java classes are for the most part serializable, in many cases caution still needs to be exercised. Consider the collections API in the* `java.util` *package. Classes such as Vector are serializable, but their contents—your classes—may not be; therefore, errors will still be thrown.*

At the point where your application makes a request of a remote method the stubs and skeletons kick in. When you first establish the RMI connection using lookup, the stub is downloaded from the server. When a remote method is invoked, the stub collects all of the arguments to the remote object. This is collected into what Java terms the marshal stream—RMI marshals all of the arguments into the stream ready to be sent off to the server. During the marshaling process, the stub determines whether an object should be serialized or a remote object reference should be passed through and puts the necessary information into the marshal stream.

Once all of the arguments have been collected together, the stub then makes a request of the lower-level layers to invoke the remote method. The stream is passed through and then the lower layers take care of the actual networking aspects. At the server end, the skeleton receives the information from the lower layers and is responsible for the unmarshaling of all the arguments. It takes the marshal stream, unpacks the information, and then calls the local server instance of the object.

Multiple Concurrent Connections

Writing an RMI server requires just as much knowledge and careful design as any other sort of network server. The major difference, as has been pointed out already, is that there is only a single instance of the remote object under normal circumstances. Then there is the issue of scalability—how many clients, how often, and for how long? Finally, you must decide the amount of robustness that your server requires.

If you strip away all the details of RMI providing remote objects, you will find that it is really just a highly abstracted socket-based server. Consider Figure 8-8, which outlines the areas of code which are used in the TCP implementation of our bank server and the RMI implementation. Notice that the details of the RMI connections are handled inside the RMI box transparently for you.

Figure 8-7
Make a call to a remote object's method.

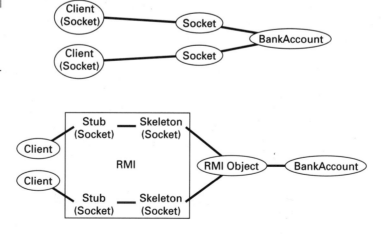

Synchronized Methods If RMI is just a big abstraction of a socket connection with some serialization thrown in (which it is), this leaves us dealing with the same issues as a TCP-based server. How do we control access to the remote objects? Well, the answer really relies on what you want to do performancewise. If each client can make a request of the same object, then it is possible that they can both access that object simultaneously. This leaves you with a choice of how to handle the problem.

One choice is to make each of the remote methods synchronized. The Java VM then takes care of the issues of making sure only one client accesses the remote methods at a time. Since your remote object class is just like any other class with synchronized methods, it follows the same rules at the server end. Calls on that remote object's methods are just like any other blocking call, so you can expect your program to act normally.

Threads Sometimes synchronizing methods presents too much overhead for the application. Another possible approach, where it is suitable for the server processing, is to make each request into a thread. Each method would start off a thread with the request information to contact the server internals.

There are a number of drawbacks with this approach. First, you can't use return values. Potentially there are many simultaneous requests with that method. As an alternative, you can use remote listeners. Once the thread has started, it finds the listener for the client (possibly involving a hashtable lookup of the listener reference based on the client's address) and sends the information back through the listener.

The second drawback is that you can build up a lot of threads, all of the same priority, slowing the machine down as it spends all its time context-switching between the threads rather than executing code (a common potential problem to all multithreaded applications and operating systems). Like multiple threads, a large number of local (to the server JVM) class instances also keep the garbage collector busy.

Finally, consider whether the overheads of synchronized methods are really all that much compared to the network latency of the rest of the system. If your remote objects are doing a lot of heavy calculations (say as a map request to a GIS, or geographical map server), then the overheads of synchronization may be minimal compared to the rest of the time spent in the transaction.

Multiple Remote Objects A halfway point between local request threads and synchronizing would be the use of local generation of remote objects. As you have seen, there is a lot of setup cost required to get a remote object registered. One design coming into fashion for high-traffic servers is to have a small single remote object registered with the RMI registry, which then creates instances of individual remote objects for each client.

For example, the remote object would look roughly like this:

```
public interface ObjectGenerator extends Remote {
  public ClientObject connect();
  public void dispose(ClientObject obj);
}

public class ClientObject implements Remote {
  public Object doSomething();
}
```

The client first makes a connection to the object implementing ObjectGenerator, then makes a request for a ClientObject; then all further transactions are made through its own ClientObject instance. This way, at the server end you get all the personalized service that a TCP socket handler might give (such as the AccountConnection class in Chapter 5, "Writing TCP Communications") with all of the benefits of remote objects and return values from methods.

Performance Issues

In designing the server, the amount of performance is always an issue. How heavy is the traffic to the site? How much time is spent by the server in processing the requests? What structure is the client/server application—two- or three-tier?

The preceding three options on how to structure the remote objects gives an idea of the variety of ways of tackling problems an RMI programmer has. There are no real favorites. Each alternative is suited to different tasks. Which you choose depends on the answers to the above questions.

Besides just how to structure the remote objects, there are much lower-level issues that also need to be sorted out. How does the implementation of RMI affect the way that you design your objects?

Serialization Issues   Throughout this chapter there have been constant references to the close links between RMI and serialization. Indeed these form quite a tight coupling. In the section "Parameters and Serialization" you saw that RMI must do quite an amount of work before determining what form the parameters must be in before even sending the data.

If the information that you are sending to the remote object is fairly limited, one possible option is to do a lot of the work of RMI yourself. That is, you can decide to not even pass objects as parameters, instead just sticking to the basic primitives and having lots of them.

Another approach that I have seen work with quite some performance enhancements is to do literally everything yourself. The parameters to each method call were just a byte array and all of the information was encoded in that array. Basically, this is a glorified binary TCP socket connection. The client then either serialized the information itself into the array or wrote in custom messages with integers, bytes, strings, etc. All RMI had to do was send the byte array across the link. No effort (and hence time) was wasted trying to determine if the parameters are remote, serializable, or anything else.

Performance improvements of the byte array approach were in the vicinity of 30 percent just in RMI overheads. Of course, this sort of approach is very limited in scope and requires a lot of extra coding on the part of the programmer (and introduces a lot of bugs). Unless you are using lots of very short, sharp requests, I would suggest that it is not really a viable option.

RMI Initialization   One thing that has been a major thorn in the side of programmers using RMI is the setup costs in making a connection. Compared to normal socket connections, this can be as much as 5 times slower. Most of this is due to the need to send stubs to the remote client and all of the handshaking required in getting a good-quality connection.

Some modifications were made to the code presented earlier in this chapter to test and print out the time it takes to send a request and get an answer and to establish connections. For comparison, also modified was the code from Chapter 5, "Writing TCP Communications," to do the same thing. For comparisons of transaction times, timing information was taken by using `System.currentTimeMillis()` at the start of the setup and again at the end. In addition to transactions, the deposit method was timed as well.

NOTE: *The two modified versions of the timing classes can be found in the code directory under the names* `TimedTCPClient` *and* `TimedRMIClient`.

In quick timing tests on a Pentium166 with NT4.0 with both client and server on the local machine, the TCP version took on average around 120 ms to connect. By comparison the RMI client took around 10 seconds. For transactions, both were returning values of either 10 or 0, which is the minimum precision available from Java under the JDK on an Intel box.

From these rough tests you can see that there is a couple of orders of magnitude difference in setup time between sockets and RMI. However, once set up, on these small transactions there is almost no difference. If your client can afford to spend quite some time in the setup process, then the greater abstraction of RMI may well be worth the effort.

RMI over HTTP   RMI has included a number of extra little features that have made it easier for applications to deal with the pitfalls of the Internet. The biggest barrier to making Java applets more usable on public web pages has been the rising use of firewalls. Generally, this has limited almost all socket connections between computers inside a company and the server that the web page was loaded on.

Realizing that firewalls were a major stumbling block to the potential acceptance of RMI, the Java team decided to implement an alternative communication scheme over HTTP. The RMI server and client could connect using an HTTP connection because firewalls very rarely stop communications on this port address (you'd never get the web page in the first place). All communications are then encoded on this channel.

By Sun's own figures, HTTP connections are extremely slow. The specifications talk of a connection time at least an order of magnitude slower than standard RMI. Our client would take more than a minute just to connect if it were using HTTP.

If our client could connect, it would face another, more important hurdle—HTTP connections are only one-way connections. That means we could not export our remote listener interface to get the balance information back. With this in mind, RMI over HTTP is very limited, and this should be taken into account when designing your applications.

Summary

This discussion has given you a reasonably lengthy introduction to RMI. There is still quite a way to go, however. Although it is useful to know how the underlying implementation of RMI works (such as its use of stream marshaling and a distributed garbage collector), what you have learned in this chapter will be more than enough for 95 percent of your applications. Java 2 has expanded RMI again with activation and a CORBA implementation of RMI. These alone are enough to fill another chapter on RMI.

Advanced RMI

In the previous chapter, you learnt how to set up an RMI server and client system. Everything that you learn is applicable to Java 1.1 and Java 2. In this chapter we will look at the capabilities that have been introduced in Java 2—activation, defining your own format for the serialization of classes, and using custom socket types (for compression, for example).

Introduction to Activation

One major disadvantage of the server in the previous chapter was that it required you to have a full server process running constantly, including all the exported remote objects in memory. You may have noticed that everything was started from a command line. If the user logged out of the system, everything that had been set up disappeared! This required a user to be logged onto the system with the server running as a process for the entire time that the server needed to be run. Although there are ways around this problem in Unix, for Windows and Mac server users it was a big problem.

Java 2 introduced expanded core capabilities to RMI in what it terms *activation*. With activation, the remote objects have become much more CORBA-like. A server can be set running, the objects exported, and then the user can log out, confident that the objects will remain available to clients.

How Activation Affects RMI Applications

Activation is a purely server-side set of APIs for RMI. As far as client-side code is concerned, it knows no difference whether the remote object is served by activation or standard RMI techniques. Changes that you need to make are purely server-side; our RMIBankClient from the previous chapter does not change.

On the server-side code, a different approach is taken to the running of the application. Naturally, there are the required implementation changes, with different APIs needed as well. In the previous chapter, a server required you to first run the RMI registry (if not automatically started by the Java code) and then start a Java application that maintains the remote objects. Closing down this application removed the objects from visiblity. Under activation, you still run this application, but all it does is register the remote object instances and then exit immediately. You no longer need to keep the application running.

Creating a New Activatable Object

Although this seems like going from back to front, our first look at activation will be by implementing a new object rather than modifying our previous examples. The simple application this time will export only a single object but still use the callback-style remote method used in the previous chapter. To illustrate that activation is working even after the initial contact, a thread will run in the remote object to send periodic events back to the listeners. A separate request to the remote object by a client will start the thread running.

SECURITY: *To complete the examples in the following sections, you will need the following permissions enabled in your policy file:*

```
java.lang.PropertyPermission "user.dir", "read";
java.net.SocketPermission "localhost" "accept, listen, connect";
java.lang.RuntimePermission "modifyThreadGroup";
```

Creating the Service Definition   To create an activatable object, you follow a similar path to the one you used in the previous chapter to create standard RMI objects. First you must create an interface that defines the methods that are going to be made available remotely. As before, this must extend `java.rmi.Remote`, and all methods must throw `RemoteException`. After the implementation is finished, you need to run `rmic` again to generate stubs and skeleton classes.

Our example this time is called `RemoteService`. It is found in package `rwjn.chapter9`. It contains three methods: two for adding and removing listeners and a third to make a request of the server, which is used to start the thread going. The request is nothing spectacular; it takes an `int` and returns an `int`—what it does with it we don't really care. The definition of this interface is given in Figure 9-1.

On the other side of the service we also need to define the `RemoteCallback` interface (Figure 9-2). This contains a single method that has an `int` as the one and only argument. Again, the value does not have any meaning for this example.

Figure 9-1
The
`RemoteService`
interface definition.

```
public interface RemoteService
  extends Remote {

  public int makeRequest(int val)
    throws RemoteException;

  public void addListener(RemoteCallback l)
    throws RemoteException;

  public void removeListener(RemoteCallback l)
    throws RemoteException;
}
```

Constructing an Activatable Object With the basic definition complete, we now need to create the implementation (`rwjn.chapter9.RemoteServiceImpl`). As with the standard RMI objects, we need to implement the interface defined in the previous section. However, instead of extending `UnicastRemoteObject`, we are required to extend the `Activatable` abstract class. All of the activation-related classes are found in the package `java.rmi.activation`, so make sure you import it.

The second requirement for activatable objects is to create a constructor with the following signature:

```
public RemoteServiceImpl(ActivationID id, MarshalledObject data)
```

The first parameter is used to pass an identifier to the superclass constructor. The second contains any data that you may need for initialization. How to use this information will be seen shortly in the discussion of the implementation of the registration class.

Figure 9-2
The
`RemoteCallback`
interface definition.

```
public interface RemoteCallback
  extends Remote {

  public void requestReply(int id)
    throws RemoteException;
}
```

The first step of any constructor is to call the superclass constructor. For activatable objects, there are four choices. The most common that you will use is the two-argument constructor of the form:

```
protected Activatable(ActivationID id, int port)
                throws RemoteException
```

The first parameter obviously matches with the first parameter of our derived class. The second is the port number that you would like to export the object on, giving you more control over the object. Generally this number is set to zero, allowing RMI to choose an anonymous port (which corresponds to the default UnicastRemoteObject constructor). Other options for the constructor let you specify whether or not the object should be restarted each time the activator restarts (the RMI demon). You may also specify a location where the classes for this object can be found. This location is any valid URL—usually a file, but it could just as well be an HTTP connection. Also available is the option to pass in your own custom socket factories for the client and server. These options will be covered later in the chapter.

Implementing the Remote Object The next step along the path to implementation is to complete all the methods required by the service interface definition. Our listeners are kept in a very simple Vector, which forms the basis of the add and remove listener methods.

When the client calls the makeRequest() method, we start our thread that sends the asynchronous information back to the client. For simplicity, an inner class was written that extends Thread and takes care of this for us. When the makeRequest() method is entered, the first thing it does is look for a currently running thread. If there is one, then it is interrupted to kill it, then a new instance is started. The thread sends to the clients the last value that was passed in as the argument to makeRequest() every 10 seconds using a sleep() call inside the run method's loop. The interrupt (or any exception) will cause an exception to exit the loop and hence the death of the thread:

```
public void run() {
  try {
    while(true) {
      sleep(SLEEP_PERIOD);

      sendEvent();
```

```
      }
    }
    catch(Exception ie) {
      // time to exit so do nothing....
      System.out.println("Reply sender caught an exception:-\n" +
ie);
    }
  }
}
```

NOTE: An interesting thing about this code is that there is a
`System.out.println()` *embedded in it. As far as I can find out, the*
information does not get printed anywhere. Debugging by `println` *of*
activatable code is not an option.

Passing Arguments to an Activatable Object Constructor   One
final class that needs to be implemented is the code to register the activatable objects with the system. Unlike classical RMI, this code is
designed to be run only once and exit almost immediately, resulting in a
completely different approach than the server start-up class used in the
previous chapter.

The start of the registration class looks fairly familiar. First we create
and set a security manager. The next requirement is a location of where
to find the classes needed. This URL should be identical to the location
that was passed into the Activatable class that we looked at in the previous section. For this, we generate it from the `user.dir` system property
and add the `file:///` prefix and also make sure that the last character
is a / (slash). This is required, and if it is missing, your code will generate a `ClassNotFoundException`.

NOTE: Some alteration of the filename is done for Win32 systems. The
drive name is removed and all slashes are changed to backslashes.

At this point you need to know if you are passing arguments in the
constructor to the remote object when it is created. Unlike standard
RMI objects, you aren't directly constructing new instances of the object.
Instead, you are providing arguments in a prewrapped form suitable for
later use. To do this, activation uses an instance of the `Marshalled`
`Object` class. The constructor of this class also takes an `Object`. This
object must be serializable so that it can be kept stored by the activation

system. Say your object wanted to take the location as a parameter to the object. You would use the following code:

```
String location = System.getProperty("user.dir");
...
MarshalledObject data =
 new MarshalledObject(location);
```

Of course, a lot of the time you would want to be sending more than one argument to your activatable object. To do this, you simply need to create a small container class that has references to all of the data that you need to pass—for example,

```
class ArgContainer implements Serializable {
  String location;
  int port;
}

String location = System.getProperty("user.dir");
...

ArgContainer container = new ArgContainer();
container.location = location;
container.port = some_port_number;

MarshalledObject data = new
MarshalledObject(container);
```

Registering the Activatable Object The next step in setting up your activatable object is to create a description of that object and pass it to the RMI system. First an `ActivationDesc` class instance is created. This represents all the information that is needed to create an activatable object. The constructor contains the fully qualified filename, the location of the file to create, and the data that is passed as the argument to the constructor.

```
ActivationDesc desc =
  new ActivationDesc("rwjn.chapter9.RemoteServiceImpl",
                     location,
                     data);
```

This code may throw an `ActivationException` if the security manager has not been set. It may be thrown for other reasons, which we'll discuss later. It is important to note that the string name of the class is used, not an instance of the class itself. Activation uses the reflection APIs to create a new instance of your activatable object on demand and also uses the location to determine how to load the class. (For example, a different `ClassLoader` would be needed if the location were on a web server rather than one sitting on the local drive.) Because of these two facts, you need the public constructor that was mentioned earlier.

At this point, you have not yet registered the object with the activation system. You have only created a description of the object that you would like to register. Two more steps are needed. First you need to register the object with the Activation system, and then you need to export the object so that anyone can find it.

Registering with activation is done by a call to the `register()` static method of the Activation class. It takes a single argument, which is the description object instance created above. In return you get a `Remote` instance, which represents the actual remote handler used by the RMI system.

Even after all of this, we still haven't finished. An object and a service exist, but nobody can access them yet because we haven't published their name to the world. The final step in the process is to register the service with an RMI name, and this is performed through the `Naming` class. Using `Naming` to bind the description that we have just created with a particular URL completes the final step. We have two options here: We can use either the `bind()` method or the `rebind()` method to do this. The former is good if you can be assured that the object has never been registered before in this instance of the RMI registry. If you can't guarantee this, then the rebind method is a safer bet. It allows you to replace an object instance that was previously associated with the given URL with a new object, or even a new instance of the same object. For safety, our examples always use the rebind method.

```
RemoteService remote_service =
   (RemoteService)Activatable.register(desc);
Naming.rebind("SimpleServer", remote_service);
```

Now you have a registered, activatable object. Combining all of the above code fragments gives you the source for the RegisterObject class that is defined in Figure 9-3.

Figure 9-3
The complete code
to register an activat-
able object.

```java
public class RegisterObject {
  public static void main(String[] args) {

    System.out.println("Activation Object registration setup");
    System.setSecurityManager(new RMISecurityManager());

    // Fetch the location and munge to proper URL format
    String cwd = System.getProperty("user.dir");
    cwd = cwd.substring(3);
    cwd = cwd.replace('\\', '/');

    String location = "file:///" + cwd + "/";

    MarshalledObject data = null;

    try {
      System.out.println("Creating the activation description");
      ActivationDesc desc =
        new ActivationDesc("rwjn.chapter9.RemoteServiceImpl",
                           location,
                           data);

      // Now register with rmid
      System.out.println("Registering with RMID");
      RemoteService remote_service =
        (RemoteService)Activatable.register(desc);
      Naming.rebind("SimpleServer", remote_service);

      System.out.println("Registration service is complete. " +
                         "Exiting");
    }
    catch(RemoteException re) {
      System.out.println("Error with remote objects " + re);
    }
    catch(ActivationException ae) {
      System.out.println("Error creating activatable objects:
"+ae);
    }
    catch(MalformedURLException mue) {
      System.out.println("Badly formed URL " + mue);
    }
    catch(Throwable th) {
      System.out.println("ARGH! " + th);
    }
    System.exit(0);
  }
}
```

Running the Activatable Object   To run an activation system takes three steps. Like standard RMI, you still need to start the RMI registry as the first step. Activation adds a second step—the RMI Daemon, rmid, must be run next. This second step is the daemon process that takes care of creating instances of the activation objects in demand to user requests. It hooks into rmiregistry and becomes the psuedo objects that the registry believes it has available.

Finally, we run the RegisterObject class. The command line requires some extra options compared to normal. This time, a property needs to be specified for the environment. The property java.rmi.server.codebase defines the code base used by the activation system to locate and create the activatable objects. This should correspond to the location parameter that you passed to the Activation Desc class a few pages ago. Again, this URL must end in the slash character. For example, a typical command line might look like this:

```
C:\book\>java -
Djava.rmi.server.codebase=\
file:///users/justin/book/
rwjn.chapter9.RegisterObject
```

Obviously it can become quite tedious to type this out every single time. It is recommended you set up a script file to automatically do this all for you. If you have access to the Java policy file, then you could always add some extra code to the start-up routine to set the system property before calling any of the activation code.

Testing the System   Implementing a test client for an activatable object is no different from implementing a standard RMI object. In fact, your client code would not know the difference. For this exercise a simple test client was constructed. The code can be found in the class ActivationClient in the rwjn.chapter9 package. Running the class, you would see the following output:

```
C:\...>java rwjn.chapter9.ActivationClient
Starting Activation Test client
Exporting local object
Fetching remote object reference
Adding ourselves as a listener
Making a request
Request returned 1
Client creation complete
```

```
Client got reply value of 1
Client got reply value of 1
```

The last couple of lines are the return values from the server code through the callback interface, indicating that the class is working. You can exit the client and restart it and still receive the same values and output. Because the client code does not know the difference between standard RMI objects and activatable ones, and because of the lack of output from the activatable objects, making sure that the activation part is working correctly can be difficult when you are writing test code for the activatable objects. This will need to be solved on a case-by-case basis.

Modifying Old RMI Code to Be Activatable

Now that you have a reasonable idea about how activation works, it is time to look at how to modify old standard RMI code to use activation. Generally, this would be the first task that you would perform with activation, rather than start a whole new application. Moving standard RMI objects to activatable is a relatively trivial task involving four steps: (1) modifying the RemoteObject class; (2) deciding what to do with arguments; (3) changing the setup; and (4) choosing either RMID or RMIRegistry.

Modifying the RemoteObject Class First you must modify the classes that implement the UnicastRemoteObject interface to now extend Activatable. Part of this process requires that you also create the constructor that fits the signature above. Your old constructor is no longer usable. Don't delete it just yet! Make sure that the new constructor code calls the appropriate superclass constructor that is needed for passing through the ActivationID reference.

Deciding What to Do with Arguments The next step is to decide what you are going to do with the arguments that you passed to the old constructor. Remember now that any per-instance and initialization information will need to be passed in through a class that is stored in the MarshalledObject instance. Decide whether that information still needs to be passed in anymore. Should you decide to pass this information, then you will have to write a serializable class and code to extract the appropriate information.

Changing the Setup   Once the code for the basic object is completed, you now need to move to the next step: rewriting the setup code. Under the standard system, the assumption was that the JVM will always be running. Now, that is not always the case. You create a description of the object, but never actually create an instance of it. Once the setup code exits, there is no more JVM instance to run other code behind the scenes.

In your old code, you would have lines that would create a new instance of the remote object and then bind that object instance to a particular RMI URL name. Now that code is replaced by the code you saw earlier in the chapter that creates a description, remote service instance, and then the bind action. Also, now your code exits upon completion of this registration task instead of staying active as it did before. Remember this, because it can have quite a profound effect on the design of your system, as you will see later when we convert the bank server code to use activation.

Choosing `rmid` or `rmiregistry`   The final change to be made is in the start-up procedure. Previously, it was assumed that you could start the `rmiregistry` through your code. This is still the case. However, in the previous example we had to run both the `rmiregistry` and `rmid` from the command line. Why?

The RMI registry is the repository of all of the bindings between a given name and an object instance. When you make the call to the `lookup()` method in the `Naming` class, that class contacts the registry on the nominated machine. It then requests a descriptor of the named object and it returns the stub to the client code.

RMID performs a completely different task: it is responsible for dynamically creating and destroying activatable object instances in response to demand. It contains a running JVM instance and uses reflection to create activatable objects. It ties with the registry so that it can create object instances on the fly in response to requests. It must do this because the client-side code does not know whether it is accessing a standard RMI object or an activatable one. It still contacts only the registry, and it is given a stub to do the talking.

If you are reading between the lines here, you should be able to see the next problem coming. Although your code could still contain the lines to create a new registry instance if one is running, there is no point. Think about the setup process. If you recall, when you dynamically create the registry within your application code, the registry lasts only as long as your application does. Exit the application and the registry dies too. Our setup class code is very short-lived—enough to register the object descriptions only, and then a forced exit. If we run `rmid` without a registry, we'd still have lots of problems because the registry would last only as long as the setup code is running. As soon as the setup code exits, so does your registry, and `rmid` becomes useless again. Of course you could always make sure that the setup code does not exit, but what's the point? Isn't the reason you are using activation so that you don't need to have a permanent application running?

Exporting Non-`Activatable` Objects In the previous chapter and in the introductory example in this chapter, we used the static `export Object()` method provided by `UnicastRemoteObject` to register a class that does not directly extend `UnicastRemoteObject` and then use it as a remote object. The same capability is available with activation. You can register a class that does not extend `Activatable` and still have it react like a standard activatable object.

Why might this be useful? Say you have a class that you've purchased but don't have the source for. You would like to make its functionality available as a remote object. You know this class doesn't extend `Activatable`. Obviously you can't make it extend `Activatable`, and Java's inheritance model does not support true multiple-inheritance, so you can't just extend both the class and `Activatable` at the same time. In this case you need to use an alternative means. A great example is our RMI bank server code. We could have a base class that implements the `RemoteAccount` interface then two separate classes with the appropriate constructors for standard RMI and activatable objects. These two derived classes would not be able to do the normal extension of `Unicast RemoteObject` or `Activatable` because they are extending the simple base class; therefore, we need to resort to other alternatives.

Extending the Base Class Exporting an object to the activation system can take one of two forms. In this section we look at the first—extending the base class to provide an activatable form of the base class functionality.

The first step is to decide exactly what in the base functionality you wish to export to the world. Once this is done, you will need to create an interface. This interface must extend `java.rmi.Remote`, just as our callback interfaces have done previously. The methods declared in this interface should exactly match the methods of the base class, noting also that `RemoteException` is also to be thrown. For example, say we wish to provide a remote `Vector` object where we can add and remove elements from the remote object. The interface would be declared as follows:

```
public interface ActivatableVector extends
java.rmi.Remote {
  public addElement(Object obj)
    throws RemoteException;
  public removeElement(Object obj)
    throws RemoteException;
}
```

Now create your derived class that extends the interface.

```
public class ActivatableVectorImpl extends Vector
  implements ActivatableVector {
}
```

Note that you don't need to provide any implementation of the methods in the derived class, so long as they exactly match the description in the base class. Next an extra constructor needs to be created that matches the profile already discussed in this chapter. This time, the constructor does not need to call the activatable superclass constructor, but you may be bound by requirements of the base class for other constructors.

Somewhere in the constructor, you need to now register the object with the activation system. Just like `UnicastRemoteObject`, `Activatable` has an `exportObject()` method too. The simplest way of registering the object is to use the three-argument version and call it as follows:

```
public ActivatableVectorImpl (ActivationID id,
                                MarshalledObject data)
  throws RemoteException {

  // Register the object with the activation system
  // then export it on an anonymous port
  Activatable.exportObject(this, id, 0);
}
```

Now your object is capable of being used as an activatable object when this constructor is called. The setup code that was shown in Figure 9-3 does not need to change. You can use this class name as the first argument in the `ActivationDesc` class just like an object that extends the

Activatable abstract class. Don't forget that any initialization arguments are passed through the `MarshalledObject` argument.

Adaptor Classes   If you are unwilling or unable to make changes or extend the original nonremote class (for example, it might have been declared final), then an alternative approach is to use an adaptor class. In this case, you create another separate class that is registered with `rmid`. This class now creates a new instance of the original class when it is created and passes all of the requests through to it.

Going back to the Vector example above, the activatable code is placed in a new class called `ActivatableVectorAdaptor` that extends `ActivatableVector`. The code does not change much from the previous section. Whereas before the base class took care of the implementation of the remote methods, this time you need to provide your own implementation. Figure 9-4 shows how this is done. Each method is a simple call to the real implementation exactly duplicating what was requested.

Changing the Bank Server to Use Activation

At first glance, changing the bank server code from the previous chapter to use activation seems a relatively trivial task. Just follow the steps presented in the previous few sections and everything works nicely. Unfortunately life just isn't that easy.

What sorts of obstacles are thrown in our way? Well, the whole principle behind activation is that objects are created only on demand. Our bank is running all the time. Even when clients are not connected to their accounts, interest is still being calculated. A thread is continuously running. Hmmm....This calls for some inventive work.

Design Alternatives

Our basic problem is that we're attempting to apply activation to an area where it really isn't suited—at least not in our simplistic application. Our application has a continuously running part, and the interface to it all running within the same VM instance.

Figure 9-4
Implementation of a
simple adaptor class.

```
public class ActivatableVectorAdaptor
    implements ActivatableVector {

    private Vector vec;

    public ActivatableVectorAdaptor(ActivationID id,
                                    MarshalledObject data)
        throws RemoteException {

        vec = new Vector();

        // Register the object with the activation system
        // then export it on an anonymous port
        Activatable.exportObject(this, id, 0);
    }

    public void addElement(Object obj)
        throws RemoteException {

        vec.addElement(obj);
    }

    public boolean removeElement(Object obj)
        throws RemoteException {

        vec.removeElement(obj);
    }
}
```

In a real banking system, this obviously wouldn't be the case. Somewhere down in the bowels of the bank would be a huge collection of big iron mainframes churning away while a heavy-duty web server formed the front end—with lots and lots of security systems in between. Typically the big iron might be IBM AS/400s running DB/2. This is a nice start, as it means we could access it by using JDBC or similar API. The activatable objects wake up, connect to the back-end database, respond to the user's queries, and then shut everything down again, waiting for the next time. Our simplistic example server is nowhere near capable of performing such tasks in its current state. As a first option, we could try to replicate this system. We could create a small database using Oracle Lite, MS Access, or similar system to form the basis of our accounts and then use the activatable objects as the front end to this—too much work for this book and it is also fairly heavily platform-dependent (particularly if we based our implementation on Access).

The second option is to split our server into two parts. The account manager becomes a separate application, which the activatable objects then connect to and make the transactions with. This is much closer to what would happen in a real system. It too will take some modification of the old system. However, there is no reason why we couldn't take the TCP-based server from Chapter 5 and implement a different client to it.

Finally, we have the option of pretending the server is running all the time. Interest calculation is pretty simple to do. There are well-known formulas for calculating compound interest. All we need to do is make sure that we know for how long the server has been asleep between calls. Using this time information, we calculate what the beginning interest rate should be, and then start the thread running again. When the activatable object shuts down, just make sure you save the time of the last interest calculation. How do you know when the activatable object is closing down? Just make sure you implement a `finalize()` method. Possibly you could even write the last time information out every time you do an interest calculation.

So that has exhausted all of the possiblities, right? Wrong. There's a final one. If `rmid` is running a VM permanently pretending to be an object to the registry, that means we can do other stuff with it as well. This leads to some interesting possibilities. To make sure that the bank back end is running all the time, we just need to make sure that any of our object types can reference it and that it stays alive after the object itself has been garbage-collected. Simple, just use a static variable in the class. If the static variable is null, create the new object and off you go.

Since this is about exploration of different ideas, we'll run with the last idea even though the second option is much more like what would happen in reality.

Reconstructing the Server Classes

Ideally we'd like to keep the amount of disruption of the code to a minimum. Taking a basic look at what we have, the following classes will need to be changed from the code that appeared in the previous chapter.

`NetworkServer` is the first to be changed. It was responsible for creating and binding the remote objects to the RMI system. Under the old code arrangements, there was also the small start-up class

RMIBankServer. Since the role of the start-up code is now fairly simple, these two will be combined into one class called Activatable BankServer.

Of course, under the guidelines above, any class that implements UnicastRemoteObject will also need to come in for some minor surgery. That means both RemoteAccount and FeedbackManager will need to be altered accordingly. As you will discover shortly, this also means some changes are needed to the AccountManager class as well.

Since we are changing only the server, this means that we do not want to change the client interface. That means the two interfaces that we wrote for the previous chapter, RemoteBankInterface and RemoteBalanceListener, will not be changed. Our new code will just import the definitions straight from the code in Chapter 8.

Implementing the New Server Code

Modification of the server code is a fairly straightforward step-by-step process. Start with the two remote object implementations, continue on to the account management system, and finish with the setup code.

Remote Objects   As you have seen already in this chapter, the first couple of steps in the code modification are to change the base class that our classes extend and to change the constructor parameters.

In the original RemoteAccount class, we passed in references to the account manager and the bank account number as parameters to the constructor. Because we have a fixed constructor parameter list, alternative arrangements are needed. Therefore we are going to take the hint provided earlier in the chapter. A small data-only class is written to hold all the information that we need. This will work fine for the account number. For the account manager, something else is needed.

As discussed a few sections ago, the alternative taken to deal with the account management is to include a static class reference and allocate it only once during the construction of the first activation of the class. Now an interesting point that we shouldn't forget here is that we have two different remote objects that are presented to the outside world. Both of these groups need access to the account manager. If both of them constructed a new instance in their respective constructors, nothing would work as expected. The input side would be sending the client updates into the accounts but on the output, because it is a separate class

Figure 9-5
The
RemoteAccount
constructor.

```
static AccountManager accountManager;

public RemoteAccount(ActivationID id,
                        MarshalledObject data)
  throws RemoteException, IOException, ClassNotFoundException {

  super(id, ((AccountInitData)data.get()).port);

  init_data = (AccountInitData)data.get();

  account_number = init_data.account;

  // Start one if it hasn't been done already
  if(accountManager == null)
    accountManager = new AccountManager(init_data.startTime);

  // Check to make sure the Feedback manager is using the same
  // instance as we are.
  if(FeedbackManager.accountManager != accountManager)
    FeedbackManager.accountManager = accountManager;
}
```

instance, none of these would be reflected in the balance output. The same instance must be accessible to both classes.

The solution to all of this is to construct only one instance in one class, and leave the variable publicly available in the other. Thus, when the RemoteAccount constructs a new AccountManager instance, it assigns the value to the static variable in the FeedbackManager class, ensuring they are always talking to the same object instance. Figure 9-5 shows how this is done.

One small contingency is that you must make sure that this is independent of the order of construction of the classes. That is, what happens if the FeedbackManager instance is created before the Remote Account? Wherever you have this sort of initialization, you must make sure it is reciprocated in all classes. The constructor of the Feedback Manager class should look almost identical to this, with just the names of the classes swapped.

Figure 9-5 also shows a couple of extra details. Notice the code that is needed in the call to the superclass constructor. We are directly extracting the port number from the marshaled object reference passed in. Following that, we properly extract the data that we need for everything else—including the account number.

Account Management   In Figure 9-5 you probably also noted the argument to the `AccountManager` in constructing a new instance of the class. This doesn't match what has been seen in every other class so far. Although the tactic of having a static variable that references a threaded class allows code to run even when the object is not currently active, there are some problems prior to this that need to be overcome.

In every other implementation of our bank server code so far, the server has been running right from the start-up time. That is, the start-up server class created an instance of the `AccountManager` and then passed that instance to the objects that formed the front end listening to the client connections. With the account manager running right from the start, interest is being calculated even before the client has connected. With activation we don't have the luxury of the account manager being already started. It only gets started the first time that someone makes a request of the activatable object. In order to maintain the same behavior as the other servers, something else needs to be done to compensate it.

To solve this requirement, we need to look back at one of the other solutions that were proposed for the server architecture. Basically all that needs to be done is a little compound interest calculation at the time of the construction of the account manager. To do this, we also want to use some other standard OO techniques. Instead of completely rewriting the `AccountManager` class from Chapter 5, we'll simply extend it and supply a new constructor with the required information.

Because of our shortsightedness before, some minor modifications are still required to the original `AccountManager` implementation. While the interest rates and calculation period were declared as private before, they now need to be made protected so that we can access them from the derived class (they are needed in the compound interest calculation). Also required is a new method to obtain the current balance of the account directly rather than waiting for the returned results of a balance listener.

The situation to date is that we now have almost all of the information required. The standard compound interest formula is given as

$$\text{Balance} = \text{principle} * (1 + \text{interest\_rate})^{\text{number\_of\_calculation\_periods}}$$

We have everything except the number of calculation periods. For this, we need to know the elapsed time from when the server was first started and how long a calculation period is. We get the first part by passing the start time into the constructor. The start time is the time that the objects were first registered, since that is how the rest of the implementations have worked. This now explains why in Figure 9-5 there was a `startTime` field in the initialization information.

Having calculated the balance as it should be now, we want to set the balance to be the time-adjusted version, not the original values set in the superclass constructor. We could add an extra setter method to the base class, but that would also require making more modifications to the internal `Account` class as well. As the goal is minimal code impact (remember, in a real system you might not have access to the source for the base class), we'll just deposit the difference between the original balance and the adjusted version. Figure 9-6 shows what needs to be done.

NOTE: *The thread for calculating interest is started in the base class constructor. That thread is started as soon as the constructor in Figure 9-6 is entered because of the call to* `super()`; *all of the calculations and setting done in this derived constructor must be completed* before *the first interest calculation is performed. That is, you have a maximum of around 5 seconds to do it. While that seems like forever in a normal system, when you have around 5 or 10 other threads and applications all demanding CPU time to start up activation, things could get rather tight. Obviously in a real bank system that is not going to be a problem because of the much longer time frames, but for other applications it is something you need to be careful of.*

Setup   Once all of the implementation classes have been completed, the setup code is the last needing to be written. You should always leave the setup code to last, as you don't really know what initialization information is going to be needed until everything is complete.

Writing the setup class is very similar to what you have seen before. Most of it is just a cut-and-paste job for each class to be registered. The only mild changes are those needed to provide differentiation information between the individual URLs for the same class instance. Start time information is taken by using `System.currentTimeMillis()` and assigned to all of the initialization class instances. Note that even though all of the activatable objects use the same class for holding ini-

Figure 9-6
The completed
AccountManager
class.

```
public class AccountManager extends
    rwjn.chapter5.server.AccountManager {

  public AccountManager(long startTime) {
      long current_time = System.currentTimeMillis();

      int num_periods = (int)((current_time - startTime) /
                            INTEREST_SLEEP_PERIOD);

      // Calculate the first account
      float principle = getBalance(0);
      float total;
      float tmp;

      tmp = (float)Math.pow((1 + ACCOUNT_A_RATE), num_periods);
      total = tmp * principle;

      // calculate the amount to deposit
      total -= principle;
      deposit(0, total);

      // Now do it all again for the second account
      principle = getBalance(1);
      tmp = (float)Math.pow((1 + ACCOUNT_B_RATE), num_periods);
      total = tmp * principle;

      // calculate the amount to deposit
      total -= principle;
      deposit(1, total);
  }
}
```

tialization information, you should always create separate instances for each `MarshalledObject` instance that is sent to each class. If you are registering two instances of the same object type under two URLs that contain different start-up information (such as the account number) you should play it cautious and use two instances of the initialization data and also the marshaled object.

The setup code is in the unpackaged `ActivatableBankServer` class. It combines the basic URL location setting code from the RMI Server class and the setup lines for creating and registering descriptions that you've seen a number of times in this chapter already.

Running the Code   Running the server-side code is not much different from anything else you have done before. Like the other activatable code presented so far in this chapter, you will need to include the `java.rmi.server.codebase` property setting and follow all of the other rules regarding CLASSPATH settings and policy files.

One minor point to note is the timing of all the start-ups. Make sure that the registry and rmid are running first. However, particularly on slower machines, you will need to wait some time before starting the code that takes care of the registration process. If you get an exception that looks something like this output:

```
Error creating activatable objects:
java.rmi.activation.ActivationException: unable to register group;
nested exception is:
        java.rmi.activation.ActivationException: ActivationSystem
not running; nested exception is:
        java.rmi.NotBoundException:
java.rmi.server.ActivationSystem
```

it simply means that the rmid/rmiregistry have not completed their start-up yet. Wait for another 5 to 10 seconds and try again.

On the client side, there is no need to change any of your code from what was used in the previous chapter. Starting `RMIClient` will start the client-side code. Choose a port number as before and connect to the server. You should be able to interact with it just as you always have.

Using `ActivationGroups`

So far all of the work you are doing with activation involves just individual object instances. The work that we did moving the bank server to an activation system relied on one assumed principle—both of the object types were running within the same instance of the VM so that the static references could be passed back and forth. While this is guaranteed because of the way that we wrote our code, such may not always be the case.

`ActivationGroups` have many different uses within the activation system. The two of main interest are (1) the way that RMI allows you to control exactly what happens with the placement of objects in VM instances and (2) the way it allows you to pass more information into the environment in which the activation takes place, such as system properties and command-line options.

Controlling the Environment

The most used function of activation groups is to control the start-up environment of activatable objects. Generally speaking, when a client first accesses an object, the activation system will create a new VM instance to run that object in. If the activatable object has special requirements, for example, a different security policy or minimum memory requirements, this information can be passed through with the use of activation groups.

There are three parts needed to control the environment:

1. An `ActivationGroup` class that represents a specific VM instance.

2. The `ActivationGroupDesc` class, which fulfills the same role that the `ActivationDesc` class did for a single object. It represents a group that has yet to be created.

3. The static `CommandEnvironment` inner class of the `ActivationGroupDesc` is used to hold a set of particular environment settings.

In combination, these three classes allow you almost complete control over the environment that your activatable objects run in.

Setting System Properties   Perhaps the most common of all the uses of the command environment control is to set system properties. This offers a useful way of keeping your typed command lines as short as possible. In the examples so far in this chapter you've had to include the `java.rmi.server.codebase` property every time that you've run the code. If you don't have some form of command line history, this can get very tiring for the fingers. Using the techniques here won't stop you from having to type the property in all the time; it just saves you from setting it elsewhere or from providing alternative locations.

Before you start, you'll want to know what properties you want to set. The two most common are `java.rmi.server.codebase` and `java.security.policy`. For the purposes of this demo, a policy file `activation.policy` has been created in the `chapter9` directory of the code. It's very simple, and it allows you to do anything to the system—not a good idea for a real production system.

The first step in setting system properties is to create a `Properties` class instance and populate it with the information that you require to be set. Next, you will need to create a `CommandEnvironment` instance to run in. For just setting properties, this can be null, as the environment does not need to be set. Next you will need to create a description of the group that you would like to use. This takes as arguments the properties list and the command environment. There are other versions of the constructor that can be used that take a class name of the group implementation and location, just as the activation description class does. However, these generally aren't used in normal day-to-day programming.

Once you have a group description you'll need to tell the system about it. To do this, you first need a reference to the system—an `Activation System` instance, that is. This can be obtained through the static `get System()` method in the `ActivationGroup` class. With the system reference you may now register your group description using the `registerGroup()` method. Returned from this is the group ID, which you might want to keep around for later use with the individual activatable object descriptions.

That is all you need to do to set up the properties for a particular object. All the code described above is shown in Figure 9-7 and can also be found in the `GroupPropertyControl` class found in the `rwjn.chapter9` package. Once you've completed the above steps you can continue with the usual activatable object setup that you've become accustomed to.

Setting the Command Environment   Another frequently required option is to modify the default environment. An example would be the initial memory heap size for better performance. To do this, you start with the same basic code setup used in Figure 9-7. This time, instead of leaving the `CommandEnvironment` reference as null, we need to create a new instance of it with all of the appropriate information.

The `ActivationGroup.CommandEnvironment` class represents everything about the functioning of the new VM instance for the activatable objects. The environment information can be set only by creating a new instance of this class. It takes two arguments: the command line used to start the Java VM of your choice and the list of arguments passed to that VM. You might want to set a different Java executable from the standard one that RMID uses—for example, one from Syman-

Figure 9-7
Code that creates
and registers proper-
ties for an activation
group.

```
System.setSecurityManager(new RMISecurityManager());


// Fetch the location and munge to proper URL format
String cwd = System.getProperty("user.dir");
cwd = cwd.substring(3);
cwd = cwd.replace('\\', '/');

String location = "file:///" + cwd + "/";

MarshalledObject data = null;

try {
  System.out.println("Creating Command environment and group");

  Properties props_list = new Properties();
  props_list.put("java.security.policy",
                 "/" + cwd + "/rwjn/chapter9/activation.policy");
  props_list.put("java.rmi.server.codebase", location);

  ActivationGroupDesc.CommandEnvironment ace = null;
  ActivationGroupDesc group_desc =
      new ActivationGroupDesc(props_list, ace);
  ActivationSystem activation_system =
ActivationGroup.getSystem();

  ActivationGroupID agi =
      activation_system.registerGroup(group_desc);

  // continue with the usual object descriptions
  System.out.println("Creating the activation description");
  ActivationDesc desc =
      new ActivationDesc("rwjn.chapter9.RemoteServiceImpl",
                         location,
                         data);
  ...
```

tec rather than the default. The arguments that are passed are those
that would be placed before the class name on a standard Java command line. That is, it is not possible to directly pass arguments to the
activatable object that a normal application would read from the `argv`
parameter of the `main()` method (since this is never called).

NOTE: RMID may add extra arguments to your list either before or after your collection of arguments. As far as I can tell, there is no way of finding out the list of all arguments passed to the system at startup.

To set command-line arguments to set the start-up memory usage and turn off the JIT, you would use the following lines of code:

```
String[] env = {"-Xms50m",
                "-Xmx100m",
                "-Djava.compiler=NONE" };
ActivationGroupDesc.CommandEnvironment ace =
    new ActivationGroupDesc.CommandEnvironment(null, env);
```

Note that the first argument is set to null, which allows `rmid` to use the standard Java runtime. The complete code for this demonstration can be found in the class `GroupEnvControl.java`.

Controlling Access with ActivationGroups

In a real-world situation, security of a server is paramount. There is no point having the best-designed application in the world just to let any cracker walk in through a back door. Any given server may have a number of objects, all performing different functions. Each object should be configured to contain only enough privileges to get the job done. For example, you might have one object being allowed to create files on the local server while another is only allowed to read and change some system properties. You can achieve this by using activation groups.

In the previous couple of sections, you saw how to set properties for a given environment. By simply defining the appropriate policy files for each object, you can create as many different activation groups as you require. With each group you associate the property file and then create the objects for that group.

Customizing Socket Types

Sometimes using the standard communications mechanisms provided by RMI is not enough. Probably the two most common reasons for RMI's wanting different socket implementations are security and compression. Below all the trappings of marshaled objects and stubs and skeletons, RMI uses vanilla TCP sockets for communications. If you don't like this, then you have the option to change it.

Setting of new socket types follows the familiar factory design pattern that you have become accustomed to throughout this book. Depending on what you are doing with RMI, there are two levels that may be taken. Both of these levels use factories; it is just a matter of how and where the factories are set. All of the socket factory-related classes may be found in the `java.rmi.server` package.

SECURITY: *To complete the examples in the following sections, you will need the following permission enabled in your policy file:*

```
java.lang.RuntimePermission "setFactory";
```

Custom Socket Implementation

The first of the factory types is that used with standard RMI. The `RMISocketFactory` takes care of all the socket code needed to produce sockets for both the client and the server side. Creating your own customized socket handling means that you first need to have a custom socket type that you wish to use. We won't go into that in this chapter apart from giving you a simple `GzipSocket` type that implements compression.

NOTE: *If you require a secure network connection, then check out sites like* `java.developer.com` *and* `www.jars.com` *for SSL and other encrypted socket implementations.*

General Socket Factory

Next we need to implement the factory class itself. `RMISocketFactory` is an abstract class, so you'll need to implement `createServer Socket()` and `createSocket()` methods. All you need to do is just return instances of your custom socket implementations. Figure 9-8 shows how we've implemented it with the Gzip versions of the socket.

Figure 9-8
Implementation
of a custom
RMISocket
Factory.

```
package rwjn.chapter9.socket;


import java.net.*;
import java.io.IOException;
import java.rmi.server.RMISocketFactory;

public class GzipRMISocketFactory extends RMISocketFactory {

  public ServerSocket createServerSocket(int port)
    throws IOException {
    return new GzipServerSocket(port);
  }

  public Socket createSocket(String host, int port)
    throws IOException {

    try {
      GzipSocket socket = new GzipSocket(host, port);
      return socket;
    }
    catch(UnknownHostException uhe) {
      throw new IOException(uhe.getMessage());
    }
  }
}
```

Having created the factory implementation, you will need to set it for use in your code. There is no restriction on when you should set the factory, although right at the start-up time would be best. As with the other factories, you may set the factory only once. If you create some RMI connections and then set the factory, only the new connections will use the new socket types.

You might think this could be handy behavior if you want only some connections to be affected, but in reality it is more trouble than it is worth. RMI uses a particular socket connection to a server, and if more objects are later referenced on that server it will attempt to use the already existing socket connection when possible. If your original connection is standard but you want encrypted connections for anything referenced after setting the factory, those later connections may well be unencrypted too.

Setting a factory is achieved through a call to the static `setSocket Factory()` method as follows:

```
RMISocketFactory factory = new
GzipRMISocketFactory();
RMISocketFactory.setSocketFactory(factory);
```

We can apply this factory to any example that uses vanilla RMI handling, such as the examples in the previous chapter. Everything would appear to be normal since, for all RMI knows, it is dealing with a stream and a socket. One point to remember though: What you do to the client you must also do to the server. If you use a socket factory in the client code, make sure that the server code also uses the same factory!

One final point: If you want to add your standard behavior to the default system settings, there is also a static method that allows you to retrieve it. The `getDefaultSocketFactory()` method will always return you the system default implementation. You could use this in combination with error handling to perform a fallback-style system where you move to different implementations if the previous version fails. Remember, the default implementation attempts two different types of HTTP connections for RMI if the default socket handling fails to connect, so keeping around that default behavior is very useful.

Per-Object Socket Creation

It was noted in the previous section that the `RMISocketFactory` is a general mechanism used for all sockets. Java also provides the capability to set the socket handling on a per-object basis as well. Per-object socket factories can be formed only at creation time or export time (which can be the same thing because creating a `UnicastRemote Object` also makes a call to the `exportObject()` method).

For per-object control, there are two factory interfaces that need to be implemented: `RMIClientSocketFactory` and `RMIServerSocket Factory`. The `RMISocketFactory` of the previous section also implemented these two interfaces, so you could use this directly if you wish (hence the ability to fetch the default implementation at any time). Creating new individual socket factories could be as simple as cutting and pasting the code from the `RMISocketFactory` and extending the appropriate interface. Two implementations of these using the GzipSocket classes are available in the rwjn.chapter9.socket package, called GzipClientSocketFactory and GzipServerSocketFactory.

If your object extends UnicastRemoteObject or Activatable, then you may use a different version of the constructor that takes the two factories as arguments. For example, to make the modifications to the RemoteAccount class from Chapter 8 (not the modified Activatable version in this chapter) to use the GzipSockets, the new constructor code would look like this:

```
public RemoteAccount(int accountNumber,
AccountManager mgr)
   throws RemoteException {

   super(0,
         new GzipClientSocketFactory(),
         new GzipServerSocketFactory());

      account_number = accountNumber;
      account_manager = mgr;

}
```

Note that the port number is set to 0 because the previous version used an anonymous port number, since it used the default constructor. The equivalent activatable code looks like this:

```
public RemoteAccount(ActivationID id,
MarshalledObject data)
    throws RemoteException, IOException, ClassNotFoundException
{
    super(id,
          ((AccountInitData)data.get()).port,
          new GzipClientSocketFactory(),
          new GzipServerSocketFactory());

    init_data = (AccountInitData)data.get();

    account_number = init_data.account;

    // Start one if it hasn't been done already
    if(accountManager == null)
      accountManager = new AccountManager(init_data.startTime);

    // Check to make sure the Feedback manager is using the same
```

```
    // instance as we are.
    if(FeedbackManager.accountManager != accountManager)
       FeedbackManager.accountManager = accountManager;
}
```

Exporting an object is not much different. In the `exportObject()` method you can just supply the two factory instances as parameters. To modify the `connect()` method of the `RMIBankClient` code from Chapter 8 you would now write the `exportObject` line as this:

```
Public void connect(String host, int port) {
....

    UnicastRemoteObject.exportObject(this, 0,
            new GzipClientSocketFactory(),
            new GzipServerSocketFactory());
....
```

Again note that we've supplied the port number of 0 to make sure of the same behavior as the previous code. The equivalent for activatable objects is:

```
Activatable.exportObject(this, activation_id, 0,
                    new GzipClientSocketFactory(),
                    new GzipServerSocketFactory());
```

Handling Error Conditions

Wherever there is a network connection, there is always a very good chance that there will be errors along the way. It could be caused by something as simple as someone tripping over the modem lead to something as complex as DNS failure to resolve a domain name. In each case, you need to know about it and deal with it.

For RMI, dealing with failure is similar to dealing with the socket factory code. There is an interface that you must implement, `RMI FailureHandler`, with a single method in it. When the server connection fails for any reason, the failure handler is called. If the method returns a value of true, then that indicates to the system that it should try again to establish a new server socket. Note that this works only for the server-side code; for the client, the handler will never be called, regardless of what happens. Of course, the definition of what is a server can be rather fuzzy too. If you export any object, then the code where that object is exported becomes a server. The RMIBankClient code from the previous chapter is also termed a server because we export that object for later use. If the method call returns false, then no attempt is made to reestablish a server socket. The default implementation always returns true.

The handler is passed the actual exception that happened and allows you the choice of deciding what to do. Java does not document exactly which exceptions might be thrown at your handler, but an educated guess would be anything that could happen when creating a server socket and any of the exceptions in the java.rmi package. In the following example implementation, if there is an UnknownHostException or RMISecurityException then a recheck is not forced; otherwise the default behavior is to always require it.

```
public class SimpleRMIFailureHandler extends
RMIFailureHandler {

  public boolean failure(Exception ex) {
    if((ex instanceof java.rmi.UnknownHostException) ||
      (ex instanceof java.rmi.ConnectException) ||
      (ex instanceof java.rmi.RMISecurityException))
     return false;
    else
      return true;
  }
}
```

Setting the failure handler is done by calling the static setFailure Handler() method in the RMISocketFactory class as follows:

```
RMIFailureHandler handler = new SimpleRMIFailureHandler();
RMISocketFactor.setFailureHandler(handler);
```

One of the messy parts of Java is that, across all of the different networking APIs, the method of handling error conditions is completely inconsistent, unlike the setting of factory implementations. As you will see in the next chapter, the URL connection does not have an error handler. However, the HTTPURLConnection-derived class does allow you to access the error information as a stream.

Summary

In this chapter you've been shown through the more advanced capabilities of RMI, and the new capabilities introduced in Java 2. While there is still more customization that you can do to an RMI system, the majority of the time you won't be needing it. The static variable trick of an activatable object is as far as I've needed to go for any production system.

The next chapter is the final chapter that examines the core of the Java networking APIs—the barely understood protocol and content handlers. Following that, the last section of the book covers one of the most useful of Sun's commercial extension APIs: the Java Shared Data Toolkit.

Customized URL Handling

One of my biggest problems in my years of developing Java applications has been the complete lack of information about how to build customized protocol and content handlers. I had to develop handlers myself, and, once I learnt how to work them, they became some of the most used items in my toolkit. Now almost everything I do uses a set of core libraries for this extended handling. I've even built large-scale application kernels entirely around this concept. In this chapter, I intend to correct the situation that confronted me so that everyone who needs these handlers can learn about them!

The combination of content and protocol handlers can be implemented in many different ways—themes and variations is probably a good way to describe the process. Making basic handler classes is relatively easy. Getting them to work within the context of the standard Java core libraries is not.

Although there is no reason why it couldn't be used, we're going to leave behind our McDuck Bank example for the duration of this chapter. Instead, we'll provide some implementations of tools that are very useful to your day-to-day toolkit as the examples.

Starting Out: URL Stream Handlers

When it comes to your day-to-day programming, the content handlers are likely to be the most important tool. However, without a thorough understanding of the protocol handlers, the content handler capabilities become a bit limited. So we'll start here first.

Protocol handlers, also known as stream handlers, form the core of Java's management of URLs. Any time a URL instance is created, the first thing that Java does is create or find an existing protocol handler. In a standard URL such as

```
http://www.foo.com:80/something/else.html
```

the first bit before the colon defines the protocol type. An interesting thing is that the Java libraries have no built-in knowledge of some of the standard protocols such as HTTP and FTP. Everything is provided through this abstract stream handler medium.

SECURITY: *To complete the examples in the following sections, you will need the following permission enabled in your policy file:*

```
java.lang.RuntimePermission "setFactory";
java.net.SocketPermission "<test_machine>", "connect";
```

Loading a Stream Handler

Our choice of stream handler for this exercise is a Telnet client. For the purposes of this book, the client will be relatively simple—just enough to establish a basic connection and display the text exchange. Even this simple program is useful because you can use it to hook to any TCP port and debug the information going into and out of that port. This is a standard debugging tactic of many a network programmer!

The standard representation of a Telnet URL is telnet://machine:port/. There are generally not any options following the basic definition.

Finding the Right Stream Handler   Before we even get started with implementing a stream handler, we need to understand how and why a stream handler gets created. This is probably a little more complex than you would imagine, as there are three different ways of achieving the same end goal.

We know from our example that the protocol will be `telnet:`. Say our `URLConnection` class is then called `TelnetURLConnection`; we need to go from the URL to the open connection. Close examination of the `java.net` package classes reveals that the class we need to extend is the `URLStreamHandler` abstract class. Given a URL, it returns a `URLConnection` instance. So now we've found our starting point.

As you read back in Chapter 3, "The `java.net` Package," you should not be creating an instance of a stream handler directly. How is it done? Well, the correct answer is, "It depends." The options you have are:

- Implement a `StreamHandlerFactory` to return the appropriate types
- Put the StreamHandler in some package and tell Java about that package
- Put it in the same package as the standard Sun JDK implementation—`sun.net.www.protocol`

Each of these options will now be considered in turn.

Implementing a Stream Handler Factory   When you first glance at the API documentation, your first guess at how to implement a stream handler would probably be the most obvious way: implement the URL StreamHandlerFactory interface. In fact, for many small projects this is the best way to accomplish the task.

The implementation of the factory is very simple; just a single interface method is needed, createStreamHandlerFactory. See Figure 10-1. This method takes a string representing the protocol part of the URL name and then returns an instance of the appropriate URLStreamHandler. It is important to note that if the factory does not understand the type of protocol requested, it should return null rather than throw an exception.

NOTE: *The null value is used by the internal implementation of the URL class to tell it that the factory does not have the answer, so it should try the alternatives.*

Figure 10-1
The
TelnetStream
HandlerFactory
implementation.

```
package rwjn.chapter10;

import java.net.*;
import rwjn.chapter10.telnet.Handler;

public class TelnetStreamHandlerFactory
  implements URLStreamHandlerFactory
{
  public TelnetStreamHandlerFactory() {
    // not doing anything here at the moment
  }

  public URLStreamHandler createStreamHandler(String protocol)  {
    URLStreamHandler ret_val = null;

    if(protocol.equals("telnet"))
      ret_val = new Handler();

    return ret_val;
  }
}
```

As you can see, there is almost nothing to it. Just check that the protocol has the right name and return the appropriate class instance. There are a few important items to note. The handler class is known only by the nondescript name of `Handler`, which tends to go against good coding practice guidelines. Apart from saying that this will save us some extra coding in the long run, we will explain this departure from good practice in the next section. Also of note is the packaging. The factory class is in `rwjn.chapter10` while the handler class is in `rwjn.chapter10.telnet`. Again, there is a reason for this, but it will be covered in the next section.

To get this running inside your application you would now create an instance of this factory class and pass it to the URL class like this:

```
URLStreamHandlerFactory url_factory = new
URLStreamHandlerFactory();
URL.setStreamHandlerFactory(url_factory);
```

This is almost enough to get you ready for work. Assuming that the Telnet protocol handler was written at this stage, everything would work just as required when you create a `telnet:` protocol URL.

Loading without a Factory   If you dig around inside the source of the Java classes that Sun provides with the JDK, you will start to understand how Java looks for classes. More digging around inside the JAR file that is used with JRE shows that all of the standard protocol handlers for loading files, FTP connections, and other protocols that are not in the `java.net` package are all in packages resident under `sun.net.www.protocol` package. That is, there are FTP classes in `sun.net.www.protocol.ftp`, file classes in `sun.net.www.protocol.file`, etc. Taking a shortcut and looking at the javadoc for the URLConnection class reveals that if you place a class in the package `sun.net.www.protocol`, then the protocol implementation will be found when needed.

Deductive reasoning suggests that if we created a new protocol handler and placed it in the `sun.net.www.protocol.telnet` package and made the stream handler implementing class one called `Handler`, we'd be ready to go. In fact, this is what happens. This is the reason we called our stream handler class `Handler` earlier in the chapter.

To use the Telnet URL in this version of the class, there is now nothing to do except create a URL instance and call the `openConnection()` and `connect()` methods in your code.

Using Alternative Packages   While the solution in the previous section looks like the ideal way of using protocol handlers, there's a catch: What if you are using a VM that is not supplied by Sun? You cannot guarantee that it will even check any package starting with sun.*. It relies far too much on specific knowledge of the underlying implementation.

A more general approach is to rely on Sun's property management capabilities instead. Java defines a system property named java. protocol.handler.pkgs that contains a list of packages separated by the pipe character (|), which it looks in to find handlers. When looking for a protocol handler, Java takes each package name in the list, appends the protocol type to it to form a full package name, and then attempts to load the class named Handler within that package.

Looking now at the code for the Telnet handler in the book packages we would need to define the system property as

```
java.protocol.handler.pkgs = rwjn.chapter10
```

Then, we'd need to create a package in the classpath called rwjn.chapter10.telnet and place the Handler class in that. Now, your protocol handlers will load just as they did in the previous package, but without relying on the underlying implementation.

Choosing the Right Way   Since there are so many different ways of loading a protocol handler, which is the best one to choose? To decide, you need to understand the order of preference used internally. First, if there is a stream handler factory loaded, then it is used in preference. If there is no factory, then the java.protocol.handler.pkgs property packages are checked, in the order that you declared them. If the previous two fail, then the sun.net.www.protocol package is checked. If all of these fail, a MalformedURLException is thrown.

NOTE: Most of this can be deduced from the javadoc of the URL constructor without having to look at the source code that comes with the JDK.

From this, you should be able to see that it is possible to override the default implementations of any of the protocol handlers provided with the Java implementation. For example, if you did not like the default HTTP handler, you could write your own and use a factory to ensure that your implementation is loaded in preference.

Before we move on to actually implementing our handler, there are a couple of "gotchas" to look out for. First the applet environment creates a number of restrictions on the basic capabilities. For example, the major browsers won't let you set a new system property by default. Why is this a problem? In an applet, there is no other way of defining the `java.protocol.handler.pkgs` property other than through `System.setProperty()`. Therefore, if you are relying on this method to load a URL protocol handler in a generic applet, you're going to be out of luck. To make this work, you are going to need a factory implementation or have everything under the `sun.net.www.protocol` package.

Factories are quite a good method of dealing with protocol handlers. Their use is explicit in the code, so that someone else knows where the nonstandard items are coming from. However, once you start building up a large inventory of protocol handlers, they can become quite a handful to manage, especially if an application requires only one or two. Assuming you are not going to be using an applet, it becomes more attractive to use the system property loading once you get above three or four different handlers.

Implementing a Protocol Handler

Now that you understand the process of loading a given protocol handler, it is time to move on to implementing one. We'll use the system property method for loading this handler so we'll start with the URL-StreamHandler implementation.

The Telnet protocol is bidirectional, which leaves us with two implementation options because the `URLConnection` class, which implements the lowest-level interface to the stream, offers two options. Either the end user can deal with the raw input stream by using the `getInputStream()` and `getOutputStream()` methods, or we can add extra utility methods into the `TelnetURLConnection` class to do all the low-level handling for us.

How the URL Classes Interact Surprisingly to many people, the `URLStreamHandler` classes do not perform the job of actually creating and dealing with the stream contents. Java has divided the job of dealing with protocol handling into two separate parts.

First, there is a container class for a particular type of protocol. This container class is solely responsible for representing how to construct a

URL connection of the kind that it knows about. This class is derived from URLStreamHandler. Second, there are the classes that actually represent a particular connection of a given URL. This class derives from URLConnection, and is usually cast to the appropriate subclass after it has been returned to the end user.

Internally, this is how the process works. First you, the end user, create a URL class instance. When you are ready to use that URL, you call the openConnection() method. Inside the URL class, the method first determines the protocol type. With this protocol type, it looks up its internal storage to see if a stream handler instance has been created for that protocol type. If it hasn't, a new one is loaded according to the rules defined previously. With this stream handler class, the method now requests of the stream handler to create a new URLConnection with the openConnection method. This connection instance is returned to the end user. It is important to note that, at this time, the underlying network connection has not yet been established, so any attempt to interact with the object (apart from setting parameters) will result in absolutely nothing happening. Only after you have called the connect method of the URLConnection do you have a live network connection to the resource specified by the URL.

Constructing the Stream Handler   Of the two classes that need to be implemented, the stream handler is the simplest. First, we extend the URLStreamHandler class. Because the class is loaded by Java using the Class.forName() method, if you provide a constructor, then it must be the default version, and public. Anything else and the class will refuse to load and throw exceptions.

With that complete, we now need to examine which methods we actually need to override. Since the openConnection() method is declared abstract, that is pretty simple. This method just needs to create a new instance of the TelnetURLConnection class and return that to the caller:

```
public URLConnection openConnection(URL u) {
  return new TelnetURLConnection(u);
}
```

The other methods of the base class can usually be safely left untouched. They assume a syntax that is very similar to the HTTP-style URL definition. Only if your protocol type is different do you normally need to worry about implementing these extra methods.

Implementing the Connection For the purposes of this exercise, the Telnet connection handler will provide many of the convenience methods rather than let you deal with the raw input stream. The definition of the Telnet specification is defined as RFC 854: *Telnet Protocol Specification* and there are a number of extensions in other RFCs for specific applications. In this version, we'll stick to only the basic capabilities of the class for convenience. There is a list of constants defining the various commands that may be used on the stream; these are publicly available, so that those wishing to use their own stream can deal with the extra information.

NOTE: *The Official RFCs relating to Telnet are:*

RFC 854   Telnet Protocol Specification

RFC 855   Telnet Options Specification

RFC 856   Telnet Binary Transmission

RFC 857   Telnet Echo Option

RFC 858   Telnet Suppress Go Ahead Option

RFC 859   Telnet Status Option

RFC 860   Telnet Timing Mark Option

RFC 861   Telnet Extended Options: List Option

RFC 884   Telnet Terminal Type Option

RFC 885   Telnet End of Record Option

RFC 927   TACACS User Identification Telnet Option

RFC 930   Telnet Terminal Type Option

RFC 933   Telnet Output Marking Option

RFC 946   Telnet Terminal Location Number Option

RFC 1041   Telnet 3270 Regime Option

RFC 1043   Telnet Data Entry Terminal Option

RFC 1053   Telnet X.3 PAD Option

RFC 1073   Telnet Window Size Option

RFC 1079   Telnet Terminal Speed Option

RFC 1080   Telnet Remote Flow Control Option

RFC 1091   Telnet Terminal Type Option

RFC 1096   *Telnet X Display Location Option*

RFC 1097   *Telnet Subliminal-Message Option*

RFC 1116   *Telnet Linemode Option*

RFC 1143   *The Q Method of Implement TELNET Options*

RFC 1184   *Telnet Linemode Option*

RFC 1205   *5250 Telnet Interface*

RFC 1372   *Telnet Remote Flow Control Option*

RFC 1408   *Telnet Environment Option*

RFC 1409   *Telnet Authentication Option*

RFC 1411   *Telnet Authentication: Kerebos Version 4*

RFC 1412   *Telnet Authentication: SPX*

RFC 1416   *Telnet Authentication Option*

RFC 1571   *Telnet Environment Option Interoperability*

RFC 1572   *Telnet Environment Option*

RFC 2066   *Telnet CHARSET Option*

Without going into detail about how Telnet works, there are a couple of background items that need to be sorted out. Basic Telnet operates in text mode using 7-bit ASCII characters; Java can operate in 8- or 16-bit mode with UTF. Another point is that this protocol handler is used to define the client side only. We're not going to give this full server capability. Also, since the code is quite large, we can't describe every single thing that has been implemented. The code is heavily documented, so make sure you check it out.

Now, on with business. The constructor takes the URL reference and keeps the appropriate information. At this stage, we don't need to do anything—that waits until the connect method is called by the end user. Inside connect we establish a socket to the destination machine and port, obtain the input and output streams, and then return to the user. A Telnet session does not really require any parameters, but we will include a timeout option. This option is used to time out the making of the initial connection. If nothing is happening on the link, the system will close the connection and notify the user of the problem.

We have some tough design decisions to make. There are a number of different ways that we can implement this URL connection:

1. We can make use of all the standard default `URLConnection` methods so that the user never knows what is going on internally.

2. Make the user cast the `URLConnection` to the `TelnetURL Connection` and use only the methods provided.

3. Give them the input and output streams and let them deal with everything themselves.

While option 3 sounds like the most attractive of the alternatives, it is also the most risky. One of the reasons that Java provides a number of predefined URL handlers is that the problems of dealing with complex protocols that are interactive in nature can quickly lead to the path of doom for an inexperienced programmer. One missed byte can cause a lot of problems. So the decision was made to mainly support option 2 with a few ideas from option 1 thrown in.

We're not going to cover exactly how this has all been implemented at this stage. This will come as we explain how the client user interface was implemented. There is quite a lot of low-level Telnet handling that would need to be covered if we were to explain it. Since the book is mainly about Java networking and not Internet virtual terminal protocol implementations, we'll limit the discussions to just the Java-specific ideas.

NOTE: *There are a lot of the basic Telnet commands that have not been implemented in this URLConnection. The main reason is that many of them require the use of socket options like MSG_OOB that are not provided in Java's default socket implementation.*

Writing a User Interface

Unlike many professional Telnet implementations, this implementation won't give you a pretty GUI interface. Telnet lives in the world of the command line, which may come as a bit of a shock to MS Windows users. So what you're going to get is the command line. Actually, we've gone even more archaic than that, to a text-based interface designed specifically for testing and debugging. At least we've got online help— just type a question mark (?) on a line by itself.

User's Guide   We're sending values and commands one at a time. The first character on each line will indicate what the command is. If the first character is a colon, then that indicates what follows is a command. The commands available are help, echo, and exit. Echo can take a second argument that requests the server to turn echoing on and off.

When the client first starts, you may supply a machine name as an argument:

```
java Telnet bogus.machine.com
```

It will attempt a connection to that machine. If the connection fails, then the Java application will exit. If no machine is specified, it will attempt to connect to `localhost`.

Sending Values Since the basic connection operates only in text mode, two methods are provided:

sendChars(String) sends text along the link-

requestOption(byte[]) passes Telnet commands

The restriction of 7-bit ASCII characters provides some interesting challenges because of the internationalization features in Java's strings. For this simple implementation, we've just stuck our heads in the sand with the hope that we don't end up with any 8-bit UTF characters coming from the string (the sendChars() method takes only a string).

Many URLConnections offer input streams to the users so that they may do their own low-level handling. For this implementation, I decided against this by leaving the default getInputStream() method to return null, to guard against any invalid commands being sent. Providing the convenience methods makes it a simple matter of working out what commands need to be sent and when, without worrying about protocol byte order.

NOTE: *There is another, potentially more difficult problem. Java's command line capabilities when acting as a console application, do not allow you to turn the character echo off. Therefore, such things as passwords, which in a real program would be replaced by empty characters or asterisks, will be echoed letter for letter for the benefit of anyone who can see your screen.*

Reading Values For the same reason that you don't have an input stream to play with, you don't have an output stream either. Instead,

I've decided to override the default `getContent()` method to return the contents of the stream. Normally this is defined to get the content of the entire connection. Telnet does not offer us any such luxury because of its interactive nature.

Dealing with this interactive nature has a very simple solution. Keep calling `getContent()` until the session ends! Each time the method is called, it will read the next chunk of data and convert it to a command or the character string. It reads only what is needed from the stream and returns the information. Determining when to stop the current process is a simple matter of stopping when a Telnet command string begins (the byte value is 255) or when there is no more data left to read.

The `Object` you get back from the `getContent()` method call can be either of two types: a `String` or a `TelnetCommand` instance. A simple string is used whenever there is plain text, and the `TelnetCommand` is returned when there is some internal command to deal with. Once you have that command, you either deal with it or ignore it. Many times you might ignore it because it is a return of a local request that has been made by the client. Other times the server sends a request, which you must respond to. Figure 10-2 shows the code used to read and process values from the Telnet connection. These take place inside a thread created specially for the purpose in the `TelnetReader` class.

Dealing with Commands   A feature of the Telnet protocol is the interleaving of commands with the character stream. Generally, this all happens at the beginning of the connection or at times when driven by user input. Once the stream reading is invoked through `getContent()` (which is covered in the next section), the protocol determines if the next item to read is a command. The command processing code is kept in the `readCommand()` private method of `TelnetURLConnection`.

NOTE: *RFC 1143 defines a method of implementing nice behavior for sending and receiving option requests. Although this code does not implement it directly, it is up to the calling code to adhere to these conventions to prevent unnecessary network traffic.*

The code of interest in this section, however, is the `TelnetCommand` class itself (shown in Figure 10-3). In many ways it is very much like a standard AWT event. Some of the commands are held internally by the connection implementation for various reasons. Sometimes the replies

Figure 10-2
Code for processing
the incoming Telnet
stream from the
`TelnetURL`
`Connection`.

```
package rwjn.chapter10;


....


public class TelnetReader implements Runnable {
  ...
  public void run() {
    Object info;
    TelnetCommand cmd;

    try {
      while(true) {
        info = connection.getContent();

        if(info instanceof TelnetCommand) {
          cmd = (TelnetCommand)info;
          if(!cmd.isConsumed() && cmd.isReply()) {
            switch(cmd.getCommand()) {
              case TelnetConstants.TERMINAL_TYPE:
              case TelnetConstants.NAWS:
              case TelnetConstants.X_DISPLAY_LOCATION:
              case TelnetConstants.ENVIRON:
              case TelnetConstants.NEW_ENVIRON:
                  connection. replyToOptionRequest(cmd, false);
                  break;

              default:
            }
          }
        }
        else if(info instanceof String)
          System.out.print(info);
      }
    }
    catch(IOException ioe) {
      System.out.println("Reading Telnet connection error: " + ioe);
    }
  }
  ....
}
```

Figure 10-3

The Telnet
Command class
implementation.

```java
public final class TelnetCommand implements
TelnetConstants {
  private boolean consumed = false;

  private byte[] data;

  private byte command;

  TelnetCommand(byte cmd, byte[] msg) {
    command = cmd;
    data = msg;
  }

  final void setConsumed() {
    consumed = true;
  }

  public boolean isConsumed() {
    return consumed;
  }

  public byte getCommand() {
    return command;
  }

  public boolean isRequest() {
    boolean ret_val = false;

    if((data[0] == DO) ||
        ((data[0] == SB) && (data[1] == DO)))
      ret_val = true;

    return ret_val;
  }

  public byte[] getData() {
    return data;
  }

  // toString is also implemented by not shown
}
```

are for these internal requests; however, we don't wish to deny that information also to the listening class. Therefore we can mark a command as being consumed and thus for interest only. Also, a convenience method is added to see if this is a reply to an option request. Usually this has special significance for either display options or other behind-the-scenes effects (such as terminal emulators).

Combining Figures 10-2 and 10-3, you can see how the two work together for processing of commands. Note the check in Figure 10-2 to see if the command has been consumed and to see if it was a reply to another message. If it was not a reply, then it must have been a request from the server for information. We could have put some good behavior in here, but for this simple implementation we have simply denied any requests by the server to gain information about the client. The list of commands that you see there is designed to handle the Solaris 2.6 Telnet daemon.

Finishing up   To tidy everything up, we've placed all of the start-up code in a class called, naturally enough, `Telnet`. This class is responsible for setting everything up and making the client run. Figure 10-4 shows the complete start-up code for this test client.

Figure 10-4
Test client start-up code for Telnet URLs.

```
public class Telnet {
  private URL url;

  private TelnetURLConnection connection;

  public Telnet(String host, int port) {
    try {
      url = new URL("telnet", host, port, "");

      System.out.println("opening connection");

      connection = (TelnetURLConnection)url.openConnection();

      System.out.println("Connecting");

      connection.connect();

      System.out.println("Starting consumer");
```

Figure 10-4
(*Continued*)

```java
      new TelnetReader(connection);
      new TelnetWriter(connection);
    }
    catch(MalformedURLException mue) {
      System.out.println("Malformed URL! " + mue);
    }
    catch(ConnectionException ce) {
      System.out.println("Unable to connect");
      System.out.println(ce);
      System.exit(0);
    }
    catch(IOException ioe) {
      System.out.println("Error with I/O " + ioe);
    }
  }

  public static void main(String[] args) {
    String host = "localhost";
    int port = TelnetConstants.DEFAULT_PORT;

    if(args.length > 0) {
      host = args[0];

      if(args.length > 1) {
        try {
          port = Integer.parseInt(args[1]);
        }
        catch(NumberFormatException nfe) {
          System.out.println("Learn to type! :)");
        }
      }
    }

    System.out.println("Setting factory");
    URL.setURLStreamHandlerFactory
      (new TelnetStreamHandlerFactory());

    System.out.println("creating client");
    Telnet telnet = new Telnet(host, port);
  }
}
```

Content Handlers

Now that you have the fundamentals of protocol handlers in order, it is time to look at the other half of the system. For every URL connection, there is some sort of information that flows either as text or binary data. Protocol handlers give us a nice, independent way of expanding the core Java-provided capabilities. There also is a nice way of expanding the process of interpreting that information flow and turning it into something usable: content. Content handlers, as the name suggests, are the basis of this approach.

In this section, we'll implement one of the most called-for features in the Java bug list on the Java Developer Connection web site—a PNG image loader.

Introduction to Content Handlers

In Chapter 3, "The `java.net` Package," you got a brief overview of what protocol and content handlers are. Although it didn't explain that much, you should now start to see the similarities between content handlers and protocol handlers. They operate on the same loading principles: factory classes or dynamic loading using system properties.

Content handlers take the stream of bytes and interpret them according to some rules. How these rules are determined depends on the URL protocol type. For example, in an HTTP connection, the appropriate handler is given to you by the underlying protocol, while the file protocol bases the choice of rules on the filename extension. A content handler is loaded only after the connection has been made.

Once a particular content handler has been loaded, it is given the URL connection to fetch an input stream from. Having received the contents of the stream, it then processes them and generates a representative object. Generally speaking, you won't call the `getContent()` method of the content handler directly. It is more likely to be done by calling the method of the same name in the URL class. This method returns an Object instance, which then needs to be cast to the right class type to be used.

Loading a Content Handler

Loading content handlers follows a similar pattern to that for protocol handlers. There is a factory interface that you can implement, or you can use the system property to load them dynamically.

Finding the Right Content Handler   With protocol handlers, determining the right handler was a very simple affair. The characters before the first colon defined the name of the protocol handler to look for. Content handlers present a more difficult task, as they are completely independent of the underlying protocol stream. Content handlers are described by the MIME type that they support. That is, to locate a particular content handler for, say, a JPEG image, you need to look for the content handler that supports image/jpeg as its type. Internally to the URLConnection class, this is how they are stored.

Java provides a number of ways around this. First, it could use the underlying protocol to give it the right hint. HTTP provides this. Part of the HTTP header includes the content type in the MIME type format, allowing the correct handler to be loaded. Because all of this takes place within the connection, the URLConnection provides a number of convenience methods to deal with the lookup process.

Simpler URL types such as file:// do not have the information directly available as part of the protocol. In this case, a different approach is needed, one that uses the name of the file to look up the appropriate type. This process is done by using the protected method guessContentTypeFromName(). Internally, this method makes a query of the installed FileNameMap. If this fails, you also have the alternative of calling the other protected method, guessContentType FromStream(), which does a search of the leading bytes of the stream to determine the file type.

File Name Mapping   We'll take a quick diversion from the main topic here to discuss how to implement a filename map, as this is also handy knowledge (more customizability). File name maps are pretty simple creatures—given a file name, they return the MIME type.

To implement your own customized file name mapping, extend the FileNameMap interface in java.net. It is recommended that your implementation also include a reference to another FileNameMap instance. Java already has a default name mapping set when you start. The purpose of providing your own mapping is to extend the default. When you set the map, you replace the standard one with your implementation. If you don't first fetch the default version and keep it around, you'll loose all that information. This default reference can be sent to your implementation through the constructor (as demonstrated in Figure 10-5) or some other method.

From our example implementation you can see that the constructor adds a list of extensions to the internal hashtable. When it comes to

Figure 10-5
A simple `File`
`NameMap`
implementation.

```java
package rwjn.chapter10;

import java.net.*;
import java.util.Hashtable;

public class ExtensionHandler
  implements FileNameMap {
  private Hashtable extension_map;

  private FileNameMap default_map;

  public ExtensionHandler(FileNameMap map) {
    default_map = map;
    extension_map = new Hashtable(10, 0.9f);

    // now populate the table with your own information.
    // These are basic ideas. Feel free to add and remove your own.
    extension_map.put("png", "image/png");
    extension_map.put("wrl", "model/vrml");
    extension_map.put("pdf", "application/pdf");
  }

  public static final String getFileExtension(String filename) {
    int last_pos = filename.lastIndexOf('.');
    String ret_val = filename.substring(last_pos + 1);

    return(ret_val);
  }

  public String getContentTypeFor(String filename) {
    // get the filename extension - see SRCSS.io.file code....
    String ext = getFileExtension(filename);

    if(ext == null)
      return null;

    String type = (String)extension_map.get(ext);

    if((type == null) && (default_map != null))
      type = default_map.getContentTypeFor(filename);

    return type;
  }
}
```

doing lookups, it first queries the hashtable for the file type. If this fails, then consult the default map that has been passed to you for the type.

Installing your newly created file name map requires first that you fetch the previously installed map, create a new instance of your class, and then set your map to be the default. The following code snippet shows how this is done:

```
FileNameMap old_map = URLConnection.getFileNameMap();
ExtensionHandler new_map = new ExtensionHandler(old_map);
URLConnection.setFileNameMap(new_map);
```

Now, whenever a file type needs to be determined, your customized mapping will be used. The best feature of the above scheme is that potentially many different parts of the application could all insert their own mapping schemes independently and the system will handle it. Then all you need to worry about is making sure they don't provide conflicts with two different implementations providing differing answers for the same file name.

NOTE: *Unlike working with content and protocol handler factories, here you are able to set a FileNameMap more than once during the lifetime of the application.*

Implementing a Content Handler Factory   A standard content handler factory is very similar in implementation to the `URLStreamHandler`. The method name and return type are different, but the basic process is the same. For our simple content handler factory that is implemented in Figure 10-6, the only type handled is `image/png`. After creating a new instance of the content handler, it is returned to the caller for use.

Loading without a Factory   By now you should start to see the similarities between content handlers and protocol handlers. Both have factories to create them and both use independent types. Also, they both have ways of being created without a factory. However, there is a small difference.

For protocol handlers, you had a choice of either using a predefined package or using your own package and an environment variable to tell Java where to look. For content handlers the choice is smaller—you may use only the predefined package:

```
sun.net.www.content.<content type>
```

```
package rwjn.chapter10;

import java.net.*;
import rwjn.chapter10.image.*;

public class ImageContentHandlerFactory
   implements ContentHandlerFactory {

   public ImageContentHandlerFactory() {
   }

   public ContentHandler createContentHandler(String mimetype) {
     ContentHandler ret_val = null;

     if(mimetype.equals("image/png"))
       ret_val = new png();

     return ret_val;
   }
}
```

NOTE: *Java 1.1 allowed you the same options as protocol handlers.
You could define an environment variable* `java.content.handler.`
`pkgs` *that would contain a list of packages to search for the appropriate
content handler. Although it was never officially mentioned in the*
`javadoc` *comments, it was supported. The source that comes with JDK
1.2 indicates that it is still available, but the compiled version of the
libraries does not appear to support it.*

The content-type subpackage refers to the major type from the
MIME type that the content handler deals with. Into this package then
goes a class whose name is the minor type, including capitalization of
the class name. Our example case, where we are going to write a PNG
content handler, has a MIME type of `image/png`. Therefore, our code
would be placed in the package `sun.net.www.content.image` and
the class would be called `png`. Note that the class name is all lowercase
because the MIME type is represented always this way. This is one of
the few times where you are not following the coding conventions established by Sun.

Implementing a Content Handler

With the package and filename business settled, we can get on with coding a solution. First, we need to establish how we're going to implement the content handler. We have an image type to load so we'll need to find the specification or a library that implements the specification. In our case, we choose the latter and obtained a copy of `libpng` (it can be found at http://www.cdrom.com/pub/png/) to serve as our starting base.

Architecture   Implementing content handlers is not as simple or straightforward as you might expect. Generally, you don't just implement one content handler. Usually there are a number of them—for example, you might do a bunch of the image formats that aren't supported by Java. In our case, our projects require more than just PNG support; they also need TIFF, TGA, BMP, PCX, and others. Because Java is relatively slow compared to native code, you don't really want to be implementing all of these handlers in pure Java either. Native code will be needed, which means needing Java Native Interface (JNI) support (and the appropriate C or C++ compiler). Finally, there is the same decision about factory versus dynamic loading of classes that you faced for protocol handlers.

In this example, we'll consider these points in reverse order. First we'll choose to use a factory to create the content handlers. Next, we've been working in a Win32 environment so everything will be built using Microsoft's Visual C++ compiler and Sun's JNI libraries. Finally, everything is built to handle multiple image types, both on the Java side and the native side. We have a single image loader that acts as the native front end to all of the loader libraries.

The common front end to all of the image loaders takes place in the code in `rwjn.chapter10.image`. This contains an image loader and buffering classes, which are generic for all image types. The classes used by the content handler are then located in `rwjn.chapter10.content.image`. Also, in order to make minimal changes to the core native library, we've implemented a separate front end in native code to do all the appropriate data manipulation for the library from the Java representation.

The Content Handler Class   As mentioned in the previous section, the implementation of the content handler is very thin. It contains only the minimal amount of code to do any processing. In effect, this means

```
package rwjn.chapter10.content.image;

// Standard imports
import java.net.*;
import java.io.*;

// Application specific imports
import rwjn.chapter10.image.ImageDecoder;

public class png extends ContentHandler {
  private ImageDecoder decoder = null;

  public Object getContent(URLConnection u)
    throws IOException {

    // create a new image decoder ready to decode a PNG image
    if(decoder == null)
      decoder = new ImageDecoder("png");

    // now decode the image from the input stream
    return decoder.decode(u.getInputStream());
  }
}
```

providing the required `getContent()` method and that is it. Figure 10-7
contains the entire source of the class. Again, note the class name `png` is
spelled in all lowercase.

When the `getContent()` method is called, the class simply creates a
new image decoder, telling it that the type is "png." We decode the image
by passing the decoder the input stream from the `URLConnection`
passed in.

You should note how our design decision regarding the Telnet protocol
handler (not to allow the raw input stream to be available) would
adversely affect our implementation here. In retrospect that probably
wasn't the best design decision, considering that we might want to combine content handlers with the stream.

Implementing an Image Decoder   The real action begins with the
`ImageDecoder` class. Inside this class we take the input stream, feed it
to the native code, and then reassemble the returned chunks of data into
a Java image. To achieve this we need three classes: the holder of all the

data processing, a class to send information to the native code (explained shortly), and one to represent an ImageProducer so that we may create a standard Java image.

We want the image decoder to work as efficiently as possible. This requires feeding data to the native code and then processing the returned data to produce an image. The problem that we face is that the raw data is in some compressed format, but the real image is presented in a row-by-row fashion. What we send to the native code does not exactly correspond to the returned decoded bytes. This means we can't have just a single method call where we send data and then get the return value as a bunch of pixels to be added to the image. It means that we need an asynchronous feed of the bytes representing the raw data stream and a separate reader getting the pixels to be placed in the image, hence the need for the third class described above. We implement it through an inner class in the decoder.

Figure 10-8 shows the implementation of the `BufferFiller` inner class of `ImageDecoder`. Note that the processing is contained in the `run()` method so that the class may operate as a separate thread to the reading code. The information is contained in 8-K blocks of data that is sent to the native code through the `sendData()` method call after they are read from the incoming stream. Remember that this incoming stream may be a web server located somewhere on the other side of the world, so the execution of the while loop may not be instantaneous.

Starting the image decoding process is a straightforward affair. In the constructor of the `ImageDecoder` class we make sure that the native code DLL has been loaded and supports the required image type that we want to decode (remember that this class serves for more than just the PNG image type). If the DLL does not support the required image type it throws an `IllegalArgumentException`.

With the setup code out of the road, the `decode()` method is used to perform all of the actions required. The `decode()` method was kept separate from the constructor so that we need to create only one instance of the decoder class for a particular image type. By having a separate method that takes the input stream each time, we save a lot of overheads, from the start-up and binding to the native code library.

Once we are ready to start decoding, we start the buffer filler class (Figure 10-8) and tell the native library to start the decoding process. Before we can continue processing the data, we need some basic information, the image width and height, so that we may create our return data structure. Now that everything is set on the receiving end, it is just

Figure 10-8
The threader buffer
sending inner class.

```java
private class BufferFiller extends Thread {
  private InputStream stream;

  BufferFiller(InputStream is) {
    stream = is;
  }

  public void run() {
    final int BUF_SIZE = 8192;
    byte[] buffer = new byte[BUF_SIZE];
    int num_read = 0;

    // copy contents of the input stream to native code
    do {
      try {
        num_read = stream.read(buffer, 0, BUF_SIZE);
      }
      catch(IOException e) {
        // error occurred reading!
        System.out.println("error reading from input stream");
      }

      // send the data.  Note that this also sends a -1 when
      // the input stream is exhausted.  This is correct
      // behavior as the -1 is used to signal the native
      // side that input has finished
      sendData(buffer, num_read);
    } while(num_read != -1);
  }
}
```

a case of looping for the number of rows expected, reading the processed data from the native code, and placing that in our image holder. Once everything is complete, we signal the end of the decoding process to the native code. Finally, we pass the image data to the default system toolkit, asking it to create an image with the data. All of this process is shown in Figure 10-9, where you will see the code of the decode method.

Interfacing to Native Code   Missing so far from the explanation is how we go from the Java code into the native library that we downloaded from the Internet. Naturally this is going to require the use of JNI. We showed parts of the `ImageDecoder` class in Figure 10-9.

Figure 10-9

The decode method of the image decoding process.

```
public Image decode(InputStream is)
  throws IOException {

  if (imageType == null) {
      throw new IOException("ImageDecoder.decode():" +
                            " null image type!");
  }

  // this is where we will place all the decoded image data
  ImageBuffer imBuffer = null;

  try {
    // perform initialization
    setImageType(imageType);

    // start sending data to be decoded
    BufferFiller bf = new BufferFiller(is);
    bf.start();

    // start the decoding
    startDecoding();

    // decoding has been started so we can now get image dimensions
    int width = getImageWidth();
    int height = getImageHeight();

    // create a buffer large enough to hold all the data
    imBuffer = new ImageBuffer(width, height);

    // temporary buffer to receive data one row at a time
    int[] tmpBuffer = new int[width];

    // now extract the image data
    for(int i=0; i<height; i++) {
      getNextImageRow(tmpBuffer);
      imBuffer.setImageRow(i, tmpBuffer);
    }
  }
  catch(InternalError e) {
    // any errors, just pass them on
    throw new IOException(e.getMessage());
  }
  finally {
    // Ensure that we perform cleanup
    finishDecoding();
  }

  // now create an image from the buffered data
  return Toolkit.getDefaultToolkit().createImage(imBuffer);
}
```

243

Figure 10-10
Method outline for
the `ImageDecoder`
class illustrating the
native methods.

```
public class ImageDecoder {


    private class BufferFiller extends Thread {};

    public ImageDecoder(String type);

    public Image decode(InputStream is) throws IOException;

    public native String[] getFileFormats();

    private native void setImageType(String type)
        throws InternalError;

    native void sendData(byte[] buffer, int size);

    private native void startDecoding()
        throws InternalError;

    private native int getImageWidth()
        throws InternalError;

    private native int getImageHeight()
        throws InternalError;

    private native void getNextImageRow(int[] buffer)
        throws InternalError;

    private native void finishDecoding();
}
```

Figure 10-10 shows the complete outline of the methods of the class
without their bodies. This will give you an idea of which methods are
native and which are not.

NOTE: *Since we're not C programmers for the life of this book, I'll skip
most of the implementation details about the native side of the house. You
can view the entire source in the* `src` *directory that is in the directory
that represents the package* `rwjn.chapter10`.

After running `jnih` through this class to produce the appropriate method names and C header files, we then create the source files for joining the library code to the Java code. Two source files are created: `readpng.c` is the low-level interface making the calls to the `libpng` functions while `decode_image.c` is the front end implementing the native interface.

You will remember that one of the goals of the library is to support more than one image format. The front-end file `image_decode.c` is responsible for taking the current image type and calling the appropriate library—without knowing exactly which libraries are to be called—at a certain time. This is achieved in C by making heavy use of function pointers to dereference the functionality from the interface.

NOTE: *The data structures and instructions on how to add new image formats are provided in the* `decode_image.h` *header file. Adding a new image format is as simple as adding three lines to the C header file and a new file for doing the translations between the function pointers and the image library.*

The final point of interest for this topic is how to deal with the sending of the data from the native code to the library. Generally speaking most of the image codecs that you run across on the Internet use files for reading and writing. This is an annoyance when your data may be coming from a socket connection from a web server somewhere on the other side of the world. One solution is to write the incoming data to a temporary file and then get the library to read that and send you the image back. This is not only slow but also inefficient, as the file must first complete downloading before the conversion process can take place. The solution that we use is to create pipes and use that as the file descriptor. The incoming data is written to one end of the pipe while the library uses the other end of the pipe just as though it were a normal FILE pointer.

NOTE: *The native code that we've supplied with this should be as cross-platform as possible. We've compiled and ran it on both Solaris 2.6 and Windows NT machines. If you get any other platforms running, let us know!*

Using Content Handlers

Now that your basic content handler code is complete, you will need an application to display the data to make sure that it works. The test class `ImageTestFrame` extends an AWT frame to provide a very simple test for the content handler and can be found in the package `rwjn.chapter10`.

Opening the Connection For the simple test application, we'll limit ourselves to using only file-based URLs. A button is used to show an open dialog; the information used to create the URL is extracted from this dialog. The first step to loading a file is to create the URL representing it.

```
FileDialog dialog =
    new FileDialog(this, "Select Image file",
                    FileDialog.LOAD);
dialog.show();

// obtain the url to the image
String urlStr = "file:///" +
                    dialog.getDirectory() +
                    dialog.getFile();
url = url.replace('\\', '/');
cp1b:url = url.replace(':', '|');
```

The extra slash and processing is needed for Win32 machines to turn the URL into a valid string. Next, an instance of the URL class is created and a connection is opened:

```
url = new URL(urlString);
URLConnection connection = url.openConnection();
```

Displaying the File Before we can go any further, it is also worthwhile to learn what type of content we are about to fetch. We need this for a variety of reasons. First, it might be used to decide how to behave with the content on the connection. For example, we might want to load any GIF and JPEG images using the standard Java toolkit methods:

```
String contentType = connection.getContentType();

if (contentType.equals("content/unknown")) {
  // unknown content type
  System.err.println("Unknown content type for " + url);
}
else if (contentType.equals("image/jpeg") ||
```

```
        contentType.equals("image/gif")) {
    // let java handle these natively
    img = Toolkit.getDefaultToolkit().getImage(url);
}
```

Having established that it is one of the types that we are interested in, we can then make the connection for the image by using the get Content() method. As you have seen previously in the Telnet implementation, this will return us the content when it feels ready and then return that as an Object. Before displaying the image, we first test whether the content type is really an Image and then render it to the screen:

```
// now use our content handlers
Object o = connection.getContent();
if (o instanceof Image) {
  img = (Image) o;
}
repaint();
```

The paint method takes care of painting the image to screen.

Content-Type Properties   Sometimes you will find that using a FileNameMap does not work sufficiently well for your needs or doesn't work at all. In these cases there is an alternative, but much more involved, method. This involves directly editing the properties files that Java uses to define MIME types.

The content-type.properties file is used to define to the system the default collection of MIME types. It can be found in <JAVA_HOME/jre/lib. The format of the file is fairly simple, allowing cut and paste additions to the known default types. For example, to add the PNG type to the file you would add the following lines to the file:

```
image/png: \
description=PNG Image;\
file_extensions=.png;\
icon=png
```

While editing this file is not difficult when you are working on a small number of known machines, dealing with web-based applications or other large-scale applications can be impossible. This file should really be used only as a last resort. Remember, upgrading your version of the

JDK may well wipe out this file and replace it with another; you may thus lose all the changes you have made. It is much better to stay with the alternatives if possible.

Summary

Well, that's about all you can learn about content and protocol handlers. Being one of the least understood areas of Java networking, they tend not to be used too much. Hopefully now you have a much greater understanding of how they fit into the system. Also a word of caution is in order: since these handlers are among the least-used areas of Java, the bugs in the Java implementations also tend to be ripe. Make sure you test your code on as many target platforms as you can before deploying it.

This ends the look at the core Java classes and how they are used. The final section of the book looks at one of Sun's commercial toolkits for adding collaborative capabilities on top of the standard Java APIs.

The Java Shared Data Toolkit

So far everything that you have looked at in this book is part of the core Java API product from Javasoft and forms part of the Java Media Framework. In the next few chapters we'll be looking at one of the applied uses of Java to provide higher-level abstract functionality for applications.

With the growth of the Internet and distributed organization, one buzzword that has managed to survive the rapid cycling of the marketing machines is "collaboration." The products built on the principles of collaboration usually fall into the category called *Groupware*. The principal aim of these pieces of software has been to aid in group participation to build something—a document, an aircraft, or a virtual community. Programs that employ collaborative concepts range from simple shared whiteboarding applications such as Microsoft's NetMeeting to Lotus Notes to military simulations (based on Distributed Interactive Simulation, or DIS protocol).

To date, all of these programs have relied on the use of fixed or proprietary protocols that you cannot just take and expand to add whatever you like. As part of the Java media framework, Sun has been developing an abstract toolkit that allows the programmer to deal only with the collaborative aspects instead of having to build low-level networking code as well. This API is known as the *Java Shared Data Toolkit,* or just *JSDT.*

NOTE: *JSDT is not part of the standard Java APIs (`java.*`) or part of the extension APIs (`javax.*`). It is a commercial product from Javasoft. Having worked extensively with JSDT and other collaborative systems including custom-written code, I'm writing about it because I think it is a very handy toolkit to know about and a great time saver. This book is covering version 1.4 of JSDT. Since it is a rapidly evolving specification adding new capabilities, be sure to keep an eye on the latest version at*

http://java.sun.com/products/media/jsdt/

What Is JSDT?

JSDT is an abstract API that can be used for providing collaborative applications very easily. It removes almost all of the details about its underlying protocols (which may be proprietary) and provides easily interoperable applications just by knowing the data that is shared between them. In the words of the JSDT introductory documentation:

This toolkit has been defined to support highly interactive, collaborative applications. It provides the basic abstraction of a session (i.e., a group of objects associated with some common communications pattern), and supports full-duplex multipoint communication among an arbitrary number of connected application entities—all over a variety of different types of networks. In addition, this toolkit provides efficient support of multicast message communications, the ability to ensure uniformly sequenced message delivery and a token-based distributed synchronization mechanism.

If you haven't managed to follow all of that, basically it is saying that JSDT is a toolkit to do such things as whiteboarding, videoconferencing, and workgroup products without knowing whether you have a TCP/IP stack, HDCL, or some RS232-based serial line protocol for doing the communications. Very cool! At the same time, you can quickly change the underlying implementation without affecting your application.

Where Would You Use JSDT?

This is an unusual question to be asking without even knowing really what an API provides. Think of any application where you might want all the users to have exactly the same view of some information. If one changes it, everyone would see the updates immediately.

One of the first things that you might think of would be a shared whiteboard. You've seen some of these products around for a while: Microsoft's Netmeeting and Netscape's Collabra, for example. These are fairly simple—you may have even written one yourself. What about some more complex ideas? Video conferencing uses shared data principles. How about a real-time viewer of a database structure or multiuser virtual worlds? All of these and many more are possible uses of JSDT. If some of these uses seem a little strange, read on to find out why.

Defining Collaborative

Our first problem is actually defining the term *collaborative application*. Depending on your view of the world, it can have many different, although vaguely similar, definitions.

For some people a collaborative application might mean taking an existing application and adding sharing capabilities—the whiteboard is a prime example. Take a paintbrush program, add in the sharing and, presto, you have a shared whiteboard application. For another user it might be a shared VRML world where you and a bunch of avatars sit around and chat in the virtual environment (or play virtual hide-and-seek). An application similar to the whiteboard might be a distributed presentation (Powerpoint on steroids). Finally, another option might be to ensure a consistent state of play in a workflow application, making sure everyone has the same copy of the document.

So how are we going to define *collaborative* for the purposes of this book? Well, the easy way is to let you create your own definition. I like to think of sharing a piece of information between two running applications, any time, regardless of how trivial or small it is, as being collaborative.

In working with JSDT over a long period, I've found uses for it I could never have imagined. I've been constantly changing my definition every time I think of a new way to use it. Basically, it is useful anywhere that you can share data—from a simple status indicator (alert levels or deadline countdowns) to interactive multimedia displays. Just think of anything that you would like more than one person to know simultaneously and that becomes collaborative to you.

Collaborative Concepts in Detail

Before we dig into the core of the JSDT APIs, it helps to understand a few of the concepts behind collaborative applications, and JSDT in particular. Believe it or not, there are actually international standards that define the terms, concepts, and general architecture of shared data applications.

JSDT is based on the ITU T.122 Recommendation for Multipoint Communication Service for Audiographics and Audiovisual Conferencing Services Definition. This standard defines a set of terms dealing with applications that share data in some sort of collaborative way.

Who's Coming to the Party?

The first step in any collaborative application is to ensure that everyone is speaking the same language. This covers a number of areas. I like to think of collaborative concepts in terms of a party (see Figure 11-1).

Figure 11-1
The JSDT party. Duke and friends are having their conversation. (*Courtesy of Sun Microsystems*)

There is a building full of rooms, each filled with lots of people—but not everyone is in the same conversation. If we want to be part of the party, we need to find out a few things before joining in.

First, we have to make sure that we are all using the same language (network protocol etc). If I'm speaking Japanese with a bunch of other party-goers, then anyone wanting to join my group needs to speak Japanese—no good coming in and opening up in Spanish because nobody would know what you are saying. Once we know that we're at least on the same wavelength, then we need to make sure that everyone is talking in the same fashion. That is, are we reliable or unreliable when we speak—does everyone really hear everything we say or just parts of it? Now that we know the way people hear us, we finally need to decide whether they hear our words, and those of everyone else in the same group, in the order that they left our mouth or in some random order.

Taking this back to JSDT terms, the group is referred to as a *session*. When you create a new session, you set the terms and conditions—the type of networking protocol, the type of reliability, and how ordered the conversation will be. Each person joining the session needs to be a *client*. In a departure from reality, a single client may also take part in many groups (sessions) simultaneously. Also, our session may or may not have a manager who can control who joins and what the participants can do once they have joined the group.

Breaking Up the Conversations

Once the client is established in a group, there are a number of things that can be done. For example, the client may just sit and listen to the controlling commands of the group, watching who joins and leaves, who creates new conversation topics, and other such high-level activities.

Have you ever noticed that once a group of people gets to a certain size, it invariably starts breaking into smaller groups that run with a common thread of conversation? This is the idea behind JSDT. A group is just a control mechanism to make sure everyone is on a common wavelength. Once within the group, you then need to establish individual conversation spaces.

JSDT defines three different conversation spaces. The first is the "all-in-brawl" space. Anybody can say anything and everyone hears it; there is no control over who you send it to, everyone gets it. This is a shared *ByteArray*. ByteArrays are just a public broadcast form of conversation.

The second form of the conversation space is like a debate. You can talk to everyone, even assigning priorities for your talk; you can send your talk to everyone else but you can't hear yourself speak; or you can just chat with only one other. This form is a *channel*. Channels are a highly reformed version of the byte array. There is much more control over whom you can send the data to and the priority of getting it there.

Finally, the last form of conversation space is like a Tupperware demonstration. Someone takes control and everyone listens while the product is demonstrated. Sometimes the product is passed around and everyone gets to look at it, so no one person has the entire attention of the audience. Other times nobody is doing anything. This best describes the *token*. Tokens can be exclusively grabbed by a single client; or multiple clients can all grab the token in a shared mode (inhibit), which does not allow anyone to take control; or perhaps nobody wants to access the token. Token control is similar to synchronizing shared data experiences, as the `synchronized` keyword does for a variable or method in Java.

Observing the Situation

Once the form of conversation has been decided, we need to deal with the organizational side of the events. Parties can be great fun but sometimes a bit of organization is needed.

In a nightclub party, a bouncer might be needed to control who comes in and out and what people can do during the party. The bouncer is a *manager*. A manager oversees which clients join the party and controls which clients can create and destroy Channels, ByteArrays, and Tokens. Also, a manager has the ability to ask for authentication any time that a client wishes to perform one of these events.

Other times a surveillance camera is needed to observe what happens. Anybody can listen into changes in any of the sessions, clients, channels, tokens, etc. These listeners follow the standard JDK event listener model. Each object has different events that can be listened to, but generally they include clients joining, leaving, destruction of an object (you can explicitly force the destruction of an object), invitations to join, and expulsion.

A very useful property is that almost every object can be listened to or managed. Every single thing happening can be monitored and controlled. This is great for adding additional security on top of the basic facilities. On top of the two array data types (not the Token) you can place whatever you like as the content message, including encrypted information. You can control how the clients joining use any sort of data object—again, encrypted challenges and responses could be used. This all makes for a very strong model for building exactly the level of control that you need in each application. In the next chapter, we'll build a system that uses password challenges for authentication.

Managers and listeners are not always required for your application. Sessions and the data types can be created with or without the managers. Listeners need to be attached only by the client that needs them. And, since the listeners use a standard event model, you can control which events you actually receive, removing any overheads of processing unneeded events.

Setting Up for JSDT

Now that you understand the basic concepts of shared data and collaborative systems, you need to get a handle on how this all fits into the world of JSDT. Just as with RMI, you can't just start coding with JSDT without going through a couple of preparatory steps.

Exceptions

The first thing you must know is how JSDT deals with exceptions. Taking a stroll through the methods, you will notice that almost all of them throw at least one exception. Most of those usually have two or more.

Method Exceptions A feature of the JSDT API is that there is a very rich set of error conditions. The number of exceptions and the breadth of errors that are covered allow some very precise program control from your point of view. The base package has 21 different exceptions alone! Not all of these exceptions are fatal to the continuing use of the shared data, but they generally indicate that all is not well with the setup.

If you don't want to have seven different catch clauses under a block of JSDT code, the clauses can be quickly compressed to a single one. All of the exceptions are based on `JSDTException` so that a single catch can be used for the lesser details. `JSDTException` itself is based on `java.lang.Exception`, so you are required to explicitly catch any and all errors that are generated from JSDT methods.

User Exceptions When it comes to supporting a distributed environment, it pays to be extremely robust in the provision of the services. Within a single machine you might have multiple clients, or even multiple listeners, all interacting with the same information. An error in one piece of code should not stop the others from working.

In highly event-driven code such as JSDT, the chances of you, the user, writing some code that causes problems and generates its own exceptions is pretty high. If you don't catch the exceptions, then they fall through to the library that generated the event. In the architecture of JSDT, one exception making its way back to the core of the library ruins it for the other listeners on that machine.

JSDT guards against errant exceptions by catching all throwable classes just inside where it calls user code. Once the error is trapped, JSDT will print out the problem and continue to operate as though nothing had happened. If you get unexpected error messages and exception stack traces, this is probably the reason why.

Class Structure

Like other third-party libraries, JSDT has its own JAR file and install procedure. There are two packages for all of the JSDT classes:

```
com.sun.media.jsdt
com.sun.media.jsdt.event
```

which are contained in `jsdt.jar`. The `jsdt` package contains all the main classes for the Java objects and exceptions we visited in the previous sections. In `jsdt.event` are all of the event structures, listeners, and adaptor classes. If you pulled the JAR file apart, you would find a number of other packages such as `jsdt.socket`, `jsdt.rmi`, and `jsdt.impl`. These are internal classes that are used in the implementation of the different networking protocols.

JSDT is a pure Java implementation of collaborative features, so all you need is the JAR file for the application to work. Installing it is simply just a matter of copying the JAR file into a convenient location (by convention into `<JAVAHOME>/lib`) and adding the file to the CLASS-PATH.

Basic Classes   It's time that we now started moving into something more concrete in the JSDT implementation and put class names to ideas. The first concept that we discussed was the session. A session is used to collect together a bunch of related clients so that they may all create a set of mutual objects of interest. Sessions are not shared data objects in themselves but act more as a grouping mechanism for shared data objects of similar interests. A session may contain any number of these shared objects.

The shared objects are Token, Channel, and ByteArray. The basic concepts of each of the objects were introduced earlier in the chapter. These three objects and the session all extend the Manageable interface. This interface declares a basic set of capabilities for managing an object, such as enabling events and controlling the clients that are working with the object. You will notice that all of these shared objects are actually just interfaces. This is so that the individual implementation can be hidden from the user.

One last class of interest at this point in time is the Client interface. This represents an individual user of collaborative services. It is used to nominate the implementing class as responsible for dealing with any authentication requests. Often you will see a single class that implements object listeners and the Client interface, maybe even one of the Manager interfaces as well. Conversely, a single application may have many individual Client classes for different activities. Clients are distinguished by the string returned from the `getName()` method. If two different class instances return the same string, exceptions will be generated when an attempt is made to join the session/object that already contains that name.

Communications Protocols   Behind the JSDT API is a clever design to remove the low-level details from the user. JSDT is all about enabling collaborative applications without having to fuss with the low-level networking implementation. However, without some degree of control over this, the programmer may run into problems due to the chosen network protocol. To alleviate this problem, JSDT comes with three different implementations— sockets, RMI, and LRMP—while adding your own is not that difficult either.

A second choice of options is also allowed when you create sessions. You can control whether the communications should be reliable (and hence slower because of the overheads) or unreliable. Also, you can have a choice regarding the ordering of information as it is being distributed—either the information is kept in the same order, or it can be swapped around as needed. Again, these choices impact speed.

Socket communications are just as you would expect. If reliable communications are requested, then TCP sockets are used; otherwise, unreliable communications use UDP sockets—all hidden from the programmer. Generally you would use socket connections where you have either speed restrictions (such as modems) or a widespread number of clients, especially around the globe across the Internet.

RMI is the second option available for the transport mechanism. This option is especially good if you are all on a local-area network, where its inherent overheads and connection times would not be a problem. Also, because it is its nature to use HTTP at the lowest level, RMI would be useful if your collaborative sessions needed to cross firewalls.

Finally we have the *Lightweight Reliable Multicast Protocol*, or *LRMP*, which is based on multicasting sockets. Essentially, LRMP is a multicast socket that has extra reliability insurance built over the top of it to make sure information is delivered. Because it is based on mcast, it has very minimal overheads and loads down the clients and networks the least. For the same reason, it makes it the ideal choice for distributing information like video or audio. To use LRMP, more third-party software is required. The implementation can be found at:

ftp://ftp.inria.fr/INRIA/Actions/webcanal

NOTE: *The LRMP implementation suffers the same restrictions as any other multicast application—you need to make sure that the routers are configured to support mcast packets. Multicast is also heavily restricted in applets so this may be of some concern if you are using JSDT in a web page.*

Choosing the protocol to use does require some careful consideration. The choice is made when you create the session object. From that point on, you cannot use another protocol. There is no capability to use mixed protocols for the same session. Or put another way, two sessions of the same name, but with different protocol types, are treated as separate entities. However, this does not restrict you to a single session in each application. It is quite common for an application to create a number of different sessions with different protocols to match the different task requirements.

Registry   In Chapter 8, "Remote Method Invocation," you saw how RMI has a registry running to keep track of all the remote objects. Looking after all the session details requires a similar structure. Similarly, JSDT has a registry that can be started either as a part of the application or as a standalone process. In this case, the registry is used to store references to shared data objects—namely, the sessions and clients. Also common with the RMI registry is the fact that you only need one instance (per protocol implementation) running on a nominated server machine.

NOTE: *Registries and servers will be discussed further in the next chapter.*

Because of the nature of JSDT, there are different registries for each of the protocols. If you wish to start the registry from the command line then you can type:

```
java com.sun.media.jsdt.<type>.Registry
```

where the type is one of `socket`, `rmi`, or `lrmp`. Usually this would be used if you were running multiple applications on the machine that used JSDT.

To include the registry in your application, you make a request to the `RegistryFactory` class. This class creates an instance of the registry on your local machine of the appropriate type. It also includes methods to check whether a registry is already running or not. We'll see how to start the registry later in the chapter when we start coding a simple application.

Manager Classes   Earlier in the chapter we encountered the concepts of the managers. In the JSDT implementation there are managers for each of the shared objects and the session. Managers are attached to the objects at creation time and the only one able to add a manager is the client that first creates a shared object.

All the managers have the same basic function: to approve what happens with the managed object. Managers are interfaces with a single method:

```
boolean sessionRequest(Session session,
                       AuthenticationInfo info,
                       Client client);
```

In place of session, you can substitute any of the shared object types. Each time a client requests something, this request method is called with the appropriate information. The manager then performs whatever actions are necessary and returns a true or false, depending on whether it approves the client doing that action.

The `AuthenicationInfo` class that is the second parameter provides some extra information about the object, the session it belongs to, and challenge setting and replies. We'll explore the class further later in the chapter.

Creating Shared Structures   As you have seen already, there are many similarities between RMI and JSDT and this resemblance continues with the need to specify shared objects with URLs (hence the similarity of also needing a registry to store these URLs and corresponding object representations).

URL Structure   Let's examine a typical JSDT URL:

```
jsdt://stard.eng.sun.com:3355/socket/Session/chatSession
```

The protocol type is defined to be JSDT so that a naming class knows where to start the search. Following this, we have the standard machine name and port number pair. The machine name is the name of the machine where you have started an instance of the registry. A port number must *always* be specified in a JSDT URL—there is no recognized default. You can use any reasonable port number except 4561, which is the port the registry listens on.

> **NOTE:** *The URL is always specified as a string, not as a* `java.net.URL` *object. You can't open this URL with the standard URL-Connection class, just as you can't open RMI URLs with URLConnection.*

The next three arguments of the URL specify what object is to be created. First there is the implementation type, which can be one of the above three mentioned types: `socket`, `lrmp`, or `rmi`. Next is the type of object you wish to create. Here you have the choice of either `Session` or `Client`. Most of the time by far, the choice will just be Session, but we'll examine in a later chapter how you can create and register your own customized client implementation. Finally, you must choose the name of the object that you wish to create. Any name can be created so long as it passes the URL syntax rules (no spaces, for example).

Creating Sessions   Creating an instance of a session now consists of passing our URL to the `createSession()` method of the `Session Factory` class. In a pattern you will see repeated through the API, two versions of the method allow for creation of either managed or unmanaged versions of the session. Calling the appropriate method returns a session object that we can then use to create shared objects.

> **NOTE:** *Sun recommends prefixing shared object names with the package name to avoid name conflicts in the registry. Generally I haven't found this to be needed, as either there are a large number of servers around or there are not that many sessions created.*

Creating Shared Objects   Once you have the handle to a session object instance, you can create the shared objects within that session. The session object contains all of the methods that are needed to create each of the shared objects.

Creating a shared object is as simple as choosing a name and then calling the appropriate `create()` method for the object type that you want. Object names are much more free-range; any name that you can express as a Java string can be used. You'll see how this is an advantage in the next chapter. There are two methods for each object—one each for managed and unmanaged varieties.

A session object also has a number of other useful methods for finding out more information. There are methods for checking if the object that you want to create already exists. Also, you can get the list of the objects that have already been joined by a client or even just a list of all the channels that already exist. Finally there are methods for adding and removing listeners to the session.

JSDT Bank Server

Now that we've had a basic look through what JSDT is, it is time to head back to our example application and implement it by using JSDT. As before, the server is the first part to be implemented. As is becoming fairly common in our example bank, we need to provide some extra classes above the basic server.

Object Organization

In our basic architecture we have two accounts on the server. The client selects an account and then passes information to the server about the transaction sometime later, and, independently, account balance information is returned to the client. In what has become a standard feature of the implementations to date, the return path for the balance has been separate from the sending path.

The RMI design in the previous chapter is common to this approach. We used two objects—one for each account—and then we created the bank client as a third remote object specifically for returning the balance information. In this chapter we will adopt a similar approach mainly as a teaching point rather than for any inherent efficiency reason. In fact, with JSDT, the design we will be using is extremely inefficient in terms of resources and objects used.

So what is the design? We'll use two shared objects—one for each bank account—and another that represents the balance information. The bank accounts will be implemented using channels, and the balance information will be a ByteArray. Again, there is no particular reason for favoring one or the other for these tasks, apart from using two different objects so you can see how they differ in behavior and APIs. Tokens can't be used because they have a boolean nature, by which they are either grabbed or not, so we can't pass any numerical information along them.

Account Object   Each of the account interfaces will be a separate shared object—that is how the client sees them. Inside the server the code also sees two shared objects; however, we also need a bunch of processing code to deal with the information that is passed along the shared object. At the client end, a client will write information to the channel, while, on the server end, there will be readers looking for changes in the channel. This means that although the client interface is relatively simple to implement, the server side needs a fraction more work. Our basic account object then shall consist of another class that contains the channel and all of the processing code for incoming information.

You may have noticed something interesting here: If the clients are only sending information and the server is only reading information from the channel, we aren't really using shared data concepts. Really all we are dealing with is a glorified socket connection. This is an unfortunate by-product of the design that we are following. At the end of this chapter we'll look at the proper way of implementing this design. Fortunately the balance information design is along the lines of the concepts we really want to show.

Balance Object   The balance object is constructed from a ByteArray. Because our account manager passes balance information out only through the BalanceListener interface, we need a class that wraps the ByteArray and the listener into a single class.

Because of the shared nature of the ByteArray, there is no need to keep track of every client that joins the server. Actually, we don't even know who has really joined the server without some extra coding. Distributing balance information is as simple as writing the balance message to the ByteArray; then all the interested clients will just read it from that same object. There is no per-client information needed.

Authentication   Since our bank client has adapted the commune approach to security in all of the implementations to date, there is no reason why we should stop now. This means that all the objects will be created without managers. If there are no managers, this can also imply that no authentication is done on each of the clients. Each object implementing the Client interface has the authentication method that was mentioned earlier. Having no authentication allows a very simple implementation—the method just returns a null.

Code Implementation

First point of call on the code implementation list is the NetworkServer class. You should remember from the previous chapters that this class is the basic server implementation that is responsible for starting up any networking interfaces. Classes for the JSDT implementation exist in the two packages `rwjn.chapter11.server` and `rwjn.chapter11.client`.

NetworkServer   Since it is the responsibility of the NetworkServer class to establish all of the communications for the server, the first thing that we will have to do is decide which JSDT implementation we should use. For this demo application we'll use the socket implementation. The second decision is what to name our objects. First the session needs a name so we'll call it *McDuckBank*. For simplicity, the two account objects will have the names "account0" and "account1" and the balance information will have the name "balance."

With that decided, the code for the constructor can flow along quite easily. The code that will act as a server in JSDT code checks whether there is a registry running and starts one if there isn't. Figure 11-2 shows how to start a registry after checking for one already existing.

As you can see, the code is very simple. In a common trait that you'll see in JSDT code, the catch clauses are often much longer than the actual working code. If we can't start the registry for some reason, then there is no point in proceeding because the objects can't be created.

Next we'll need to create the session objects. Taking a look at the documentation shows that we need to pass an instance of a `Client` object as one of the parameters. Further inspection of the documentation for

Figure 11-2
Code to start the
JSDT registry.

```
try {
  if(!RegistryFactory.registryExists("socket"))
    RegistryFactory.startRegistry("socket");
}
catch(NoRegistryException nre) {
  System.out.println("Couldn't start the Registry " + nre);
  System.out.println("Exiting - bye!");
  System.exit(1);
}
catch(RegistryExistsException ree) {
  System.out.println("The Registry is already running.");
}
```

the other shared objects that we are going to create also reveals the need for a `Client` reference. We have two options:

1. Have the `NetworkServer` implement the `Client` interface itself and then call each of the create shared object methods with `this` as the first argument.
2. Create another class that implements the interface and pass that class through. The first situation is the most common variant seen. It is generally used if there are only a few objects that are going to be created and no authentication needs to be done.

Creating a large number of objects or having authentication required generally favors having a separate class. In our application I've chosen the second option for the server because the client uses the first option. This class is called `ServerClient`. The implementation of `Server Client` is given in Figure 11-3.

NOTE: *A third alternative is to create an inner class inside the Net-workServer class, but this is very rarely seen or used.*

Figure 11-3
The `ServerClient` class implementation.

```java
package rwjn.chapter11.server;


import com.sun.media.jsdt.*;

public class ServerClient
  implements Client
{
  // The name of the client to return
  private static final String CLIENT_NAME = "Bank Server";

  public Object authenticate(AuthenticationInfo info) {
    return null;
  }

  public String getName() {
      return CLIENT_NAME;
  }
}
```

Figure 11-4
Creating a session
object.

```
private static final String SESSION_URL =
  "/socket/Session/McDuckBank";

...

// The constructor definition
public NetworkServer(int port, AccountManager mgr)
{
  Session session = null;

  // establish the registry as per example 11.1

  // create the client
  Client server_client = new ServerClient();

  // Now lets put together the URL - localhost and create the
session
  try {
    String url = "jsdt://localhost:" + port + SESSION_URL;

    if(!SessionFactory.sessionExists(url))
      session = SessionFactory.createSession(server_client,
                                             url,
                                             true);
  }
  catch(JSDTException je) {
    // I could catch all of the exceptions individually but that
    // would involve more lines of code than real application.
    System.out.println("Error creating a session " + je);
    System.exit(2);
  }
```

With the client class instance created, we can now continue establishing the rest of the shared objects. Before we can create any of the shared data objects, we need a session object. This is created with a call to the createSession method of the SessionFactory class, which is shown in Figure 11-4.

One item that may have slipped past your gaze is the third parameter of the createSession() method. The boolean value is used to specify whether the client should automatically be joined to the session when it is created. The act of creating a shared object (or getting a reference to an object if it already exists) in JSDT is not the same as joining. Frequently you will create the object and automatically join it, but other times you might delay the join operation. Before you can do anything with a shared object you must join it. Listeners will not receive events and you cannot send information over a shared object without having first joined it even though you may have a reference to it.

With the session object that we now have, we could create the shared data objects directly, but, as always in good OO design, we won't do this directly. Instead this will be left to the account classes themselves so that they can hide the implementation of the type of object that will be used. The only public information that we will have and be able to use is that the Java class representing the balance information will be a BalanceListener that can be registered with the AccountManager. Apart from that, we'll pass all of the relevant information that is needed to create the shared objects to the account classes.

The implementations of these three classes will be looked at shortly. All we need to do to finish the NetworkServer class is write the lines to create instances of all of these classes.

```
// once we have a session we can now create two objects for the
// transaction listeners and one for the balance information.
new TransactionListener(session,
                        server_client,
                        account_manager,
                        0);
new TransactionListener(session,
                        server_client,
                        account_manager,
                        1);

BalanceOutput balance =
 new BalanceOutput(session, server_client);

// create the connection manager and register the listener
account_manager.addBalanceListener(balance);

// Just a quick announcement
System.out.println("Server ready");
}
```

There is no need to keep references to our TransactionListener classes. Internally they are referenced as listeners to the shared objects, which means that they will always have one reference so long as the shared object exists.

Listening to Transaction Requests   Once the basic server is finished, we can start work on the classes that listen to the requests from the clients. Passed in to the class are references to the current session, the client for the server, the account manager and the account number. The first two are needed so that we can create our shared object, the second so that we can pass the requests on to the bank (making the transaction request useful), and the final parameter so that the class knows which account it is representing.

As was mentioned earlier in the chapter, we will be implementing the transaction shared object as a channel. Shared objects have listeners that can be attached to them to tell if information or state of the object has changed. Channels provide an extra way of receiving the data—the `ChannelConsumer`. This interface is used as a callback method when a new piece of information arrives on the channel. It is the preferred way of dealing with a channel.

An alternative way of dealing with the channel is to treat it as a form of stream. There is a blocking method called `receive()` that can be used to read data from the channel. Using this involves an extra thread and extra overhead processing code. This way of receiving information is best used when it is known that a piece of data is about to arrive—for example, combining it with a Token for more complex interactions and receiving information only if a token is grabbed. Generally speaking, consumers are a better approach to take because a single consumer can handle multiple channels simultaneously with minimal extra coding.

Channels operate like a UDP socket. All information is packetized and sent as individual pieces of information at the high-level end. The encapsulation device is the Data class. It contains a byte array that is the information and some ancillary information like the channel, sender, and priority of the message. When the consumer is informed, we must process the message just like we do the UDP packet. Actually, most of the code here and in the client has been pinched from the UDP implementation of the bank. We are even using the same `Keywords` class that was used for the UDP implementation.

The constructor of the TransactionListener, shown in Figure 11-5, is very simple. It creates the channel from the account number it has been given and adds itself as a consumer.

The `createChannel()` method is probably going to need explaining a little. Apart from the client reference and the name of the channel to create, there are three boolean conditions:

Figure 11-5
The constructor of
the Transaction
Listener class.

```
public TransactionListener(Session session,
                           Client client,
                           AccountManager manager,
                           int acc)
{
  account_manager = manager;
  account = acc;

  String name = "account" + acc;

  try {
    Channel channel;

    channel =
      session.createChannel(client, name, true, true, true);

    channel.addConsumer(client, this);
  }
  catch(ConnectionException ce) {
    System.out.println("Connection Error " + ce);
  }
  catch(NameInUseException niue) {
    System.out.println("The name " + name + " already in use!");
  }
  catch(PermissionDeniedException pde) {
    System.out.println("Sorry - you can't do that!");
  }
  catch(JSDTException je) {
    // The rest of the exceptions aren't really important.
    System.out.println(je);
  }
}
```

1. The reliability indicator. If it is true, then a reliable connection is set up (TCP if the socket implementation is used). If it is false, an unreliable connection (UDP for the socket implementation) is set up. Unreliable means that all of your data may not arrive at all of the clients attached to this channel. Not every client loses the same data packet either!

2. The orderliness of the values. Assuming that a consumer receives every packet, this condition determines whether or not information that you get is in the same order that it was sent. You might want

this if you have an unreliable channel running audio information, for example, where you don't want packets out of order (or the information can be unordered and the out-of-order packets can be dropped).

3. The auto join feature described in the previous section.

Once some data has been received at the server by this class (remember it implements the ChannelConsumer interface), there needs to be some processing. The message format is identical to that used for the UDP bank implementation and we won't show that again, so Figure 11-6 shows the important details for the JSDT implementation.

Of interest will be the bit shifting that is done. We've permitted partial dollar amounts to be used in the transactions. Since we represent these with floats and the byte array consists of individual bytes, we need to get the floats into the array somehow. One option would be to create a DataOutputStream from the byte array and then read the values out. Considering that we have only 5 bytes to read in the entire message, I think this is an unnecessary overhead. We also know well that the amount is going to include at most 2 places after the decimal point. A

Figure 11-6
Processing the information received.

```
public synchronized void dataReceived(Data data) {
    byte[] msg = data.getData();

    // The message format is
    //   msg[0] = command
    //   msg[1] = MSB    4 byte ints
    //   msg[4] = LSB
    int value = (((int)msg[1] & 0xFF) << 24) |
                (((int)msg[2] & 0xFF) << 16) |
                (((int)msg[3] & 0xFF) <<  8) |
                 ((int)msg[4] & 0xFF);

    float amount = value / 100.0f;

    switch(msg[0])
    {
      case Keywords.DEPOSIT:
          account_manager.deposit(account, amount);
          break;
    ...
```

quick multiply by 100 makes the amount an integer which can be quickly written to the byte array (and conversely quickly read and reassembled from it too).

Another item to watch for is the `synchronized` keyword sitting in the method declaration. With high-volume streams and a single consumer for multiple channels, it is entirely possible that the `data Received()` method could be called more than once simultaneously. Making the method synchronized prevents any problems occurring from reentrant code calls. It should be used on everything except the most trivial of cases.

Balance Listener   Now that we can place information into the bank, we need to finish by sending the results back to the client. While the transaction requests were implemented using a Channel, the balance information will be sent out over a shared ByteArray. ByteArrays are much simpler objects by design. There are no options about creating one—there is a ByteArray and that is it.

In the transaction listeners we were listening to information coming from the bank clients applications. In this class the tables are turned and we are now only interested in sending information out—writing values to the array. Constructing the object, which again is done in the constructor of our class (shown in Figure 11-7), is almost the same process as for the channels.

Probably the major difference between the ByteArray and Channel is in constructing them; a properly constructed byte array (that is, the `byte[]` version) is needed in the constructor. A small byte array is created as the token placeholder to have information placed in it.

NOTE: The need for the array of bytes has always mystified me, and I've never received a really good, clear answer as to why it is needed. The code never uses it, as the `setValue` method always has a new byte array written to it each time a message is created and the reading also produces a new array each time. The need for the byte array in the construction is expected to be removed in the next release of JSDT.

One more thing to point out in the constructor is the last two lines, where two streams are created. Streams are created here and reused for every update that is sent out, saving on time and memory usage. For this example the DataIn/Output streams are used to write infor-

Figure 11-7
Constructing a
shared ByteArray.

```
public BalanceOutput(Session session, Client client)
{
    server_client = client;

    String name = "Balance";

    try {
        byte[] msg = new byte[1];
        shared_array =
            session.createByteArray(client, name, msg, true);
    }
    catch(ConnectionException ce) {
        System.out.println("Connection Error " + ce);
    }
    catch(NameInUseException niue) {
        System.out.println("The name " + name + " already in use!");
    }
    catch(PermissionDeniedException pde) {
        System.out.println("Sorry - you can't do that!");
    }
    catch(JSDTException je) {
        // The rest of the exceptions aren't really important.
        System.out.println(je);
    }

    // create the output stream for the outgoing data.
    bank_byte_output = new ByteArrayOutputStream();
    bank_data_output = new DataOutputStream(bank_byte_output);
}
```

mation to the underlying `byte[]`. There is technically no difference
between this and the channel. Either approach could be used with
either of the data types. The streams are used this time to illustrate
the alternative possible approaches to reading and writing data to the
shared objects.

The second part of the BalanceOutput class is the implementation
of the BalanceListener interface and the updateBalance method. Writing out the values to the byte array should look rather familiar, as it
is identical to the code used for the UDP server. The only difference is
where the values are written to—a ByteArray rather than a
DatagramPacket.

```
public synchronized void updateBalance(int account, float balance)
{
  try {
    // start the array at the beginning again
    bank_byte_output.reset();

    bank_data_output.writeByte(Keywords.BALANCE);
    bank_data_output.writeInt(account);
    bank_data_output.writeFloat(balance);

    // Fetch the contents and send it off
    byte[] msg = bank_byte_output.toByteArray();

    shared_array.setValue(server_client, msg);
  }
  catch(IOException ioe) {
    System.out.println("Error sending balance information " + ioe);
  }
  catch(JSDTException je) {
    System.out.println("Error sending balance information " + je);
  }
}
```

That's it for the server code. Compiling these four classes
(NetworkServer, ServerClient, TransactionServer, and
BalanceOutput) with the starter class, JSDTServer, will be enough
for our JSDT implementation of the server.

Running the Server

After compiling the code, running the server is a trivial task. Assuming
that you have your class path setup to point to the JSDT JAR file (which
you should have done already to compile the code), then it is simply a
matter of typing the first line below:

```
c:\>java JSDTServer
server ready.
```

When you see the second line it indicates all of the setup is complete and the bank is ready for transactions. Killing the server is just
a matter of killing it with CTRL-C as you would for any other Java
application.

JSDT Bank Client

Having made most of the design decisions while implementing the server, you will find that completing the client implementation becomes pretty straightforward. Do what the server did, only do the other half—where you read in the server, write in the client.

Client Design

Like the server, any piece of code that wishes to use shared objects must have a Client to pass. The first design decision is how should we construct our client. Since the BankClient is an abstract class and we only use one of them in the client application, it makes sense to include the Client interface directly into the BankClient code implementation.

Just as the server returned `null` for the authentication method, so will the client-side code. Also, we'll use a different name to be returned for the client name—the highly original "Bank Client" is our name.

Listening for balance information also needs to be dealt with. Since this comes through a ByteArray, we'll need to also implement a ByteArray listener as part of our bank client code too. This listener will process the account balance updates and pass those along to the appropriate pieces of user interface.

Implementing the Client

As in previous implementations, the first place to start is the connect and disconnect routines. Once the network connections have been established to the server, a small general-purpose command writer method is constructed and methods that call it (for outgoing transaction requests), followed by the methods to read in the balance updates and process them, are written.

Connecting to the Server   Connecting to the server follows the same basic pattern. First we call the `disconnect()` method to remove any previous connections. Following that, we start to establish a session. Since the bank client is a client-side application which does not "export" shared objects to other applications, there is no need to start a registry. Instead, we need to make sure that the session JSDT URL points to the right machine that is acting as the server. Since this information is provided as an argument to the connect method we have to assume the best.

Creating a session looks suspiciously like the code in Figure 11-4. The only real difference is in how we construct the URL. Figure 11-8 shows how it is done for our client-side application.

Figure 11-8
Client-side code for establishing a server connection.

```
public void connect(String host, int port) {
   disconnect();

   String name = null;

   try {
      StringBuffer buffer = new StringBuffer("jsdt://");
      buffer.append(host);
      buffer.append(':');
      buffer.append(port);
      buffer.append(SESSION_URL);

      String url = buffer.toString();

      // If the session does not already exist it means that the
      // server is not running. Print an error message and exit.
      if(!SessionFactory.sessionExists(url)) {
         System.out.println("The server is not currently" +
                   "running on" + host);
         return;
      }

      // So create the session and join it
      session = SessionFactory.createSession(this, url, true);

      // Now create the objects in the session.
      name = "account0";
      account_a =
       session.createChannel(this, name, true, true, true);

      name = "account1";
      account_b =
       session.createChannel(this, name, true, true, true);

      byte[] msg = new byte[1];
      name = "Balance";
```

Figure 11-8
(*Continued*)

```
      balance = session.createByteArray(this, name, msg, true);
      balance.addByteArrayListener(this);
      balance.enableListenerEvents(this,
                              ByteArrayEvent.VALUE_CHANGED);
  }
  catch(ConnectionException ce) {
    System.out.println("Connection Error " + ce);
  }
  catch(NameInUseException niue) {
    System.out.println("The name " + name + " already in use!");
  }
  catch(PermissionDeniedException pde) {
    System.out.println("Sorry - you can't do that!");
  }
  catch(JSDTException je) {
    // The rest of the exceptions aren't really important.
    System.out.println(je);
  }

  // everything is OK so register ourselves as a listener.
  current_account = account_a;

  System.out.println("Remote connect complete");
}
```

JSDT has some interesting behavior when it comes to creating shared objects. If you are the first one to call create<Object> then the JSDT code internally sets up your machine to be the "server" to all of the other potential clients. It literally creates the shared object. Any other client that then tries to create the same object is returned a reference to that shared object.

It is quite obvious that if the server is not running we don't want to let the client attempt to connect. On the basis of the behavior expresssed in the preceding paragraph, that would imply that if no bank server were running, then the first client attempting to connect would suddenly find itself as a psuedo-server for the accounts. I say psuedo-server because to the bank client code it only acts with the objects to write the information; it never really performs any serving of the requests that get sent by other clients.

We can also use this behavior to our advantage to determine a few things about the status of the server. For example, if the session is not available, then the server probably hasn't started. So, the first thing that our code does is check whether our session exists. If it does not exist, then there is no point in attempting any further connections, so the method exits immediately.

Having established that our session does in fact currently exist, we take a naïve view of the world and blindly attempt to obtain references to all of the other shared objects. The lesson to be learned from this is, with the current code, wait until the server shows the message that says it is ready before even attempting to connect the client interface with it.

Last on the list of things to note about the connection routine is the lines about registering as a listener and the enable events for the ByteArray. The order in which these lines are written is very important. First you create the ByteArray reference, then you add a listener to it, and then you modify the list of events that are allowed through. If you attempt to filter the events that come through before adding the listener, it will throw a NoSuchListenerException at you. It will be explained later in the chapter why we are enabling only certain events.

Sending Requests to the Server   With the objects created, sending information to the server becomes the inverted process of Figure 11-6. We create the usual private `sendCommand()` method that is responsible for collating the right information, formatting it, and dispatching it to the server.

```
private void sendCommand(byte cmd, float amount) {
    // round to an int - make sure cent values are kept
    int value = (int)(amount * 100);

    byte[] msg = new byte[5];

    msg[0] = cmd;
    msg[1] = (byte)((value > 24) & 0xFF);
    msg[2] = (byte)((value > 16) & 0xFF);
    msg[3] = (byte)((value >  8) & 0xFF);
    msg[4] = (byte)(value & 0xFF);

    Data data = new Data(msg);

    try {
      current_account.sendToOthers(this, data);
    }
    catch(JSDTException je) {
      System.out.println("Error sending transaction request " + je);
    }
}
```

As you can see, it is a two-step process to send the information. First everything is written to an array of bytes, then it is wrapped into the Data class instance and posted on its way with the `sendToOthers` method. There are three versions of the sendToX methods: `sendTo Client, sendToOthers,` and `sendToAll.` The names pretty much suggest their behavior. We've used the sendToOthers variant, as we have no need to get the information back. Alternately we could have used the sendToClient version and used the name of the bank server. However, this would require either hardwiring of the bank client name or some convoluted process of getting the list of all the client names and performing substring checks for the word "server" in them. Either is not pretty and since the clients only send information on the channel without reading it in, the sendToOthers option is reasonably safe under the current assumptions.

Sending a transaction request becomes trivial then, as our old favorite, the `deposit()` method, shows us:

```
public void deposit(float amount) {
   sendCommand(Keywords.DEPOSIT, amount);
}
```

Processing Balance Information In the constructor of the method you saw that we added this class as a listener for byte arrays. Obviously the first thing that we do is implement all of the methods required of the listener with empty methods. The only method of interest to us is the one used when the value changes.

JSDT implements its event listeners in a very similar way to the AWT classes. With this comes the ability to select those events you want to know about, which is the point of the enableListenerEvents line in the constructor. By enabling events we are specifically disabling all the others. We are really only interested in knowing about the value of the array changing, so that is all that we enable. The byteArrayValueChanged method now becomes our focus of attention.

Like the server code, the code to process the balance messages is a direct copy of the UDP implementation. The new message arrives in the format of an event, which we then use to trigger the processing as shown in Figure 11-9. Although the event itself contains reference to the ByteArray, we choose to ignore the event object completely. When we created the connection earlier, we kept a reference to the byte array. We can then just ask this reference directly for the array of bytes that forms

Figure 11-9
Processing the bal-
ance message.

```java
public void byteArrayValueChanged(ByteArrayEvent event) {
  byte[] msg = null;

  try {
    msg = balance.getValue();
  }
  catch(NoSuchByteArrayException nbae) {
    // Oops - someone destroyed the byte array on us!
    System.out.println("Error reading balance object");
    return;
  }

  ByteArrayInputStream byte_input =
   new ByteArrayInputStream(msg);
  DataInputStream in = new DataInputStream(byte_input);

  byte  command;

  try {
    command = in.readByte();
  }
  catch(IOException e1) {
    System.err.println("Error reading data from input");
    System.err.println(e1);
    return;
  }

  // if it is the balance. From here on it is identical to
  // the UDP code.
  if(command == Keywords.BALANCE) {
    int    account;
    float balance;

    try {
      account = in.readInt();
      balance = in.readFloat();
    }
    catch(IOException e2) {
      System.err.println("Error reading data from input");
      System.err.println(e2);
      return;
    }

    // send this to the listener
```

Figure 11-9
(*Continued*)

```
if(listener != null) {
  if(account == 0)
    listener.accountAChanged(balance);
  else
    listener.accountBChanged(balance);
  }
}
....
```

the message. We could ask the event for the ByteArray and then get the array of bytes, but this is an extra method call that we don't need.

Disconnecting from the Server   Having finished with our bank transactions, we take the final step and close the connection to the server. For JSDT-based applications, this is a relatively simple affair. For each of the shared objects we just announce that we are leaving.

On first reading of the javadoc you might be confused by the number of methods that appear to be usable to leave the object: `leave` and `destroy` both look likely candidates, and the session also throws in a `close` method as well.

The destroy method (part of the `Managable` interface) is chosen when you want to force the destruction of the object completely. This is often used in the server code when it is about to exit or it determines that nobody is left listening to the object (other than itself). Any clients that still have listeners on the object are forcibly removed from it.

The leave method indicates that the particular client is no longer interested in being joined to that object. If your code retains a reference to the shared object, you can always join it again later. If you compare this to the close method of the session, the close completely destroys what that reference is used for. If you want to rejoin the session at a later date, you will need to go back to the SessionFactory for a new reference.

The final piece of code to show for the implementation is the `disconnect()` method:

```
public void disconnect() {
  // Destroy the objects
  if(session != null) {
    try {
      account_a.leave(this);
      account_b.leave(this);
```

```
          balance.leave(this);
          session.leave(this);
        }
      catch(JSDTException je) {
          System.out.println("Error disconnecting " + je);
        }
      }
      // set the remote object references to null so that the GC
      // can garbage collect them if needed
      current_account = null;
      account_a = null;
      account_b = null;
      session = null;
    }
```

Running the Client

Once you've compiled the code and the start-up class
(JSDTClient.java) start the server first. Wait for the server ready
message and then start the client. Connect to the server with the same
port number as the server uses. This defaults to 8000 as has been used
in all the other servers (except RMI). You should now be able to use the
client just as you have for all the other servers. One point to note is that
you cannot use localhost as the server name. Because of a bug in JSDT,
you must use the real name of the machine.

Now try starting a second client up on another machine. What happens? Hmmm.... A NameInUseException is generated. A quick look at
the client-side code reveals the problem—all of the clients are returning
"Bank Client" as their name, even on different machines. JSDT makes
no differentiation about where the client name is coming from; all it
cares about is the name it calls itself by. The way to avoid this problem
is to affix the name of the machine as part of the string that becomes the
name of the client.

To make the new client name, we add a constructor to the class (none
of the other implementations have needed one). In the constructor we
find out the name of the machine and append it to the name string:

```
// The name of the client to return
private static String CLIENT_NAME = "Bank Client";

public JSDTBankClient() {
  try {
```

```
        InetAddress address = InetAddress.getLocalHost();
        CLIENT_NAME += address.getHostName();

    }
    catch(UnknownHostException uhe) {
        // Argh! But ignore it anyway.
    }
}
```

With this code in place we can now happily run multiple clients accessing the bank server from multiple machines. We still have a problem
with multiple clients running on the same machine. In this trivial application, it does not really matter, but in real systems it could potentially
cause some problems. The only real way around this problem is to
attempt to create a session and, if you get the NameInUseException,
start tacking numbers on the end of the string in a loop until you stop
getting errors. This is a nasty kludge but there is no other real solution.

Alternative Design Notes

While we were looking at the design of the server, it was mentioned that
the design of the server with all of the shared objects is not really the
best. Now we look at the most efficient solution for the problem. In the
most efficient design of the project I would use just a single shared data
object—a Channel. All of the information is encoded on this channel and
the listeners can filter the messages that they want to hear.

The first part of the exercise requires the creation of the generic message format, which we basically have already done, thanks to the bor-
rowed UDP code. After this, we need to send out the message. Remember the extra versions of the sendToX methods that the channel has?
This is where they start coming in handy. Channels allow us to direct
our data to the right place, which is very convenient because we don't
need to worry about filtering.

Server Modifications

The first step in the implementation is the server. If there is only one
server (and there is), then when it sends out messages, it is sending to
everyone else except itself. Where the balance listener code was created

and used the `setValue` method of the byte array we can now substitute our Channel and use the `sendToOthers` method of the Channel to pass out the balance information.

Another by-product of all this would be the reduction in the number of classes needed. Now, we could create a single class to replace the Client implementation, the Channel Consumer for incoming information, and the BalanceListener for sending the balance information back to the clients.

Client Modifications

On the client side, things could be a little more difficult. We really only want to send information to the one machine—the server. Well, each machine is represented by a client name. The server has the client name "Bank Server." One way of approaching the problem would be to have the sendToClient method hard-code the server name. For example,

```
account_channel.sendToClient(data, "Bank Server");
```

While this might be adequate for a small system, it is not sufficiently generic if we decide to change the name of the server's client. If we stick to the convention that the name of the server always ends with the word "Server" and no other names are to end in this word, then we can do a few more things to provide a generic solution.

Looking at the Manageable interface again reveals the listClient-Names method. This is particularly handy in this situation. Once we have created the Channel we can then list the names of all the clients that are currently joined with this channel. Since the server is the one that always creates the original object, it is guaranteed to be joined to the channel and hence to one of the names that are returned in the list. We simply loop through the array of the client names (they are all strings), searching for the name that ends with "Server." Once we've found it, we keep a reference to it, and every time that we use the sendToClient method we substitute it in the string reference for the client name.

Summary

So far you have seen a basic introduction to the Java Shared Data Toolkit. With what you have learnt to date, you can implement most simple applications. Even applications up to whiteboards and the like can be implemented with just this basic knowledge. Basically, if you can get the data into an array of bytes, you can share the information with others quickly and simply. This could go as far as serializing whole classes to the array if needed.

In the next chapter we'll examine how to include more control over what happens within a shared object. Also, a look at the underlying architecture implementation will help immensely in your understanding of what JSDT is under the hood.

Advanced JSDT— Gaining Control of the Situation

Now that you are familiar with the basic JSDT concepts and have seen JSDT in action, it is time to move on to learn more about the advanced side of the toolkit. One of the great things about JSDT is that you need to use only a minimal amount of the API to get the desired results. With the basic capabilities presented in the previous chapter, I have implemented more than 10 different applications right up to a fully collaborative whiteboard that includes file transfer and text chat. I never needed any more than this to make these applications do what I need.

This chapter is about adding more control over the basic application capabilities. Some examples of this control might be to moderate who is joining the shared party, or to allow only certain operations for different people. In the process we will dig into the implementation and examine a few interesting points about the internals of JSDT.

Project Outline

In order to illustrate a lot of the concepts in this chapter, it is most practical to build another application. The purpose of this application is purely to demonstrate what can be done to control the user(s) of shared objects. The GUI doesn't look like anything special—just a bunch of text values with some menu items. We are really interested in what is going on behind the scenes.

The application consists of a server and client as usual. The server acts like a privilege handler, much like the Unix-style user system. This system has many different groups of privileges that allow the users to do whatever they like, right up to wizard levels for creating and destroying the session. The user interface produces these effects as a row of each of the object types with the list of all the objects in existence at the time. From these objects you can then perform the various operations—if you are permitted. There is also a large selection of dialogs for sundry tasks.

Authentication Schemes

An aspect that we might wish to consider in the design is the different ways of structuring the authentication system. With the session manager there, every request to create, destroy, and join an object requires authentication. There are at least two possibilities for implementing the authentication scheme:

- *Authenticate every request every time.* Each time the session manager receives a request it calls the `authenticate()` method on the client. The client is then required to respond with its current access level and password for that level. If this matches the required password for that level, the process is allowed and the client finishes the task. This requires a lot of networking overhead because of the piles of authentication taking place.

- *Keep a list of all clients as they join.* Each client starts with the lowest level of privileges. If clients request an operation above the current known level they are asked to authenticate themselves. If a client then passes back a correct level and password equal to or higher than that required, the client is permitted to continue and the permission table is now set to the new level for that client. Compared to the first scheme, there are a lot less overheads. Authentication is made only on an as-needed basis. However, what we gain by saving in network bandwidth, we lose in flexibility. In this scheme privileges can really change only when users want to do more than they currently can. Of course the system can always return a lower access level than the previous one, but the changes are noted only when a request is made for a higher level. Potentially, clients could be operating on levels higher than they've set.

There are other arrangements that could be constructed. For example, authenticate when a client joins and use that for the rest of the time that client is joined. No adjustments can be made while that client is connected. The reason for pointing all this out is that we want to construct the authentication managers on both the client and the server to be as flexible as possible. With the authentication method we can pass any arbitrary object, so this allows another level of complexity—making sure that the correct schemes are used. Also, the main goal is to produce a system that relies only on the server side granting or denying requests. There should be no code in the client side artificially restricting privileges to make up for what the server can do. And, of course, the whole lot is to be implemented by using the JSDT security mechanisms only.

NOTE: *In this application we are not really in major paranoia mode with security. I am attempting to illustrate the JSDT mechanisms for authentication. Everything we are doing is inherently weak. There is no encryption of passwords; even the list of passwords is open to anyone with a copy of Mocha. Besides, if I did too much here U.S. export restriction laws might affect us. :)*

Server Outline

The basic server consists of two parts: (1) maintaining a list of all the privilege levels and what operations each level may perform and (2) monitoring each object that is created and ensuring the correct behavior based on what the user has set for privilege levels. The privilege levels are defined as follows:

Privilege Level	Actions Allowed
Peasant	Join an object and observe values
User A	Create a Channel
User B	Create a ByteArray
User C	Create a Token
Administrator	Create all Objects
Programmer	Destroy Objects

This design implies a number of basic parts. First, a class is needed to act as the privilege manager. Almost all of the classes on the server will need to have access to this class. The second is a class that is the manager for the session. This controls the high-level capabilities like creating and destroying individual shared objects. Finally code is needed to handle the start-up routines.

Compared to the client, the server is pretty basic. It doesn't have to do much other than monitor attempts to do things and either accept or reject them. It is not really the main focus of what could be derived as useful code for your applications. We can use it as a vehicle for testing authentication strategies.

One fundamental restriction that we will need to place on the application is to restrict it to a single session at a time. Another restriction that we'll place will be to limit the byte arrays used by the Channel and ByteArray to just a single byte, which is a value. This is purely for demonstration purposes to show that you can change the values.

Early on, this points out one of the flaws that JSDT has. If you create a managed session, you can't force a particular client to join in read-only mode. There is an option to set this from the client-side code in channels only, but there is no mechanism for enforcing the policy on a managed session.

Client Outline

Compared to the server, the client is much more complex. Not only must it represent the contents of the session and the values as they change, but it must also allow us to create new items and delete others.

First there must be code to deal with the requests. A manager is needed to keep track of the current authentication level and deal with passing the information back to the server every time it requests an authentication. For this, the Client implementation, dialog boxes for the selection of levels, and passwords all must be in close contact.

Second, there need to be some GUI components that are used to display each of the object types and their values. The GUI must then also include listeners for changes in the session to add and remove new objects from the UI component on demand.

Finally there is the supporting infrastructure: error dialogs, menu bars for controlling the application, and a window to put everything in. These become the wrappers. What is really of interest is the panel for displaying the current state of all the objects.

Implementing the Application

For the first version of the application, we are going to start with the first of the authentication schemes mentioned earlier. Each time a request is made of the session manager we'll fire off an authentication manager. The only times when we don't are when a client is joining (we'll always let them join) and when an attempt is made to destroy the session by someone other than the server (which we will deny). On the client side of the equation we will allow the user to change the privileges and then store those. Next time an authentication is needed, we'll send off the last input value to the server. The client will always start with zero privileges set.

The Server

We'll start with the server because it is the easier of the two parts to build. Also, we need it to define a number of the data structures that the client-side code will use. This follows the golden rule of network design—design the server first and let the clients simply use the bits that the server defines for them, rather than try to shoehorn the client requests into the server code.

Before we start, just some mild housekeeping is in order. Following the precedent set in the previous chapters, the server code will be located in the package `rwjn.chapter12.server`. This time there won't be any anonymous package start-up code. That will be included in the server-packaged classes directly.

Authentication Management   Most important on the list of things to construct is the data structure for the authentication. If we don't know what this is and how it is going to work, building the rest of the server suddenly gets much more complex. For the authentication system we are going to need three classes: the password/level container, the database of the password level information, and an abstract definition of the password container class. This last item is needed so that we can come along again at a later date and use a different password authentication database.

Starting with the class containing the password returned from a client, we see we need to hold the name of the level chosen and also the password to that level. Another factor in the design consideration is that we want to define all of the levels that are available as part of this class. This allows the client to be completely independent of the server and any requirements to hard-code levels. From this we can deduce that we're going to need to set the password and level, fetch those back and give a list of all the types of levels.

We define all of this information in the `LevelAuthentication` class, which is defined in Figure 12-1. A fairly obvious security requirement is that once the password and level have been set, we don't want to change them. A couple of different approaches are available: using methods that throw exceptions once set or using a constructor. For this case I chose the constructor approach, as I decided that we'd need to be creating a new instance of this class every time we wanted the level to change so we'd need to call some constructor anyway. We might as well save ourselves an extra method call by doing it all at once.

There are a couple of things to note about the methods. First, note that the `getPassword()` method is restricted to package private access only. This is so that only the server code can access the password. No one else has any need to get that information. Second, there are two constructors. The first provides an ability to create a new instance just by knowing this class. The first parameter is one of the values listed in the public static part at the top of the class. A second constructor was pro-

Figure 12-1
The class outline of the `Level Authentication` class.

```java
package rwjn.chapter12.server;

public class LevelAuthentication
        implements Serializable {

    public static final int PEASANT = 1;
    public static final int USER_A = 2;
    public static final int USER_B = 3;
    public static final int USER_C = 4;
    public static final int ADMIN = 5;
    public static final int PROGRAMMER = 6;

    public LevelAuthentication(String levelName,
                                String passwd)
        throws UnknownLevelException;

    public LevelAuthentication(int level, String passwd)
        throws UnknownLevelException;

    String getPassword();

    public static String[] listLevels();

    public boolean equals(Object val);
}
```

vided for users who might use the `listLevels` method and then wish to construct a class from that without matching the level name string to one of the `int` values. Finally I've overridden the `equals` method so that we can do some comparison operations later on for equivalence of the password/level pair with known valid values.

Why does this class implement `serializable`? The object is what we are going to be passing back and forth between the client and server as part of the `client.authenticate()` return value. That means any object that we want to send must at least be serializable. With our class being so simple (just a `string` and an `int`), there is no need to define our own serialization methods.

Next we'll define the authentication database abstract class. It is a very simple interface. If the authentication level checks out correctly, then return a true value. If it fails, then return false. Figure 12-2 shows the outline of the interface.

Figure 12-2
The AccessTable interface for defining generic authentication capabilities.

```
package rwjn.chapter12.server;


public interface AccessTable {
  public boolean checkAccess(LevelAuthentication level);
}
```

On basis of the interface we now implement the real authentication database. For this exercise we are creating a separate class from any other mechanisms. In other designs you might want to include it as part of some broader scheme. The class is called `SimpleAccessTable` and implements basically only the interface defined in Figure 12-2. There is not too much else to the class. Internally we keep a database of levels and passwords in a hashtable, with the key being the password. This database is populated in the constructor of the class by using a simple `for` loop:

```
int i;
LevelAuthentication level;
String[] level_strings = LevelAuthentication.listLevels();

for(i = 0; i < level_strings.length; i++) {
  try {
    level = new LevelAuthentication(i, PASSWORD_LIST[i]);
    privileges.put(PASSWORD_LIST[i], level);
  }
  catch(UnknownLevelException ule) {
    // should never happen!
  }
}
```

Note that we use the LevelAuthentication class even here to define the list of levels, and we have an internal string array of corresponding passwords. If we change the number of levels in LevelAuthentication we might be in trouble, but I wanted to have some reasonable password other than "level1," "level2," etc.

Checking a person's password is also a straightforward affair. We simply retrieve the password, fetch the object from the hashtable, then if it exists do a comparison of the two objects. If these all check out then we're fine to return a true value.

```
public boolean checkAccess(LevelAuthentication level) {
  String passwd = level.getPassword();

  LevelAuthentication real_access =
    (LevelAuthentication)privileges.get(passwd);

  if(real_access == null)
    return false;

  return real_access.equals(level);
}
```

Session Manager   With the basic authentication system sorted out, dealing with session management issues falls into place pretty quickly. If we are to watch and confirm every shared object that is created, we'll need to have a manager on the session. This is the only place where we can enforce this.

If you've been wandering around the javadoc for these packages you might have noticed a bunch of listener and adaptor classes for all of the shared objects in the com.sun.media.jsdt.event package. Listeners work just like that. We can't use them to enforce the authentication scheme. They get called after the event has happened. This is where the various manager classes become useful. They step into the middle of the process and get called just after a client makes a request, but just before it is approved and all the listeners receive the change event. If the manager does not approve the change (returns false) the process halts and no events are sent to the listeners.

In order to act as a manager, our server class, SecureManager, must implement the SessionManager interface. Inside the sessionRequest method is where all the dirty work of confirming or denying session activities take place. The javadoc commentary on this method states:

```
The following privileged operations could occur:

    CREATE a ByteArray within the managed Session.
    DESTROY a ByteArray within the managed Session.
    CREATE a Channel within the managed Session.
    DESTROY a Channel within the managed Session.
    CREATE a Token within the managed Session.
    DESTROY a Token within the managed Session.
    JOIN a managed Session.
```

These types of acts are defined as constants in the AuthenticationInfo class. We need to deal with every one of these by saying either yes or no to each action, regardless of whether we are really interested in it or not. Handling this is usually done in a large switch statement. Luckily for us, we can break the functionality down into one of three behaviors:

1. Destroy the session. Prohibit this to anyone but the server client.

2. Join the session. Everyone should be allowed to do this.

3. Create or destroy objects in the session. This we need to confirm every operation has the correct privileges so we authenticate the client.

This makes life very simple for us. Figure 12-3 shows the code needed to implement this strategy.

We start the method by retrieving the action that occurred and also creating a boolean, which is our exit condition, to be set at false. The default behavior is therefore set at deny everything, for the security conscious. So we deny all and then override that to allow an action. As you can see, there is not really that much to the server-side code. To authenticate an action, we call the `authenticate` method of the client with our authentication information instance. The return value from that is what the client sent in return, which we cast to the appropriate type. If the authentication database approves of the action, then the all clear is given and the method exits, allowing that action to take place.

A point to notice is the line for the SESSION_DESTROY case. Notice that we don't use the reference equality comparison (==). Even though we are operating the same VM instance, we are not necessarily guaranteed to get the same reference twice when referring to a client or any JSDT-based object for that matter. `JSDTObject`, which is the base class of all the shared objects, overrides the basic methods of `Object` so that these sorts of comparisons are valid. The `equals()` method checks for the two client instances being the same client.

NOTE: *The JSDTObject class cannot be found in either of the two public packages. You can find it in the* `com.sun.media.jsdt.impl` *package.*

Apart from the sessionRequest method, the only other method in the class is the constructor. As you might have noticed, Figure 12-3 included a couple of undefined variables: `server_client` and

Figure 12-3
Implementing a session manager with the sessionRequest method.

```
public boolean sessionRequest(Session session,
                              AuthenticationInfo info,
                              Client client)
{
  boolean valid_action = false;
  int action = info.getAction();

  LevelAuthentication auth_object;

  switch(action) {
    case AuthenticationInfo.DESTROY_SESSION:
        valid_action = server_client.equals(client);
        break;

    // All of these have the same behaviour
    case AuthenticationInfo.CREATE_CHANNEL:
    case AuthenticationInfo.DESTROY_CHANNEL:
    case AuthenticationInfo.CREATE_BYTEARRAY:
    case AuthenticationInfo.DESTROY_BYTEARRAY:
    case AuthenticationInfo.CREATE_TOKEN:
    case AuthenticationInfo.DESTROY_TOKEN:
        auth_object =
(LevelAuthentication)client.authenticate(info);

        valid_action = access_table.checkAccess(auth_object);
        break;

    case AuthenticationInfo.JOIN:
        valid_action = true;
        break;
  }
  return valid_action;
}
```

access_table. Server_client, as its name suggests, is a reference to the client that is used by the server. This is passed in as a parameter to the constructor. Also passed into the constructor is the reference to access_table. This is an instance of the AccessTable interface that was defined back in Figure 12-2. The flexibility of keeping these two references as interface definitions can now be seen. We can change the authentication tables and implementation without disturbing the process of the authentication.

Starting the Server With all the functional areas of the server complete, all that remains is the start-up routines. Most of this you have seen already. We create a class called `ManagedJSDTServer`. In this we place our usual static main method to start the application. Then, in the constructor we place all the code necessary to start the JSDT code and accessory code. This is presented in Figure 12-4.

Figure 12-4

The constructor code used to start the server.

```
public ManagedJSDTServer(int port) {
  Session session = null;

  server_client = new ServerClient();

  // Check for a registry existing and create one if not.
  try {
    if(!RegistryFactory.registryExists(SESSION_TYPE))
      RegistryFactory.startRegistry(SESSION_TYPE);
  }
  catch(NoRegistryException nre) {
    System.out.println("Couldn't start the Registry " + nre);
    System.out.println("Exiting - bye!");
    System.exit(1);
  }
  catch(RegistryExistsException ree) {
    System.out.println("The Registry is already running.");
  }

  // Now let's put together the URL - localhost and
  //create the session
  try {
    StringBuffer url_buffer =
      new StringBuffer("jsdt://localhost:");
    url_buffer.append(port);
    url_buffer.append('/');
    url_buffer.append(SESSION_TYPE);
    url_buffer.append("/Session/");
    url_buffer.append(SESSION_NAME);

    String url = url_buffer.toString();

    Client client = new ServerClient();
    AccessTable access_manager = new SimpleAccessTable();

    SecureManager server_manager =
```

Figure 12-4
(*Continued*)

```
          new SecureManager(client, access_manager);

      if(!SessionFactory.sessionExists(url)) {
        session =
          SessionFactory.createSession(url, server_manager);
        session.join(client);
      }
    }
    catch(JSDTException je) {
      System.out.println("Error creating a session " + je);
      System.exit(2);
    }

    // Just a quick announcement
    System.out.println("Server ready");
  }
```

A quick review of the code will reveal a fair amount of familiar code. In fact, most of this is just cut-and-paste of code from the previous chapter. The only lines that have changes are those where we actually create the session. When you create a managed session, there is no automatic join process like there is for unmanaged sessions. This time we need to explicitly join the session. Although there is no need for it in this case, it is useful to join just in case we wish to do something.

What's Missing?   The server that you now have is relatively complete. It does the main tasks of starting and monitoring the appropriate session. From all of the above code, the only noticeable missing feature is an explicit exit capability for the server. This is relatively trivial to add in. Just construct an exit method in the class and make sure that it calls `session.destroy()` with the server client. This will pass and the clients will receive this information and act appropriately.

The Client

Having the authentication structures defined in the server makes the design of the client side much easier. With this information, we can now sketch out the rest of the design of the client code. First, there must be a class to keep track of the current level that has been requested. Next, we know that we can have a session listener class that is used to keep track of shared objects and render those to screen. Also, from this information we can say that we'll introduce UI objects that implement each of the different shared object listeners, so that each time a new shared object is created we can just create a corresponding UI object. Finally, we know that we can create a completely separate authentication mechanism and a mechanism for creating/destroying the shared objects.

Authentication Management   In implementing the client-side authentication mechanism, we will follow the lead set by the server side. We will design a base interface that contains the basic capabilities, then we will produce an implementation of this for each required scheme. The basic interface is defined in Figure 12-5.

Notice that the `getCurrentAccess()` method returns an `Object` rather than a `LevelAuthentication` class. This allows the implementation to be completely independent of what the authentication classes are. Since the `authenticate()` method of a client returns an `Object` too, we are pretty safe with this option. The interface uses a string for the level because—I know from having implemented this—I'm going to be using the strings from the `listLevels()` method in a dialog and then forwarding the selected value straight to the method.

On top of our interface from Figure 12-5, we must now build an implementation. Again, following the server, we'll call this `Simple AccessHandler`. Compared to the server code, this is even simpler. We need to implement the two methods of the interface and store the information. The simplest way to do this is to make a new instance of the `LevelAuthentication` each time the password is set, store this reference internally, and return it when asked to provide the access level. Earlier in the chapter it was stated that the server starts with zero priv-

Figure 12-5
The client-side interface for defining generic authentication capabilities.

```
package rwjn.chapter12.client;


public interface AccessHandler {
    public void setAccessLevel(String level, String passwd)
        throws UnknownLevelException;

    public Object getCurrentAccess();
}
```

Figure 12-6
Code to show a dialog for changing the level information.

```
public static void changeAccessLevel() {
  JOptionPane.showMessageDialog(frame,
                                access,
                                "Select Access Level",
                                JOptionPane.QUESTION_MESSAGE);
  try {
    access_handler.setAccessLevel(access.getLevel(),
                                  access.getPasswd());
  }
  catch(UnknownLevelExceptionRule) {
    // should never happen!
    // but should loop until we get valid levels
  }
}
```

ileges. We can't just keep a null reference around to indicate this problem because that might cause problems with the JSDT authentication schemes. Instead, we'll create a bogus instance of the authentication class with a zero-length string as the password. That way, any attempt to do things will result in an instance of JSDT's `PermissionDenied Exception` being generated and the user needing to supply a password.

Last, we need to provide a dialog that provides this capability to the user. To implement this, we'll create a method that pops up a dialog asking for user input and then fills in the appropriate information. Figure 12-6 shows the code needed to do this.

Before going on with things, I need to explain this `access` variable that's suddenly appeared. This is a class (`AccessLevelPanel`) that extends a `JPanel` for providing all the user interface items for the task. Figure 12-7 shows a screen shot of the dialog. At the top there is a choice

Figure 12-7
The dialog for selecting the user access level.

Figure 12-8
The dialog for select-
ing the server and
port number.

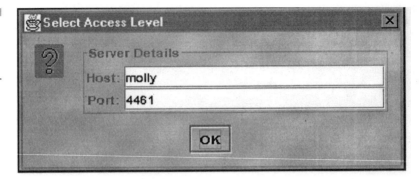

box for all of the levels provided and the text field; at the bottom is really a
`JPasswordField` for typing in your password. These are what are
queried in the two lines forming the `setAccessLevel` method call. Figure
12-8 shows the server connection dialog. Note that it is almost identical to
that used for the bank client user interface used in the earlier chapters.

NOTE: *There are some minor problems with Swing. The dialog is
smaller than the combo list, which means that the list won't paint outside of the borders of the dialog. This results in the list being truncated
at about TokenUser. You can use the arrow keys to navigate up and down
the list contents if necessary.*

Shared Object UI Component   Next on the agenda is developing the
UI components used to represent the shared objects. For this task, I've
chosen to go with three separate classes—one for each of the shared
object classes. These classes are just a simple Jlabel for the representation. There's nothing fancy about the design, although it wouldn't take
much to add an image to them. Each label prints out the name of the
object and the current value as follows:

```
<object name>(value)
```

For tokens this just prints out one of the four states: GRAB, INH,
AVAIL, or GIVE. This information is based on the status of the token.
Figure 12-9 is the source for the button.

   All of the labels follow a similar pattern. In the constructor a check is
made to see what the status is. The status is then rendered to the text of
the label. Note how we have made each label responsible for listening to

Figure 12-9

The source to pro-
duce the label.

```
public class ChannelLabel extends JLabel
    implements ChannelConsumer
{
  private String channel_name;

  public ChannelLabel(Channel channel, Client client) {

    try {
      channel.addConsumer(client, this);
      channel_name = channel.getName();

      if(channel.dataAvailable(client)) {
        Data data = channel.receive(client);
        dataReceived(data);
      }
      else {
        setText(channel_name);
      }
    }
    catch(JSDTException je) {
      setText(channel_name);
    }
  }

  public void dataReceived(Data data) {
    byte[] value = data.getData();
    StringBuffer buffer = new StringBuffer(channel_name);
    buffer.append('(');
    buffer.append(value[0]);
    buffer.append(')');

    setText(buffer.toString());
  }
}
```

its own data representation. This frees us from the duties of doing it at a
higher-level class with the extra management issues involved.

These labels are not affected by any of the authentication issues.
They are created only as a result of a new object being added to the session, and only listen to the values as they change.

Shared Object Column   Once we have a label, we need to then collect
all the labels for that shared object type together. The next step in build-

ing our collection is to create a column of similar objects. Since the easiest way to store this data is in tabular form, we'll use the properties of Swing's JTable. To create a customized column our collection class will extend ColumnModel.

The column model that we've implemented for this example comes in two parts: (1) a base class representing all JSDT shared objects and (2) derived classes for each type of shared object. In the base class we keep all the common functionality, such as listener code and ability to add and remove objects in a generic fashion. In the derived classes we deal with handling particular object types.

Since this is not a book on Swing, we won't deal with the implementation intricacies of JTables. One interesting point to note, however, is that because everything is an abstract class, setting up session listeners for the processes of adding and removing shared objects on a per-column basis means that the base class cannot also extend SessionAdaptor. Instead we have to provide all the method implementations and let each base class override only the methods that it needs.

An example of the ChannelColumn model implementation is given in Figure 12-10. Note that the derived class is responsible for adding itself

Figure 12-10
Channel column—
the implementation
of the column model
for the channel.

```
public class ChannelColumn extends JSDTObjectColumn {
  private Session session;
  private Client client;

  public ChannelColumn(Session s, Client c) {
    super("Channels");

    session = s;
    client = c;

    int i;
    int size = 0;
    String[] item_names;

    try {
      // join as a listener
      session.addSessionListener(this);

      // first load all the channels
      item_names = session.listChannelNames();
      if(item_names != null)
```

Figure 12-10
(*Continued*)

```
            size = item_names.length;


     }
     catch(JSDTException je) {
         // Ouch! Don't do anything.
         return;
     }


     for(i = 0; i < size; i++)
        createChannelLabel(item_names[i]);
}

private void createChannelLabel(String name) {
    Channel channel;
    ChannelLabel label;

    try {
        channel = session.createChannel(client,
                                         name,
                                         true,
                                         true,
                                         true);

        // create the label and then add it to the column
        label = new ChannelLabel(channel, client);

        addObject(label, name);
    }
    catch(JSDTException je) {
        // ignore it and continue on
        System.out.println("Error grabbing channel: " + je);
    }
}

public synchronized void channelCreated(SessionEvent event) {
    String name = event.getResourceName();

    createChannelLabel(name);
}

public synchronized void channelDestroyed(SessionEvent event) {
    String name = event.getResourceName();

    removeObject(name);
}
}
```

as a listener to the session, rather than the base class. This is so that you can see everything happening; it also associates the event filtering with the process so that it is more explicit to the reader of the code. The addObject and removeObject methods seen in the last two methods of the example come from the base class and are responsible for talking with the underlying table and column model implementations to make sure the screen is updated correctly.

NOTE: *In another concession to reality, we always* `autojoin` *and create reliable, ordered channels.*

Viewing a Complete Session Following the completion of the column implementations for each of the shared data types, we naturally follow on to the code that is going to bring them all together—the Table code. The data in the table is represented as an implementation of a `TableModel` based on the `AbstractTableModel` base class.

A number of different models of data representation were tried before settling on a final design. In the end it was elected to have a table model instance represent only one session. Once a session is left, then the table is discarded. Creating a new session requires creating a completely new table model instance. The column model implementations of the previous section also reflect this design decision (see the parameters of the constructor in Figure 12-10).

Our table model implementation is pretty simple compared to what it could have been under other designs. Since the columns are individually responsible for listening to their own shared data types, there is no need for the table to also be a session listener. The table is simply responsible for starting off the columns and then answering any queries asked of it by the Swing rendering processes.

Interacting with Shared Objects So far, all of our code has been responsible for viewing the objects. Our client code also needs to be able to create, destroy, and edit these same objects from some sort of GUI front end. An easy solution to this problem would be to create a menu bar and then embed all of the code in the menu handling. This leaves us with some problems if we want to expand the code later to use, say, pop-up menus or other interaction devices. To cater to these requirements, all the real interaction with the session is left to a static class called

`FunctionManager` which contains one method per action that needs to be performed.

Interaction with the shared objects is through a two-step process: (1) a menu item representing the required action is made and (2) the event handling code then makes the appropriate call to the function management. Inside this class, dialog boxes are presented to the user to make the same choice of actions. An example of the dialog is presented in Figure 12-11, which shows the selection of a byte array before a value is edited on it. After performing the appropriate UI interactions, the function manager then goes away and makes it all official by performing the appropriate calls to the JSDT session and objects.

Since this is a proto-debugger, it is possible that the client code could be entering into a session some time after it has been established. One aspect of Figure 12-10 that has been glossed over is the code in the constructor. Notice that the first thing that code does is request all of the currently existing channels and display those as items in the column. The internal interaction management also needs to handle this case. Another possibility is that someone else adds items to the session other than your client so these need to be accounted for as well.

Inside the FunctionManager class we also need to deal with the lookup problems of objects. Getting the list of names of each shared object type is a trivial exercise. Fetching the objects named in this list isn't. If you should decide that you want to create an object just as we have been doing all along in the examples, say a channel, and then lose the reference to it (it was only through a local variable), you are pretty well stuffed for any further interaction. Any attempts later on to fetch that object using a `Session.createChannel()` call will result in a `NameInUseException`.

How did that happen? Well, a client has created a named object but

Figure 12-11
Dialog for selecting a ByteArray for further processing.

never said it was leaving the object. Now along comes another client, which is really the same one, that has the same name and attempts to attach to the object. JSDT, not knowing where the client really comes from, assumes that you're trying to create a new connection and bounces it because the name is identical to a client that has already joined the session. This is important to note because it is something very fundamental in almost all JSDT implementations that you are bound to run across. There are two ways of avoiding this problem—make sure that the autojoin parameter is always set to false, or make sure you keep a reference to the object when you first create it, say in a hashtable where the key is the name string.

For this implementation, we've selected the second option, as it matches well with another point that you're about to discover. The function manager also implements a session listener so that it may keep abreast of changes in the session by other clients. When your client creates an object through a call to FunctionManager, it also receives notification of that object being created through the listener interface. This is a rather interesting source of generation of NameInUseExceptions. In the code I have this (ignoring exception handling):

```
public static void createChannel() {
  // get a name from the user through a dialog
  createChannel(user_supplied_name);
}

private static void createChannel(String name) {

  if(channels.get(name) != null)
    return;

  Channel ch = session.createChannel(client,
                                     name,
                                     true,
                                     true,
                                     true);
  channels.put(name, ch);
}
```

then later on in the listener code I have

```
public synchronized void channelCreated(SessionEvent event) {
  createChannel(event.getResourceName());
}
```

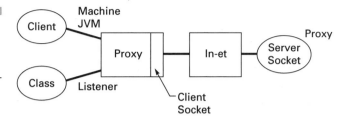

Figure 12-12
The architecture
of JSDT's
implementation.

This code results in a `NameInUseException`. Why? The answer is not immediately obvious, but has to do with the underlying implementation of JSDT. Figure 12-12 explains some of the architecture of JSDT's implementation.

What effectively happens is that the menu calls the public `create Channel()` method. This then calls the private version, which makes a call to the `session.createChannel` method. Internally the implementation then notifies all of the session listeners on the local proxy and also goes out to the network to notify any other clients. Now, the proxy sends all the session listeners the message that an object has been created, so the `channelCreated()` method is called in response. Not knowing any better, it also attempts to create a new channel because the hashtable does not contain an instance of the named channel. The listener code thinks that some other client has created an object. The next call to `session.createChannel()` that results generates our exception. Why? Because at this point, the code has not yet returned to the original `session.createChannel()` call made and hence the channel has not been entered into the hashtable (which is why our check previously returned nothing). The only real solution to this problem is to provide a check in the listener code that compares the string names of the creating client (available as part of the event) and the local client name and proceeds only if they are different, like this:

```
public synchronized void channelCreated(SessionEvent event) {
  if(!client_name.equals(event.getClientName()))
    createChannel(event.getResourceName());
}
```

NOTE: *This is an acknowledged bug in JSDT 1.4. A fix will be forthcoming in version 1.5.*

Pulling It All Together   Finally, we have all the pieces together. All that is needed now is some GUI glue to bring it into a single user interface. The class responsible is called JSDTDebuggerFrame. This is a JFrame that creates the menu bar, the FunctionManager, and the table. The problem is that the table is created as a result of someone creating a new session.

JSDT provides no method of notification that a new session has been created. Also, this interaction is driven from the menu code, which interacts only with FunctionManager. A quick fix to the problem is to create a listener callback structure and have the frame code implement it. When the GUI requests that a new session be created, the frame code simply creates a new table and adds it to the frame. Problem solved. Our basic code outline would be something like the following:

```
public class JSDTDebuggerFrame extends JFrame
    implements SessionCreationListener {

    private Client client = null;

    private JSDTSessionTableModel table_model;

    public JSDTDebuggerFrame() {
        super("Session Debugger");

        AccessHandler access_handler = new SimpleAccessHandler();

        client = new MenuClient(access_handler);
        MenuBar menus = new MenuBar(access_handler);

        FunctionManager.init(this, client, access_handler);
        setJMenuBar(menus);

        setSize(400, 200);

        JPanel panel = new JPanel();
        setContentPane(panel);
    }

    public void sessionCreated(String url) {
        table_model = new JSDTSessionTableModel(url, client);
        TableColumnModel column_model =
         table_model.getColumnModel();

        JTable table = new JTable(table_model, column_model);
        table.setAutoCreateColumnsFromModel(false);
```

```
table.setRowSelectionAllowed(false);
table.setColumnSelectionAllowed(false);

//Create the scroll pane and add the table to it.
JScrollPane scrollPane = new JScrollPane(table);

//Add the scroll pane to this window.
setContentPane(scrollPane);

repaint();
    }


    . . . .

}
```

Everything looks all right, but JSDT keeps generating these annoying NameInUseExceptions whenever you try to create an object. What could still be wrong with the code? Wasn't everything fixed? Yes, maybe, but your problem comes from a little forgetfulness. Basically, we've got the FunctionManager creating instances of shared objects and we also have column models creating exactly the same object—both of them have been given the same client instance! Therefore, when one tries to create an object, the other also tries to create it with the same client name and you end up with an exception.

Luckily the solution to the problem is really simple—just create two different clients that have different names. For example have an int as a parameter and use that in the client name string generation. Or, as this example did, make two completely different classes with different names, and pass one to the FunctionManager and the other to the table when it is created.

Now we're all happy and we end up with a user interface looking like Figure 12-13.

Running and Implementation Notes   Both the server and the client code have main functions in their respective code. Unlike the other examples in this book, the example in Figure 12-13 doesn't have a simple, nonpackaged class to run everything. First you need to start the server:

```
c:\> java rwjn.chapter12.server.ManagedJSDTServer
Request to join for Debugger Server
Server ready
```

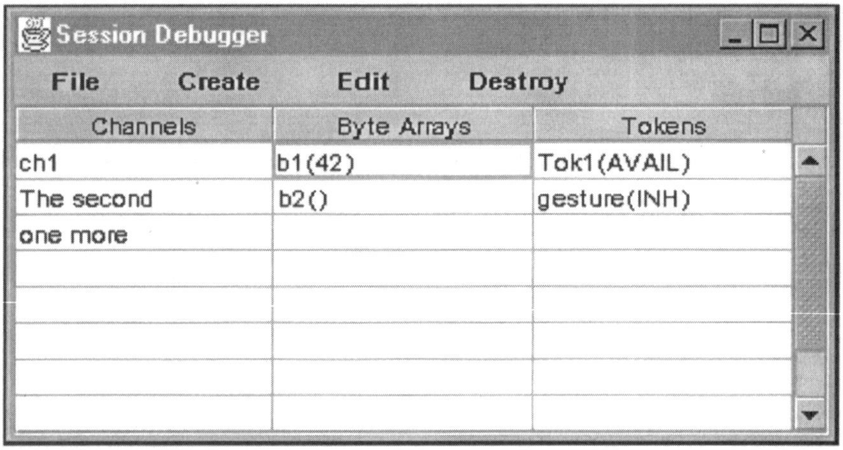

Figure 12-13
The completed user interface.

After you see the server ready line, it should be fine to start the client code:

```
c:\>java rwjn.chapter12.client.JSDTDebuggerFrame
```

which does not produce any output unless you get some strange exception happening.

Before moving on to other areas of JSDT, we present a few notes about some of the implementation aspects that might be of use. First, if you look closely at Figure 12-13 you'll notice that channels don't have any values printed next to them. Channels don't save events sent through them. If you join a channel and check to see if data is available, it will always say there is none. There is no buffering of the last sent value for you to read. If this is important for your work, then you are going to need to implement some much more complex logic on the server side. Luckily, Chapter 13 shows you exactly how to do this.

The second note is about the choice of user interface. Most of the dialogs were put together in a hurry using JoptionPane and require you to answer, usually, a couple of different dialogs to get something done. A smoother example would create a bunch of custom dialogs that do everything in one hit.

Finally, watch out for Swing repaint problems. During the development, more than one apparent bug was due to Swing not repainting or behaving exactly the way you expected. In the end we implemented everything right down to CellRenderers to get the display to work nicely and correctly.

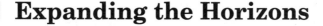

Expanding the Horizons

While the preceding exercise has given you a lot more experience in using JSDT, there is a lot more to learn about. In this next section we'll go through some of the more commonly asked questions and techniques used in implementing JSDT applications.

Challenge-Response Authentication

Don't be fooled into thinking the authentication model presented in the previous exercise is the only way of doing authentication in JSDT. It is probably the simplest of systems that could be implemented. If you require more or stronger authentication, JSDT provides other options.

Typical strong authentication systems these days rely on a challenge-response system. The server sends a challenge to the client that then must process it and reply with an appropriate response. For the strongly security conscious, this authentication system might be in the form of a public key encryption system. The server sends a pass phrase, which the user's application then encrypts with its private key. The server then attempts to decrypt the returned message, using the stored local public key for the user. If everything matches, the process is allowed to continue.

Revisiting the AuthenticationInfo Class   To work out how to implement this challenge-response system using JSDT, we need to revisit the `AuthenticationInfo` and `Client` classes again. Looking at the documentation for `AuthenticationInfo`, you will find two methods—`getChallenge()` and `setChallenge()`. Ah—the perfect methods. `setChallenge` allows you to set a challenge piece of information. It takes any object so long as it is serializable. This allows you to put in any sort of challenge that may be of use. Typically this is just a `String` instance, but you could use anything.

SECURITY: *Just remember that whatever you use as the object is subject to the same security problems as any other item that has been serialized unless you have your own customized socket implementations that include other lower-level security mechanisms.*

Once you've set the challenge, a client may fetch that challenge with the `get()` method. The object is then cast to the appropriate type before the system continues with whatever processing and response is required.

Now that you can get and set a challenge, you need to actually pass that from the managing class to the respondent. This is where the Client interface comes in again and serves double duty. Although you might have thought that the client only implements the interface so that it may respond to authentication requests, it is also used to request authentication directly. Having set a challenge in the AuthenticationInfo instance you call the client's `authenticate()` method with that instance and wait for the response. With the return value of the method you can then do your processing to determine the required action.

Implementing a Challenge-Response System   The following example, although very simple, illustrates how to use the challenge system provided in JSDT. The first action is to define what we'll do for authentication. The typical example used is to return an uppercase version of a string that was sent in all lowercase. Not very intelligent or secure, but enough to show the principles.

The first step is to set up the authentication system. This requires the use of a managed shared object. For example, we would start with a managed session such as the one presented in Figure 12-3. Notice that we've been passed both of the required pieces of information—the Client and the AuthenticationInfo. To the AuthenticationInfo we would modify Figure 12-3 to look like the following:

```
private static final String QUERY_STR = "encode this string";
private static final String RETURN_STR = "ENCODE THIS STRING";

public boolean sessionRequest(Session session,
                              AuthenticationInfo info,
                              Client client)
{
  boolean valid_action = false;
  int action = info.getAction();

  info.setChallenge(QUERY_STR);

  switch(action) {
  .....
```

Then we need to request the client to authenticate, just as we did before:

```
case AuthenticationInfo.DESTROY_TOKEN:
 auth_object = (String)client.authenticate(info);
```

The final test of whether to allow the action is then a basic string compare:

```
valid_action = auth_object.equals(RETURN_STR);
```

On the client implementation side of the situation, we now need to completely change the implementation that was presented in the debugger clients. This time the body of the `authenticate()` method must grab the string, change it to upper case, and return it:

```
public Object authenticate(AuthenticationInfo info) {
  String input = (String)info.getChallenge();
  String output = input.toUpperCase();
  return output;
}
```

With these small modifications, you now have a completed challenge-response system. Just remember that your challenge can be anything and it gives you tremendous power and security.

Can I Put in More Control?

Although there seems to be quite a bit of control that is available to the programmer, there is always the requirement for even more control. For example, it would be nice to allow people to join in read-only mode. However, in short, the answer is that what you've seen above is the maximum amount of control that can be forced on the system.

The Channel class does allow a small amount of additional control. When you join a channel explicitly [as compared to using the `autojoin` feature of the `createChannel()` method], you may give it a mode for read, write, or read/write. However, this still relies on you, the programmer, for implemention in any libraries that you distribute with the application. Unfortunately, there is no way of using a manager implementation to allow a client to join in a read-only mode.

Shared Serialized Objects

One of the more common ideas that you might use is to share an entire class rather than just an array of bytes. For example, you might use this technique to represent a geographic coordinate. The class is serialized to the shared data object (ByteArray or Channel), and then, at the receiving end, the user would ask the item for the location in the type of projection that it wants.

Making a class serialize over a shared data object is a case of taking the pieces you have learned already in this book and putting them together.

Writing the Shared Object   The first task is to write the object to a stream so that we may extract the raw bytes for sending. Since both target shared object types use arrays of bytes as the data type, you will need a `ByteArrayOutputStream`. Into this you can then write the object, as the following code example shows:

```
try {
    // Create the output streams
    ByteArrayOutputStream bos = new ByteArrayOutputStream();
    ObjectOutputStream oos = new ObjectOutputStream(bos);
    oos.writeObject(some_object);
    oos.flush();

    // Turn the result into a Data object.
    Data data = new Data(bos.toByteArray());

    // Send serialized object to all Channel Consumers.
    channel.sendToAll(client, data);
}
catch(IOException e1) {
    System.out.println("Error creating object output stream.");
}
catch (JSDTException e3) {
    System.out.println("Error sending object over Channel.");
}
```

In this example we've put everything into the single try/catch block. You may of course elect to break it up more finely. It is suggested that a fine-grained approach is more appropriate in this instance because some nonfatal errors can be generated. In our code above, the nonfatal errors would result in the entire operation failing.

Reading the Shared Object   Reading in the shared object is just the reverse of the previous example: First create the streams needed to read the data and then use the serialization to reconstruct the object. Since the class read and returned is just an Object you will need to cast it to the appropriate type before using it.

```
public synchronized void dataRecieved(Data data) {
   byte[] msg = data.getData();

   try {
     ByteArrayInputStream bis = new ByteArrayInputStream(msg);
     ObjectInputStream ois = new ObjectInputStream(bis);
     Object info = ois.readObject();

     // now cast the object to the appropriate type
     // and use it

   }
   catch(IOException e1) {
     System.out.println("Error reading object input stream.");
   }
}
```

One technique that I have found useful with this system is to make sure that the class with the above method in it also has listeners attached to it. The idea is that, as soon as the object is read, the local application listeners would be notified of the new information. You would probably place this just before the exception catching, or after that if needed.

Summary

In this chapter you have seen how to implement authentication on top of standard JSDT objects. The idea has been to create as many components that may be useful for debugging or displaying the contents of shared objects. The design has been such that you could take any of the items presented here and use them within your application almost immediately.

Where to next? The design has been fairly limited in its capabilities on the user interface side. With the basis presented here, there would not be much more work to turn this into a full JSDT debugger. A feature that might be useful would be to allow you to look at any byte in the array, and the sender of the last update. Also useful for debugging would be the ability to save the data to a file, maybe even to perform full transaction logging.

The next chapter will show you through a full JSDT application that takes everything you have learned so far and more to build a full collaborative application. It takes your standard, basic, shared whiteboard and turns it into a very useful conferencing tool.

13

Sharing Your Thoughts

In a different style from the rest of the book, this chapter will build a complete application from the ground up. From the experience gained in the past couple of chapters, the application will create one of the most common building blocks of a collaborative application—the shared whiteboard. However, this whiteboard is a lot more complex than what you might have seen on various people's web pages.

System Design

Although the book is concentrated on the networking aspects of any application, there is always a user interface to consider. That user interface might be in the form of configuration files or something graphical. In all cases, this must be part of our overall system design. No point having the world's best network server if it is impossible to attach something usable to it. This chapter will discuss mainly the networking aspects of the design, but it will also check out the GUI side as well (written by my partner in coding crime, Cameron Gillies).

The following is a set of requirements for the application:

1. The application outline is to create a collaborative sketching tool allowing users to create either open or moderated groups.

2. Anyone is free to create a group and name it either as moderated or open. The sketching tool will provide both a shared whiteboard and a chat facility.

3. Creating a moderated group gives the user who controls the session the ability to approve or disapprove a new user joining that group.

4. The shared whiteboard should offer as much capability as can be provided in Java 2 graphics.

5. A user joining a chat some time after the commencement of the group should have all the current drawing details available on screen. This is not a requirement of the chat information.

Code Layout

With the above design statement and a good knowledge of JSDT and Java 2, we get a reasonably good picture of how to construct the application. It really sounds like a distributed application where anyone may be the controller of what happens.

Because JSDT allows anyone to create a shared object and manage it, there is no central "server" as such. However, requirement 5 above means that some machine needs to be listening to everything that happens and listening for new users to send updates to them. Another requirement imposed by JSDT is that we nominate at least one machine to act as a registry for everything that happens. To keep life simple, the machine that has the registry will also function as the recording server for update information.

NOTE: *The statement about no central server is not, strictly speaking, correct. There is a central server hiding in the underlying implementations. If you terminate the first JSDT process, i.e., the one running on the machine whose name you have used in the JSDT session URLs, then the JSDT collaboration is over.*

On top of the server code, we need to provide a client-side system. While it is possible to write most of the JSDT code directly inside the GUI component interactions, this makes our code less flexible. As in our designs to date, it should be possible to change the implementation of either the GUI code or the networking implementation without requiring a rewrite of the other. To achieve this, a separate API will be created to deal with all of the shared data interactions.

On the basis of the above thoughts, we end up with three basic parts: GUI code, client-side API and networking, and a server application. Figure 13-1 outlines the parts of the APIs and the application and how they relate together in a simplistic fashion.

Client Code Design

The most complex part of the application, in terms of code, is on the client side. Although we talk about client-side code, it is important to remember that, as far as the JSDT API is concerned, there is no such thing as a server. We have code that acts a bit like a server, but to JSDT all it appears to be is another client joined to a shared session.

As part of our design effort we must try to keep this in mind. All of the code used to send and receive messages can be used in both the

Figure 13-1
Simplified API
structure.

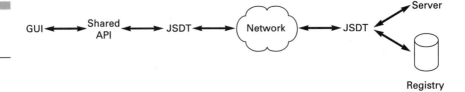

server code and client code. A good fundamental OO design should allow this to happen. The following sections outline the main high-level design considerations. It also leaves a fair bit of the detail design information out. In large-scale systems, making that fine break between detail design and implementation documentation can be quite tricky. We'll include quite a lot of the low-level design information when we talk about the implementation. Just in the shared data code there are close to 70 classes, so you can see we are going to be leaving quite a bit of the information out.

Code Architecture   Another point to keep in mind is that we'd like the code to be as modular as possible. This code consists really of two independent parts—a chat application and a whiteboard application—that happen to exist in the one GUI framework. You should be allowed to take one of these pieces of code and use it in your own application, or take both of these and put them into a bigger framework of shared data.

Although there are two separate parts, we would like them to act in a coordinated way. To the user (and the user interface), joining a group should seamlessly join them in one action. Making this a reality requires a little bit of coding glue, which is implemented in the Shared Data interface. Figure 13-2 outlines how the various high-level objects interact together on the client side.

As you can see, the GUI code is effectively two separate parts. Each part directly interacts with its shared data item, but the higher-level GUI, such as menu bars and dialog boxes, interacts with the common SharedData interface.

Interacting with each of the shared data interfaces is done through the usual method calls. Method calls are used by the GUI code to send information to any other people on the channel. Receiving information from other users is done through an event listener mechanism that you are familiar with. There are event listeners for almost everything from getting a draw line command to requesting that the user confirm that someone is allowed to join the session.

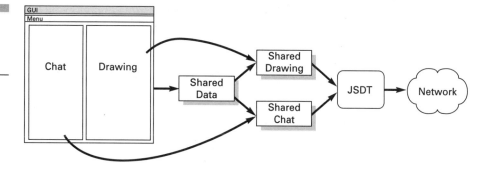

JSDT Objects With each object representing a shared piece of information, we've got a couple of design choices to make. First, we need to decide exactly how to hook into JSDT. We've got all of these different shared objects and ways of handling information over them. Having decided that, then we need to take care of the method of collating this information and getting it to the user interface in a proper form.

For the first task, we have a range of options. Do we allow the user to connect to any session? Once in a session, how do we decide which of the shared data objects contains a drawing channel? Then, if we make it through all of this, which sort of shared object should be used?

Starting with the last question, we decide by looking at the data and how information needs to be sent. Since we need to send more than just a yes/no answer, that rules the Token out, leaving just the ByteArray and Channel. A look again at the requirements says that we must be able to send data to a particular client when it first joins the group. As the Channel is the only object that you can do this with, then that becomes the choice. An alternative design would be to use byte arrays for all of the current actions and then use a specific, known channel name for sending start-up information to a particular client. This adds unnecessary complexity to the system so it has not been used.

Moving on to the first question, we could allow the user to connect to any session, but dealing with the shared object question becomes a problem. Also, in terms of the user, that sort of information is usually too "complex." If you look at all the common commercial systems, very rarely do they even offer the user the choice of what server to connect to, not to mention a port number or session information. To keep things simple on the user side, we will allow them to connect to any server that they wish, even a port number, but on that server the session names will always be fixed. This allows quite a bit more freedom on our part than naming individual groups would.

A follow-up question now arises: Should we have many sessions or a single session for all the shared objects? For this there is no definitive answer. As JSDT allows arbitrary names to be used to name a shared object, we could use naming conventions to nominate each of the channel types. Any names that the user interface sees would have this extra information filtered from the name strings. As far as scalability is concerned, there don't seem to be any problems that we haven't yet encountered. While a session is not likely to have more than, say, 20 objects, increasing the number of shared data object types at the API level (that is, more than just shared drawing and chat, not JSDT shared objects) would lead to a corresponding increase in the number of shared objects registered with a particular session.

For this design, we've opted for the other approach of having a separate session for each API-level object. The main reason behind this is to maintain the full separation of data for each object. With each object having its own session, it would be possible for us to split the load between different servers if needed (not that this isn't possible with the above alternative). Each section of the application is responsible purely for its own data without having to rely on external information such as naming conventions.

Having answered the first question, we have automatically answered the second. We don't need to worry about which JSDT shared object is useful to us because we know that everything within our named session belongs to our code.

Shared Object Interaction   Moving one step up the design chain, we now come to designing how we are going to interact with the objects. Within each session, we shall be creating new channels on the fly, in response to user requests. A JSDT channel is exactly equivalent to the group that the user sees. When users open a dialog to connect to a channel, they are given a list of the current groups that exist and are given the option of joining one of them or creating a new one. These lists of the names are taken directly from the session. Choosing a name then creates that channel on the client-side API code, which we must then interact with.

Our first step in interacting with a channel is extracting data from it. As you have seen previously in this book, for a channel that is done through the `ChannelConsumer` interface. We'll implement a consumer class that does our processing of data and then passes it on to the user interface code.

Generally speaking, the channel consumer is the code that will cop most of the traffic in terms of events going to the user interface. However, a lot of other important support code is needed too. The users have the option of creating a new channel that they can approve or deny to a user joining their channel. This requires the user interface to become involved, so another listener is needed. On the JSDT side of the house, this is implemented through the `ChannelManager` interface. This channel manager will approve or deny on the basis of the user interface feedback. Obviously, some blocking on this will need to be implemented while we wait for the approval to come back from a dialog.

A final piece of nice-to-have code is some notification that a user has actually joined or left a group. You see this in many of the other groupware products out there—even systems like IRC have this. A user joins and a message is sent to all users that person X has joined (usually followed by a flurry of "hi X" messages). With the manager code, only the person who originally created the channel as manager will know that a person is wanting to join the system; none of the other users would know. Our nicety code is implemented by using a `ChannelListener`, looking for joining and leaving events. This information is then relayed to the user interface, again through a listener interface.

Summarizing all of this information, we end up with an architecture that looks somewhat like Figure 13-3. This figure outlines the main parts of the JSDT API that are used and how they interact with the application. Note that this system applies equally well for both chat and drawing. They use exactly the same architecture, just different low-level processing.

Figure 13-3
The JSDT client-side implementation.

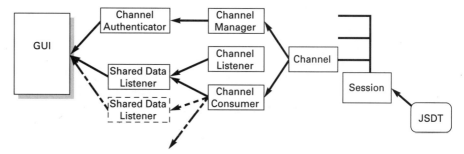

Client Identification   As you saw in the previous chapter, keeping track of client names and ensuring uniqueness can be quite difficult. Unfortunately, this application makes life even more difficult in this regard. This time we don't have multiple clients on the one VM instance accessing an object, but we have potentially multiple clients acting on the one machine running multiple copies of the application. Another major factor is that in these sorts of environments, users don't like being given a name like "Shared Chat Client Case." Users like to choose a nickname based on a personality they like to project or on the local login name. We need to account for this in the design. JSDT offers us a couple of options.

Our first option is to encode the user name in the name returned by the client that accompanies the data when it is sent. This requires having a predefined format that guarantees both uniqueness and usable names. Since JSDT allows any string to be used as the name, this requires us to impose some limitation on it so that we may include formatting characters in the string. Also, because a nickname is held as part of the client's name string, in order to change a nick, the user must first exit the session and then rejoin with the new name and client.

A second option is to write and include a customized client interface. JSDT allows us to do this with the `ClientFactory` class. By implementing a `Client` and `ClientListener` interfaces, we may create custom clients with the registry. This custom client could be used to return a username only and guarantees uniqueness. A quick check to see if a client exists in the registry is all that is needed to guarantee uniqueness. Depending on what systems you've used, uniqueness is a good thing or a bad thing. Sometimes uniqueness is used maliciously to spoof another character or provides the user multiple views of the scene (multiple copies of the application open on the one channel). One minor hurdle that this approach presents is that, in combination with the rest of JSDT, you can't add the same client more than once to a given shared object. If you have a user who wishes to have, say, two machines with the same user ID running concurrently (perhaps one for a presentation and another for local manipulation), this requires you to again do something with the standard name returned from the URL. Also, it is really easy to rebind a new client to a given URL, so a malicious user who knew what to do with JSDT could easily boot the other user off and assume that user's identity.

For several practical reasons (like less code to write), we've gone with the first option.

NOTE: *In more than 12 months of coding JSDT and JSDA (JSDT's predecessor), I have yet to find a real use where custom clients are better than a standard client with some encoding in the name.*

The username for this application will use the format:

```
<header>:<application_name>:<localhost_name>:<user_nick>
```

The header is a shared object-specific header allowing multiple clients to be used on the one machine and application instance. The application name is, as it suggests, a way to define uniqueness for a given application on the command line. The hostname is used to define the host that this user is running from for identification purposes if needed.

Server Code Design

The server code design does not share many similarities with the client code. Apart from knowing exactly what messages are created, the server has a completely different function and therefore does not need to use the client-side API. At the same time, there is not much user interface to consider. We rely on a much flatter collection of classes to achieve the design.

As an example of the differences between the server and the client code, a server does not need to confirm whether a user has joined or left. It certainly wants to know about exactly when they join and leave, but nothing else. Along a similar vein, their user interface is really the JSDT network. That is, the server sees a new user arrive, takes a snapshot of the current picture, and sends that to the client that has just joined. Another final requirement of the server is logging. Most servers want to have some form of logging for statistical information at least.

Code Architecture In the previous section we mentioned that the server design was much flatter than the client-side code. Looking back at Figures 13-2 and 13-3, you'll see a good deal of branching at each level. Many different parts of the application all want a piece of the pie. For the server side, this is completely different, as it has only one task: monitor everything that happens. If you compare the previous figures with those presented in Figures 13-4 and 13-5 you'll notice quite a dif-

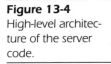

Figure 13-4
High-level architecture of the server code.

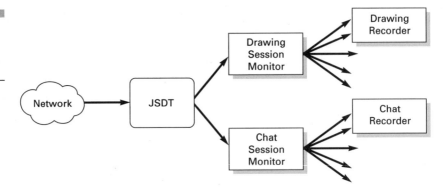

ference. Note that the information passing is almost entirely in one direction—outward from JSDT into the recording system.

The main focus of the client code was on a single channel within a session. It did not care when new channels were created by other users. On the server, Figure 13-4, the opposite is true. It really wants to know about every single channel that is created within the session so that it may record what is happening.

Of course, there is another reason too. Think about what happens when all the users leave a channel. Under JSDT, even if there are no users currently connected to a channel, it will still exist. After a couple of days in operation, you end up with a server that contains hundreds of unused channels. Even worse might be users joining an interestingly named channel to find no one else there. The server will be responsible for pruning unused channels and so needs to know everything that is going on within the session. Attaching a SessionListener to the session when the session is created will be the answer to watching the channel. When a channel is left empty, the server code will destroy that channel.

If we have a monitor watching the session, we shall also need something to watch over each channel to determine when it has no users left. A ChannelListener will be needed to watch for the user levels. A recorder class will take care of all the information relating to a particular channel. It handles all of the processing that needs to be done, including responding to the user joining, if needed.

A channel listener will not give you all of the information. Like the client-side code, a ChannelConsumer is needed to record the actual messages that take place on a channel. These messages are then stored on the server side as in-memory objects so they may be passed back to any joining clients. At the same time, a message may be written to a log file.

JSDT Objects Since all of the choices about which parts of JSDT to use have already been made on the client side, life is pretty simple for the server designer. As you have already seen in the previous section, a collection of listeners is added at the session and channel levels to watch over what is happening. The real difference between the client and server code is what we are interested in. For the server code we are not interested in the content of a particular group's messages, but in the fact that such a group exists in the first place.

The focus of our server code is to maintain a listening watch for everything that happens. When we see a new object being created, we immediately hook it and attach the appropriate monitoring code. Once a monitor has been created, the core server may ignore its existence completely. It doesn't care about small details like naming conventions. The server should never be creating shared objects.

As a response to this requirement, in the server side implementation of the JSDT objects, the structure is much flatter. Figure 13-5 shows that now the GUI code is replaced by an optional logging system as the output. After establishing a channel and any listening interfaces, the server stops at that level. It doesn't need to provide any more levels of abstraction as it acts as a data sink. The only time it acts as a data source is when a new user joins a given channel and even then it is only a one-to-one communication.

For every rule there is an exception. Although the server should not create anything, it will need to establish the sessions. While it is possible for the code to run without the server, we are using it to establish certain ground rules. The main rule is that we want to establish a fair playground. If any client creates the session (assuming the registry is always running on a known "server" machine), then that client has the opportunity to introduce a managed session. Introducing a managed session then gives that particular client the right to refuse the creation

Figure 13-5

The JSDT server-side implementation.

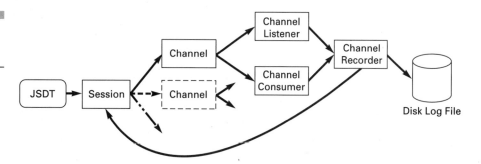

of a channel. An operator who is particularly malicious could selectively stop certain people from establishing groups or potentially even stop people from joining up at all. Having the server establish the registry followed very quickly by the sessions ensures the level playing field for all users.

For the server, this is the one time where reality must intrude. On the client side, we've designed this lovely API that abstracts the user away from the JSDT implementation. On the client side, we could quite easily implement the system using RMI or sockets. On the server, this is a completely different story. While it is possible to create some abstract server core, the functions that the server requires are too closely wedded to the underlying API. Any levels of abstraction would provide quite unnecessary overheads and would be very thin wrappers on the session- and channel-specific behaviors. In this case, we've built a custom server specifically married to the underlying network implementation for practical purposes rather than maintain (and ignore) OO religious convictions.

Client Identification   One area that we do need to be particularly careful of is the Client implementation for the server code. Because all the authentication of users is done at the client, everyone joining a managed session requires approval by that person, *including the server.*

We could get around this in a couple of ways. First, we could establish a certain naming convention and check for the server before passing authentication requests to the user interface. A server is automatically allowed to join. The other option is to use the same encoding of the client name and pass everything to the user interface, thus allowing the manager the choice of whether to allow server logging or not.

While the second of these two options seems like the ideal choice, in fact it actually causes us quite a number of problems. If the server is not able to monitor a session, who provides the updates to new clients joining the session? We're certainly not going to burden every single client with recording and logging facilities. Also, who would take care of pruning out the unused sessions? Does every client attempt this, or only some? So this makes the choice fairly easy—have a special encoding of the server and filter the names before it gets passed to the user interface code.

Server Logging   In our never-ending quest for a good design, server logging now comes to our attention. In an ideal world, anything should be able to act as a server log. We could write the standard plain text, impossible-to-read log files, but why not give the administrator the option to output directly to a nicely formatted HTML file (or PDF files or a syslog facility or…)?

The server logging will be based around a very simple architecture. A set of base interfaces will be established that define the required methods, and then the user can implement whatever logging system is required. At the start, a property is checked for the names of the classes to be loaded for logging. If the class implements the correct interface, it is installed and used.

NOTE: *Something that constantly amazes me is that, even though it is very simple to add small changes at the start of the design, people never think about something as necessary as this and thus end up with a rigid, nonextensible system. A small amout of thought at the start and an extremely flexible/customizable system results. Java in particular makes this so easy that it is a poor design that does not allow this flexibility right from the start.*

Code Structure

In terms of the implementation of the code and how it is divided up, we have four sections:

1. Client-side API and implementation
2. Server-side implementation
3. Events and associated listeners
4. User interface code

Package Structure This nicely breaks up into the four packages. The Chapter13 package contains all the GUI code, `rwjn.chapter13.shared` contains the client-side code, `rwjn.chapter13.shared.event` is the listeners and event data structures, and finally `rwjn.chapter13.shared.server` contains all of the server-specific code.

To keep track of the various properties we'll create the `white board.properties` file to locate all of the configuration information in.

Class Hierarchy In accordance with our goal of maintaining good design practices, we will examine a few areas that can benefit from

Figure 13-6
The Client
implementations.

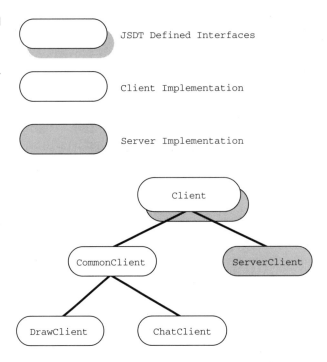

reusability. Presented are a couple of drawings that describe the class hierarchy where appropriate in the application. In each of these, a very simple system is used to get the basic ideas across. We've avoided a full UML description because that is overkill for what needs to be shown.

In Figure 13-6 you can see the organization of the client information. CommonClient will provide most of the real implementation of the client processing. The two derived classes are used for start-up settings and keeping the complete separation of the two sets of functionality. As you can see, the server's Client implementation does not need all of this functionality and has its own separate class.

Figure 13-7 illustrates the arrangements of the incoming processing classes. The consumer obviously is used to gather the raw data from the channel. The next level up is used to process this raw data into a more understandable form. At this stage, it takes the raw byte stream and turns it into instances of the event classes. Everything is stored as an event on both the server and client sides to ensure that they both view the information the same way. Notice that we have also included the ChannelListener hierarchy in the same figure. This is used to illus-

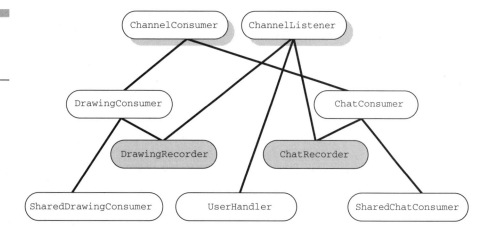

Figure 13-7
The information
processing
arrangements.

trate that the server-side recorders also act as controllers of the channel's life. As soon as this listener sees the channel destruction events, the recorders stop the recording process and start the cleanup and exiting process.

Message Encoding Because channels use arrays of bytes to transfer information we need to write all of our data in this way. We have two options—serialize classes to a stream which is then sent to the byte array, or write a custom protocol.

A quick appraisal of our requirements shows that, for the chat side, we have strings as the data. For the drawing side, there is quite a lot more data to be sent: color, line thickness, coordinates, and more. As the two are not interdependent, we could quite easily take two different approaches here, but for ease of understanding, we'll implement both, using the same philosophy.

What is the main concern in any drawing package? Answer: *Speed*. The more speed the better. When you add a network as the back end to drawing, this becomes even more critical as it is the limiting factor on ensuring your screen looks exactly the same as everyone else's. The quicker you can get something off the network or onto it, the quicker the code can return to dealing with more mouse events etc.

Applying a little bit of prior knowledge here, we know that the method calls from the API side will include everything as primitives, basically, with a few minor exceptions. Serializing these to a stream actually becomes more of a pain than it's worth. You would need to wrap all of the information into a class instance and serialize that, or you would have to wrap each primitive into its own class representation. A third alternative, of course, is to write the values directly to the stream where possible. Unfortunately, a lot of the bytes consumed in this approach are wasted. Values for most items rarely exceed 255—one byte's worth of information. Nowhere in the system do we use floating-point numbers, so generally speaking, we're really using only one byte in four that is written to the stream.

In accordance with our need for speed, we've implemented a customized protocol that writes the bytes to the stream. The overheads of serialization are quite enormous compared to the information that is actually transmitted. For small data systems like this, just using serialization can mean an order of magnitude or more reduction in speed.

This is not the place to describe every single byte ordering for each message, so instead we'll quickly summarize. The first byte is the type of command. Location values are written as 2-byte values per coordinate, limited to X, Y values relative to the drawing area's (0, 0) position (top left corner). Color values are written as 3 bytes, one representing each color component value from 0 to 255. Strings are written by giving a 2-byte length value and then the bytes of the string (from `String.getBytes()`). The 2 bytes obviously limit string lengths to 64 K characters, but that seems like a fairly good limit. We couldn't see a user typing that many characters without hitting the <enter> key somewhere in there.

Events Finally we approach the issue of events. The events are what keeps the JSDT code connected to the user interface code. There is not enough space to discuss every event type here, so we'll do some broad summaries. The class hierarchy for the events is presented in Figure 13-8.

Events are there to keep information and overheads minimal. A nice structure of base classes keeps the number of listeners and methods to a minimum. The data in the events is used to represent information in the most efficient way for getting it drawn to the screen. Where we had two competing implementation choices, the one which more closely represented the AWT `Graphics` class was chosen. Also, the information coming out through an event has not lost anything compared to the method call in the shared data APIs used to generate them.

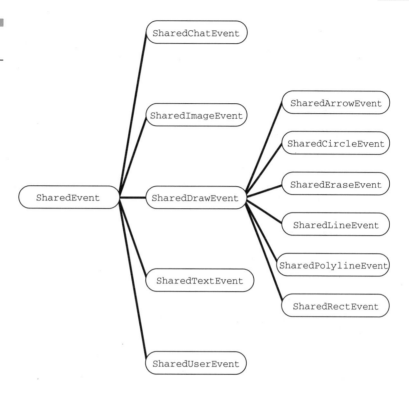

Figure 13-8
Event class structure.

Implementation

That concludes the design phase of the application. Now we move onto making everything a reality. The implementation is broken into three parts. First there is the client-side code, then the user interface, and finally the server. As our design above has suggested, if we implement the client-side code correctly, the server side becomes much simpler. Much of this arrangement has been illustrated over the last few pages. What we shall try to concentrate on is the implementation as a whole. At last count, there were some 80-odd classes in this application alone.

The client API is the largest of the pieces of code to be written, although the GUI code comes a very close second. Since so much depends on having the API code written, we'll start with that, then move to how the user interface interacts with the information, and finally to how you handle the server.

As we have done so far in this chapter, the following descriptions will tend to remain neutral of the particular implementation for chat or drawing. We aim to discuss the structures and why it was built this way. Where necessary, the discussions will highlight requirements of one or the other parts and any particular problems. For this project we are pretty fortunate in that both collaborative parts are very similar in design and implementation.

Client

Figure 13-7 illustrated the classes used in the implementation of the message processing. The client-side code is really about two things: sending messages to others and receiving messages from others. The bulk of the code goes toward these aims. Gluing these two parts together is a range of support code such as maintaining the list of listeners, JSDT clients, initialization code, etc.

Sending Events   Earlier we discussed how to write information to the channel. We decided to use a custom-written protocol in the byte stream. Writing something to a stream of bytes is useless if you don't know how to interpret those bytes. To make life easier, we'll follow the lead set previously in this book. At the bottom of the stream handling, there is an interface that defines all the numerical values as constants. These interfaces are remaining as package-level definitions and are in the `Data Constants` class names.

While it may sound like a bad idea to hide away these values inside the package, it is all in the name of ensuring accurate message handling. In order to fill the apparently missing pieces, publicly accessible reader and writer classes are provided. You simply need to pass your raw data to the writer class, which returns a correctly formatted stream. On the other end, because of the listener nature of the JSDT code, you only get informed when a correctly processed message is received. Assuming that the reader and writer are speaking the same language, you should not need to be involved with any low-level processing of the stream.

Writing values to the stream is implemented in the two producer classes: `ChatProducer` and `DrawingProducer`. A user makes a call to create the appropriate message type and is returned the complete formatted byte array. Figure 13-9 shows the implementation of the request to draw a rectangle.

Figure 13-9

Illustration of producing a byte array in the producer classes.

```
public byte[] drawRect(int x,
                       int y,
                       int width,
                       int height,
                       byte lineWidth,
                       byte fillStyle,
                       Color drawColor,
                       Color fillColor)
{
  ByteArrayOutputStream bos = new ByteArrayOutputStream();

  bos.write(SQUARE);

  bos.write(fillStyle);

  bos.write((byte)drawColor.getRed());
  bos.write((byte)drawColor.getGreen());
  bos.write((byte)drawColor.getBlue());

  writeLocation(x, y, bos);
  writeLocation(width, height, bos);

  if(fillColor != null)
  {
    bos.write(HAS_FILL_COLOUR);
    bos.write((byte)fillColor.getRed());
    bos.write((byte)fillColor.getGreen());
    bos.write((byte)fillColor.getBlue());
  }
  else
  {
    bos.write(NO_FILL_COLOR);
  }

  bos.write(lineWidth);

  return bos.toByteArray();
}
```

As you will note from the code in the figure, there are some calls to a `writeLocation()` method. Each producer contains a number of internal helper methods for simplifying common tasks. For the drawing producer, there are convenience methods for locations and integers. You remember that we previously stated that we limit the number ranges. If you took the standard streams, and if you wrote an `int`, the result would be all 4 bytes written to the stream. For our application that is unnecessary, so the convenience method writes only the lower 2 bytes to the stream.

For further explanation of what might seem to be an odd decision, you might also want to take a closer look at the code. That `ByteArray OutputStream` doesn't look quite right either. That is because we've gone and implemented our own version rather than use the standard `java.io` implementation. There were a number of reasons for this. First we wanted to keep the handler code as lightweight as possible. There was no need to generate IO errors, because we wouldn't get any (most messages are less than 40 bytes in length). Next, we were going to be responsible for writing every single byte to the stream. That is, we weren't going to over-lay a basic byte stream with a data output stream or file output stream or any of the other higher-level writing code. Next, for historical reasons, we found a lot of variant behavior in some of the stream handling, and most of the overheads of the extra methods were not needed. It was more important to our system to have a very lightweight implementation that did exactly what we needed rather than use system defaults.

Another option that we added to the producer classes was alternate, convenience versions of the method calls that took the event instances as the source of the data. This was done primarily for the server-side code that had to deal with both eventualities.

Image Handling   An area of particular interest that you haven't been shown yet is image handling. A feature of our shared whiteboard is the ability to set the background image. Now, for the guy that originally sets it, everything is fine. Simply open a dialog and then use `Toolkit.getImage()` to load it from disk into the background of the whiteboard. What about the other users? They are almost guaranteed that they won't have the image located in exactly the same directory, or even have the image at all. We want it all to happen transparently with-out the user needing to go to some external piece of software to make sure everyone has the same image.

Handling this situation was as simple as creating just another event. This time, the event data mainly consists of the file contents. When a user sets a background image, everyone receives an event that gives that image. Strictly speaking, this is not quite true. We transport the contents of the file to the client and then let the client UI load the image from a temporary file on the local disk.

Why bother saving the file to disk? Of the choices that we have, it was the option that consumed the least bandwidth (and therefore resulted in the fastest transfer). Image file formats are generally highly compressed. While it is possible to either serialize the raw AWT `Image` or extract the contents of the image with an `ImageConsumer`, these will always lead to larger amounts of data to be transferred. If we read the contents of the file from disk on the source end and then save it out on the receiving clients, it also gives the client the opportunity to decide how to load the image. Leave the graphics code to the UI, not to the networking.

So that an image loads properly on the receiving end, we need to know what file type it is. File type is generally determined by the file extension. If the raw stream of bytes from the file were the only thing that the client code received, loading the image would not be a particularly pretty process. To make life easier, the protocol for the image includes the file extension as the first few characters. This allows the code on the client side to create the temporary file with the correct file extension, making image loading much easier.

Creating the client temp file uses the `createTempFile()` method of `java.io.File`. Figure 13-10 shows how we process the image event type and generate a temporary filename pattern. Because we don't care where the file is located, we've used the single-argument version of `createTempFile()`. The single-argument version places the file in the system's temporary directory. The first string argument for this is the file pattern's prefix followed by a second string, which is the file extension to use (the image type in our case). The resulting filename will be `sds` (for Shared Data Service) with some random number/character combination followed by the proper file extension for the image type, which was retrieved from the data byte array.

Receiving Events It might seem that the receiving of events is just the reverse process of sending them. Simply extract an array of bytes, send the values to some class that returns the right event type, and then post it off to the listeners. While this is one way of looking at it, it is certainly not the optimal solution.

Data arrives from a channel through the `ChannelConsumer` interface, which we must implement. This gives us one level of classes. However, we know that both the client and the server do different things with the data once it has been processed. It makes sense to process the data as soon as we get it and pass it on to the required server or client code. One method of doing this is to register another listener directly

Figure 13-10
Implementation of
the file writing code
for the shared image
processing.

```
private void processImage() {
  try {
    SharedImageEvent evt;

    int size = input_reader.readByte();
    byte[] message_array = input_reader.readBytes(size);
    String file_ext = new String(message_array);

    // create a temp file that has the pattern
    //"sdsXXXXX.<file_ext>"
    File output_file =
      File.createTempFile("sds", file_ext, null);
    output_file.deleteOnExit();
    FileOutputStream fos = new FileOutputStream(output_file);

    size = input_reader.available();
    message_array = input_reader.readBytes(size);
    fos.write(message_array);

    evt = new SharedImageEvent(output_file.getAbsolutePath());
    processImageEvent(evt);
  }
  catch(IOException ioe)
  {
    // ignored
  }
}
```

with our first level of consumer code. Once the data has been processed, immediately call the listener. On the other hand, both the client and server need to do something with the data. The client needs to send it out to some user interface code for display while the server wants to keep it locally for storage. The idea of needing listener code on the server seems like we need to write a few too many classes. Besides, the consumer code has everything processed already. What to do becomes the old six of one, half a dozen of the other scenarios.

Saving on overheads and providing the cleanest solution (at least in our opinion) is usually what we opt for in implementation. By further extending the consumer class with another level, we can achieve the goals of both the client and the server. The server implementation is passed the values to be stored directly without the listener management overhead, and the client implementation sends the events straight out to the user interface.

In Figure 13-10 you saw an example of how this works. The `data Received()` method takes the array of bytes and reads the first byte. On the basis of this value, the appropriate private processing method is called (for example, the `processImage()` method presented in Figure 13-10) and illustrated in the code in Figure 13-11. Processing the data becomes a case of reading the bytes and creating an instance of the appropriate event. Dispatching that event is made by calling the appropriate abstract send method. Each of the derived classes implements these send methods. The server-side code stores the values internally in the derived class while the client-side code makes an immediate call, passing those events to the listeners.

NOTE: *One nice side effect of this system is that the server-side code stores the events exactly as a client would receive them without all the listener processing overheads. You can trace exactly what is sent to the client-side code just by tracing the events. Also, data storage on the server side is simple. The event class holds everything that you really need to know about without having to create any extra server-only code.*

Figure 13-11
Initial processing and dispatching of event data.

```
public final synchronized void dataReceived(Data data) {
    int length = data.getLength();
    byte[] msg = data.getData();
    input_reader.setStream(msg, length);

    byte command = -1;

    try {
        command = input_reader.readByte();
    }
    catch(IOException ioe) {
        System.out.println(ioe);
        return;
    }

    try {
        switch(command) {
            case CIRCLE:
                processCircle();
                break;
```

Figure 13-11
(*Continued*)

```
        case SQUARE:
            processRect();
            break;

        case LINE:
            processLine();
            break;

        case ARROW:
            processArrow();
            break;

        case TEXT:
            processText();
            break;

        case POLYLINE:
            processPolyline();
            break;

        case CLEAR:
            processClear();
            break;

        case ERASE:
            processErase();
            break;

        case SET_IMAGE:
            processImage();
            break;

        default:
            System.out.println("Unknown command " + command);
        }
    }
    catch(Throwable t) {
        System.out.println("Drawing consumer exception");
        System.out.println(t);
    }
}
```

NOTE: *The* `input_reader` *is one of our custom* `ByteArray`
`InputStream` *implementations. We simply reuse the current instance
and reset the stream—something that you can't do with the standard
implementation. This saves object allocation overhead and helps to make
the processing faster.*

Creating Groups No collaborative application is complete without
the ability to select and join a group of people. We've set up the public
shared APIs so that you may customize the user interface as much as
you like. Creating an instance of either `SharedDrawing` or `Shared`
`Chat` is just the beginning of the process.

The two public shared classes contain a lot of code that is common. Creating an instance does not do much except initialize a few data structures.
The first thing that a user would expect to do is nominate the server to
connect to. This can be set through the `setServerInfo()` method, where
you may specify the server and port number. Once you have done this, you
need to instruct the class to connect to that server with a call to the
`connect()` method. There is no requirement to begin by setting server
information because default values are set through the `whiteboard.`
`properties` file and the internal data management classes.

With a connected server, you now want to actually do something. Connecting to a server, however, does nothing more than establish a
`Session`. We need to create or join a particular channel within that session. Because we want to be nice to the user, and our requirements state
it, we create a method, `listChannelNames()`, that returns an array of
all the currently existing channels in that session. The user interface
should display this and allow the user to select to join a preexisting
group or create a new one.

Once the user has selected a channel or decided to create a new one,
one of two methods must be called. If the user wishes to join an existing
channel, then the `joinChannel()` method should be called with the
name of that channel. If the channel does not exist, and the user would
like to have it as a managed channel, then the `createChannel()`
method is called. This contains both the channel name and a reference
to a `ClientAuthenticator`. This interface is designed to work as our
callback when a new user wishes to join the channel. Finally, the
`joinChannel()` method can be used to create a new channel that is not
managed.

Figure 13-12
Code to create and
join a new channel.

```
public void joinChannel(String name)
  throws ServiceUnavailableException, AlreadyJoinedException {

  if(chat_session == null)
    throw new ServiceUnavailableException(NOT_ACTIVE_MSG);

  if(current_channel != null)
    throw
      new AlreadyJoinedException("Currently joined to " +
                        current_channel.getName());
  try {
    current_channel = chat_session.createChannel(chat_client,
                                                 name,
                                                 true,
                                                 true,
                                                 true);

    // create consumer for the channel
    consumer = new SharedChatConsumer(listeners);

    // add the consumer as a listener to the channel
    current_channel.addConsumer(chat_client, consumer);
    current_channel.addChannelListener(user_handler);

    user_handler.setChannel(current_channel);
  }
  catch(JSDTException je) {
    throw new ServiceUnavailableException(je);
  }
}
```

The implementation of joining a channel requires a little bit of work. Not only do we have to create the channel, but we also need a channel consumer, a listener (for notification of users joining and leaving), and potentially a channel manager too. Figure 13-12 shows the create Channel() method used to join a user up.

You will see from the code in the figure that we also reuse the references to most of our listener type classes. All that really changes is the Channel reference itself.

Moderated Groups At the start of the chapter, one of our requirements was to be able to create a group where the creator can control who may join. In terms of the underlying implementation, this is achieved through a `ChannelManager`. Getting this information out to the user interface for confirmation requires a small amount of work.

The first task in implementing the management scheme is deciding how to notify the user interface. (We are assuming that the `Channel Manager` part is trivial to write, as you've done this before in the previous chapter.) Since the channel manager requires a yes or no answer from the user, the UI code must return a boolean, no matter how we query. What needs to be decided is exactly what form this query should take, and what should be passed to the UI.

Our inspiration for the form of the authentication mechanism comes directly from the manager interface used by JSDT. The main aim of our "manager" code is to place a dialog or similar device in front of the user and ask the user to say yes or no to a person's joining. We really don't need much information for this process—just the user name and perhaps the machine that the user is logged into. JSDT's manager interface puts all sorts of extra information in there for authentication back to the original caller that our code does not really need. Therefore, we've gone with a very lightweight interface mechanism, shown in Figure 13-13, called `ClientAuthenticator`.

Figure 13-13
The `Client Authenticator` interface implementation.

```
package rwjn.chapter13.shared;
public interface ClientAuthenticator
{
    /**
     * Grant permission to this client to join. The implementor is
     * request to either grant or deny the named user joining this
     * this channel. Returning true allows the client to join,
     * false will prevent them from joining.
     *
     * @param name The name of the user that wants to join
     * @param host The host name of the user's machine
     * @return True if the client is granted permission to join the
     *      channel
     */
    public boolean grantClientJoin(String name, String host);
}
```

ClientAuthenticator is a Java interface that contains a single method, grantClientJoin(). For arguments we are passing two strings that describe the name and machine the client wishes to join from. Other options such as creating an event-style encapsulated class were rejected because the extra overhead wasn't considered necessary.

Implementing the management system falls to the ChannelUser Manager class. This class implements the ChannelManager interface and forms the connection between the authenticator method call and the JSDT code. A channel manager really has only one action type to authenticate: AuthenticationInfo.JOIN. If anything else is received, it is rejected (manager returns false).

Because everything passes through the manager on its way to joining a channel, we need to make a couple of quick checks before calling the registered authenticator. First, even our own client that creates the channel and manager must be approved. Therefore the first thing that we do is check that the requesting client is the same as the local client (passed in through the class's constructor). For this we perform a string compare of the two names returned by the Client.getName() method. Using the equals() method does not work for these comparisons, so the only valid check is to use the names themselves. You can see how this works in Figure 13-14.

Mentioned previously was the decision to allow the server to join without authentication. After checking for the local client and that the request is to join, the code then looks to see if the incoming client is the server. CommonClient has a static class method that allows for this check. If it returns true, then the server is given automatic privilege to join and the checking system exits. If it doesn't return true, then we finally make the call to the authenticator. Whatever value is returned from this is returned from the manager to JSDT.

Once all of this is complete, we need to get one of these beasts from the user interface. In the shared class API, we have a joinChannel() method used for joining a preexisting channel. Because the act of creating a moderated channel is a different task, we've created a new method called createChannel(). This takes the channel name and a reference to a ClientAuthenticator. Because the authenticator is like a manager rather than a listener, we can only have one of them. If there was a previous authenticator set, then it is replaced by the new one, even if they are the same class instance. If the channel name already exists, JSDT will not let you create the channel with a manager, so we catch these exceptions and throw our own NotOwnerException. Similarly,

Figure 13-14
The `ChannelUser Manager` implementation of the authentication mechanism.

```java
public boolean channelRequest(Channel channel,
                              AuthenticationInfo info,
                              Client client) {

  int type = info.getAction();
  boolean approve = false;

  if(local_client.equals(client.getName()))
    return true;

  switch(type) {
    case AuthenticationInfo.JOIN:

        String name = client.getName();

        String username = null;
        String host = null;
        try {
          if(CommonClient.checkServer(name)) {
              approve = true;
              break;
          }
          else {
            username = CommonClient.getUserName(name);
            host = CommonClient.getHostName(name);
          }
          try {
            approve =
              authenticator.grantClientJoin(username, host);
          }
          catch(Throwable th) {
            System.out.println("Channel authenticator error\n" +
                      th);
          }
        }
        catch(InvalidSettingException ise) {
          // approve already set to false, so just exit the switch
          System.out.println(ise);
          break;
        }
        break;
  }
  return approve;
}
```

creating a moderated channel requires an authenticator, so we check that we do have a valid reference before doing anything. If it is not valid, then we have an `IllegalArgumentException`.

`SharedData`: A Uniform Interface Having two separate interfaces for both drawing and chatting can be a bit annoying from the coding perspective. It also means that you need to do a lot of double handling of information about such events as joining and leaving groups, being notified of users, etc. As a purely convenience measure, a class was created to handle all of this in a single interface.

The `SharedData` class acts as a uniform front-end for not only the basic handling of the chat and drawing interfaces, but also for some of the management side too. Much of our low-level setup information is kept in a public `SessionData` class in the server package. We really don't want the user playing with this directly (we didn't have much choice in making it public or package private so the `SharedData` class forms the front-end, providing all the access and keeping everything working correctly.

In general, most of this class is pretty uneventful; most methods simply replicate the methods that are defined in the two individual shared classes. The one area of interest is handling the user authentication scheme. If you had taken the natural approach to this and called the `createChannel()` methods in each class as we do for the other methods, then the process of a user joining the channel would end up with the authenticator code being called twice every time a user joined—once for the chat system and once for the drawing system. This is not really the best thing to do, as the user would get frustrated having to say yes/no twice for every joining user. To make life simpler, we've done a little bit of extra legwork in the common interface.

Combining the two calls into a single output for the UI is just a matter of a little trickery. Firstly, we make the `SharedData` class implement the `ClientAuthenticator` interface. When the user interface code calls the `SharedData.createChannel()` method, instead of passing the `ClientAuthenticator` reference from the parameters, it now takes a copy of that reference but passes itself in as the authenticator. This is so that our code gets called rather than the user interface implementation.

In the `grantClientJoin()` method we now start a little fiddling with the information. What we want to do is pass the authentication request onto the UI if we have not seen it before (approved it prior to this), but not pass it on if we have seen this request before (while returning the same answer). This way we are agnostic about where the request came from in the first place, avoiding the ordering question of whether it was chat or drawing that called the method last time. Keeping track of who has and has not joined is taken care of by two hashtables—one for approvals and one for rejects. The hashtable keeps the name/host pair as key and value, respectively. When an authentication request first comes in, it checks the request hashtable for the given name. If the hostnames also match, then it allows the user to join. The same operation is then repeated with the rejected user list, only this time a false is returned if they match. When both of these checks fail, the real authenticator reference passed in originally is now called. Before returning the value to the JSDT system, entries are placed in the appropriate hashtable. To help you understand what we've just said, look at Figure 13-15, which contains the code for the above explanation.

Figure 13-15

The grantClientJoin implementation in the SharedData class.

```
public synchronized boolean grantClientJoin(String name, String host)
{
    String machine = approved_users.get(name);

    // first check the current hashtables
    if(machine == host)
      return true;

    machine = rejected_users.get(name);

    if(machine == host)
      return false;

    // neither of these worked so let's ask the UI
    boolean ok = authenticator.grantClientJoin(name, host);

    if(ok)
      approved_users.put(name, host);
    else
      rejected_users.put(name, host);
    return ok;
}
```

NOTE: *A problem with hashtable use is that, if two users have the same name but are on different machines, it will cause problems. A hashtable replaces the given key with the new value if you pass it the same key with a different value—the case when you have the same user name but two different machines. Generally this is not a problem, as you want all users to have different names, but we don't check for it anywhere else so it could always come into play.*

An important thing to note is that we've made the method call synchronized. One problem that you are bound to run into is that the two channel managers will both receive the authentication request at the same time. Both will then attempt to call the above code. If the method were not protected like this, it is quite possible that while the user is clicking on the dialog, the method would be called again by the other manager and a second dialog would result. Even screen lockups are possible, with the GUI rendering code of Swing causing the application to freeze.

Finally, a little bit of housekeeping is in order. Users can leave and join any channel they like while the application is running. If the user creates a moderated channel, then later exits and creates a new moderated channel, we don't want the old list of approved users hanging around. In the `createChannel()` method we need to clear the two hashtables to make sure that we don't get any problems. Note that we don't do this until a new channel is created, because it is possible that the user might exit but the channel may continue to operate. Although this is impossible under JSDT's socket implementation, a different underlying implementation may well allow it.

User Interface

Having finished the client-side APIs, we now turn our attention to the user interface. We're not going to talk in too much detail about what we've done, just a few salient points and some screen shots.

The user interface is a single frame that contains both the chat and drawing parts (Figure 13-16). Operation of the main shared data principles of creating, joining, and leaving groups and the server are in the File menu. A menu of options is also provided. You can see that the chat and drawing sections contain equal amounts of screen real estate. On the left is the chat area and on the right is the drawing area.

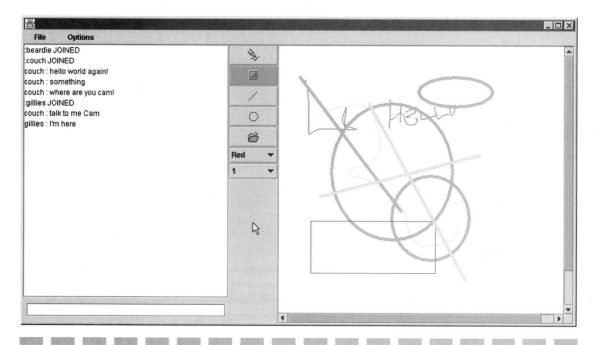

Figure 13-16   The main user interface.

Joining the server pops up our now very familiar server dialog that you've seen in the other projects. Joining a group pops up a dialog that contains the current list of groups (Figure 13-17). A separate text field at the top allows you to type in the name of a new dialog and a check box allows it to be managed or not.

The Chat Area   On the left side of the main window is the chat area. A close-up of this is provided in Figure 13-18. On the top is the contents of the session. The text area contains all of the text that the users have written, and information about users coming and leaving as well. Although both windows receive the user status messages through their listeners, we've decided that only one really needs to show this information. In this case, the chat area shows all the status information while the drawing area ignores everything.

At the bottom of the large text area is a small text field. This is where the users enter their comments. When a user hits enter, the text is taken and broadcast to the world. So the user may follow the conversation, the text is also echoed to the main area. In common with standard practice, the user name is always prepended to the message that is displayed.

Figure 13-17
The group join dialog.

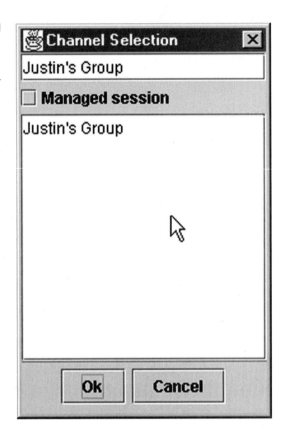

The Drawing Area Opposite the chat area is the drawing area. This looks like your standard simple paint tool. However, we also include an extra few features. Everything that you put in this window is automatically shared with the rest of the users in that group. As has already been mentioned, there is the facility to set the background image. The toolbar (shown on the left side of the image in Figure 13-19) has a button with the open folder image on it. Pressing this brings up a standard file open dialog allowing the user to select a picture. Once set (if it loads correctly), this is then sent to all the other users, as previously noted.

After some time in the chat environment, the scribblings always become too cluttered. Selecting the clear option from the Options menu allows you to clear all of the drawing, leaving just the background image. This will clear everyone's window, not just your own so you need to be a little careful in using it.

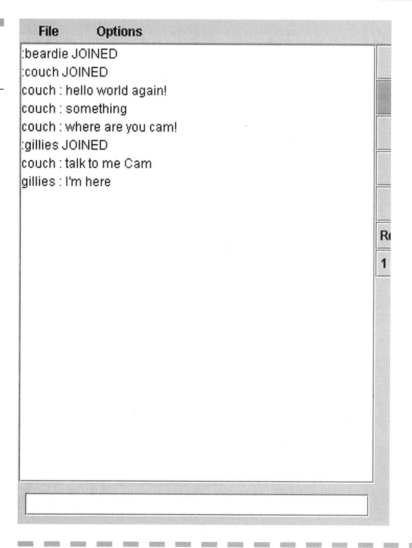

Figure 13-18
Close-up of the chat area portion of the main screen.

NOTE: *The drawing area implementation supplied with the book does not implement the full set of functionality provided by the* Shared Drawing *class. Missing are text and an erase event. Check the author's web site for future updates.*

Server

Finally we turn our attention to the server-side code. At this point in time, it is technically possible to run the client code in standalone mode,

Figure 13-19
The drawing area window.

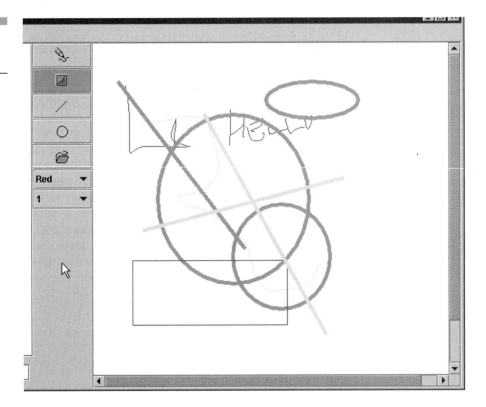

so long as the server machine has the registry running on it (it would need to have been started in standalone mode from the command line). The server may be slowly implemented and checked for correct operation while the client code is running.

Earlier in the chapter, you saw a breakdown of the code structure in Figure 13-5. The written code follows very closely the structure laid out in the diagram. It consists of four parts: start-up code including session and user input management, session listeners for the channels, recorders for each channel, and the logging system.

Channel Recorders   Like the shared channel consumers of the client-side code, the server-side recorders extend a base consumer class. Unlike the client code, the server code only uses the information for storage and updating of individual late-joining users. Another dissimilarity is that the two are very different in nature. In fact, if it were not for the logging, there would almost be no need for the chat recorder.

One of the main differences between the client- and server-side extensions of the consumer classes, is that the server side also implements the `ChannelListener` interface. Channel listeners are important for tracking the number of users currently connected. If you remember the earlier discussion about the need for a server, the prime reason was for managing the channels and pruning dead ones. Channel listening is how we do this.

User information about joining a channel is passed through the `channelConsumerAdded()` and `channelConsumerRemoved()` methods and events. Looking at the definition of the `ChannelListener` interface you might be wondering why we did not use the `channelJoined()` and `channelLeft()` methods, as they seem to be the ones that make more sense. Remember that we need to send updates to the client code when it first joins. Because of network traffic or application load, it is quite feasible that there will be some delay between a client joining the channel and it adding a consumer. When we send updates, we want to be guaranteed that the client will receive them. This can be assured only when we know that a consumer has been added, not when the consumer joins the channel. For the same reason, we use the consumer removed event to keep track of the number of users. A client that is joined but has no consumer is virtually useless in the context of this application.

Looking first at the chat recorder, you will see how we manage the user tracking (the drawing recorder contains a lot more inside the same method implementations). Code for this section is shown in Figure 13-20. When a consumer is added, all we need to do is simply increment our user counter. When the user leaves, we decrement it. Once we know a user has left, we should always check to see the number of users still connected. If we find that we only have one left, then it must be time to ditch the channel. As was mentioned earlier, we close the channel when there is one user left because that one user is our server-side listener—this class. To do this we fetch the channel and the server client (references aren't kept by the class), and then call the `destroy()` method on the channel. Of course, not included in the code in Figure 13-20 is writing the activities to the log file.

NOTE: *Because of the frequency of users joining and leaving the channel, we are not concerned about the counter getting into a form of race condition with the operational code—as the counter example of Chapter 4 illustrates.*

Figure 13-20
Code for managing
and tracking users
connected to the
server.

```
public void channelConsumerAdded(ChannelEvent evt) {
    listener_count++;
}

public void channelConsumerRemoved(ChannelEvent evt) {
  listener_count-;

  // if there is only one listener left then that must be just
  // the server. At this point in time destroy the channel

  if(listener_count == 1) {
    Channel ch = evt.getChannel();
    Client client = ServerClient.getServerClient();

    try {
      ch.destroy(client);
    }
    catch(JSDTException je) {
      System.out.println("Cannot dispose of chat channel");
      System.out.println(je);
    }
  }
}
```

NOTE: *An alternate scheme to using the counter is to just call* list
ConsumerNames() *and look for a return value of length 1. Since this is
the server code, it will be an extremely fast operation.*

Drawing Recorder Recording the actions of users on the drawing
side requires quite a different implementation from the chat side.
Although the basics of user tracking are the same, the rest isn't. When
users join a shared drawing, they expect to be updated with the latest
information. Keeping track of that information is as simple as recording
every single event in a big data structure such as a list.

Although this basic approach seems fair, there are two factors that
require some modification of it. First, we have to deal with clear events
removing all of the drawing actions that have taken place, leaving just
the background image. The second is the background image itself, where
only one of them is ever set. It would be a waste of bandwidth to trans-

mit every image over the network to a client when you first join, as only the last one is displayed.

As a result of some fortunate design of the `DrawingConsumer` base class, implementing the above functionality is actually quite simple. The base class has four different methods for passing processed data to subclasses:

```
protected abstract void processPrimitiveEvent(SharedDrawEvent
    evt);

protected abstract void processImageEvent(SharedImageEvent
    evt);

protected abstract void processEraseEvent(SharedEraseEvent
    evt);

protected abstract void processTextEvent(SharedTextEvent evt);
```

The erase event may contain either an erase or clear action, so some checking is needed here before blindly acting. As you can also see, the image also has its own method for allowing that functionality to be handled simply. Having this information and knowing what we have to do, we can write the code easily. Any time that we get a primitive or text event, we add that to the list of events. If we get an image event, we replace the last image with the new one. If we get a clear event that wipes out the list of the drawing primitives, we add an erase to that list. The only other point of consideration is that we really should keep the list of events in the order that they are received. This ensures that, when we send the information out, the new user's screen looks almost identical to that of everyone else. The implementation of this is shown in Figure 13-21.

Now, how do we look after the sending of updates to the client? We need to send the entire contents of the event list as well as the last image. In a busy group, there could be hundreds of events to send out. Just running through and sending those events out inside the recorder class consumer added event probably isn't the best way of doing things. This really requires a thread.

The `DrawingRecorder` class is already pretty crowded. Not only does it extend the `DrawingConsumer` class, it also implements the `ChannelListener` interface. While we could also make it implement `Runnable`, this would make things even worse. However, a better argument can also be found. If we have multiple people joining over a short

Figure 13-21
The implementation of the event recording mechanism.

```
private ArrayList event_list;

private SharedImageEvent last_image;

protected void processPrimitiveEvent(SharedDrawEvent evt) {
  event_list.add(evt);
}

protected void processImageEvent(SharedImageEvent evt) {
  last_image = evt;
}

protected void processEraseEvent(SharedEraseEvent evt) {
  if(evt.clearAll)
    event_list.clear();
  else
    event_list.add(evt);
}

protected void processTextEvent(SharedTextEvent evt) {
  event_list.add(evt);
}
```

period of time, there is going to be a number of these thread instances running. If we implemented all of this in the recorder class proper, keeping track of the state of each thread could turn out to be a real nightmare. A separate class for sending the updates is needed. In our case, the update class is called DrawingUpdater.

Sending updates to a given client is not much different from the client-side code. We take the event (everything is stored as the event class instances), turn it into an array of bytes, and then send it to the client using JSDT. The difference between client and server update code is that, instead of calling the channel's sendToOthers(), method we call sendToClient() to send it directly to the named client. There is nothing particularly special about the sending code, so we won't show it to you here.

When creating the update class, we need to pass it the list of events. While it seems like a good idea just to pass the reference to the ArrayList straight in, in reality it isn't. On a busy list, by the time you start sending updates out to a client it is probable that one of the other users has also sent a new item out. When the server picks this up, it is added to the event list. If you pass that list in directly to the update class, those newly arrived events will also be sent to the client. Since we know a client has joined because of the consumer added event that started the update process, we know that the user is also going to be receiving these new events anyway. To avoid this, we take a snapshot of the current list of events at the time the update was started and send only those to the client. The run() method exits only after all of this—list of events and the background image (if one is set)—has been sent.

There is one final matter of importance here. As you are now aware, we could be sending data to the client as an update at the same time that all the other users are also sending out information. In order to reduce possible out-of-order defects, we set the priority of the update messages to the highest we can get. At least this way we give that client a fighting chance of having all the image in place before the general melee of everyone's events also arriving.

Session Management   Most of the day-to-day running of the channels and recording information is handled with the recorder classes that you have just been looking at. Before these can do their work, we need something to create instances of them. This is the job of the session monitor classes. The session monitors attach themselves as listeners to the appropriate session and look for the creation of new channels.

When a monitor adds itself as a listener, it is interested in only the channel events, so it disables everything else. Because the monitor doesn't do anything else, it extends the SessionAdaptor class and overrides only the channelCreated() and channelDestroyed() methods. When the listener is informed of a new channel being created, it starts a new instance of the recorder class, as shown in Figure 13-22. It then adds that recorder as a consumer and places the class instance in a hashtable keyed by the name of the channel. Although strictly speaking this last step isn't necessary, it allows for some other management-type activities to be quickly implemented.

Main Server   The main functional aspects of the code are now complete. All that remains is a bit of management code for getting everything started and looking after any other issues such as restarting or exiting the server.

Writing the server code follows the fairly standard lines that you have seen to date. Start the registry, create the sessions (no managers), attach the session listeners, and then listen for user input from the key-

Figure 13-22
Monitoring channel
activities in the ses-
sion monitor classes.

```
public void channelCreated(SessionEvent evt) {
  String res_name = evt.getResourceName();

  try {
    Channel ch =
      session.createChannel(client, res_name, true, true, true);
    DrawingRecorder recorder = new DrawingRecorder(ch);
    ch.addConsumer(client, recorder);

    // now store it in the hashtable
    recorder_log.put(res_name, recorder);
  }
  catch(JSDTException je) {
    System.out.println("Server cannot attach to byte array");
    System.out.println(je);
  }
}

public void channelDestroyed(SessionEvent evt) {
  String res_name = evt.getResourceName();

  // remove the recorder from the hashtable.
  recorder_log.remove(res_name);
}
```

board. Because the session listeners act on feedback directly from
JSDT's core, once they are attached, the thread of execution that has
done the setup work can finish at this point. So long as the application
does not exit (through a call such as `System.exit()`), the server will
keep itself performing everything as needed. Remember that our server
does not create any of the shared objects; it only responds when new
ones are created by the clients so the entire activity of the server is
externally driven. The main server code is contained in `rwjn.`
`chapter13.shared.server.SharedDataServer`, but there is a small
launcher class containing just the main method called `Whiteboard`
`Server` that does not belong to any package.

Real servers don't just sit there blankly. If they are not running as a
daemon process, then the console input should be able to handle some
form of user input for control purposes. For this server we have quit,
restarted, and called on the obligatory help command. Typing in one of
these commands will call the appropriate method in the server code.

Restarting the server forces the sessions to be destroyed and all items to exit and then be recreated from scratch. This is a bit of a controversial decision because restarting the server code forces the clients to behave badly, as we've pulled the rug out from under their feet. It could be argued that the server should just exit nicely, leaving the sessions running and then rejoin them. The problem with this is that when the server rejoins the channels, it is in an inconsistent state with the clients. They have more information displayed than the server has stored. If new clients joined they would not have the same picture as everyone else. The safest solution is to kill everything when the server exits, thereby at least guaranteeing a consistent state for everyone.

On the structural side of the server, we've got a standardized interface for all server components. Although this server is only one item, theoretically a number of servers that all implement this interface can be written and combined into one superserver. All of the command line processing can then call individual servers without knowing what the real underlying server implementation is. Although an apparent overkill in this situation, the code came from a much larger server that contained may different disparate services.

Running Everything

Once all the code is completed, you need to run everything. First, on the setup side, make sure that the file `whiteboard.properties` is in a top-level directory (or JAR file) that is in your classpath. If your classpath points at the `code` directory, then this is where the properties file should be kept, not in the `rwjn` or `chapter13` directory.

SECURITY: *In order for the code from this chapter to run, you will need the following permission enabled in your policy file for both the client and the server:*

```
java.io.FilePermission "c:/temp/*", "read,write";
java.net.SocketPermission "*", "connect";
java.net.SocketPermission "localhost",
"connect,accept,listen";
```

Server   To start the system, you need to run the server code. Change into your code directory, type the following, and see the response:

```
c:\code\>java WhiteboardServer
Creating Drawing session
jsdt://localhost:4461/socket/Session/draw_session
Creating Chat session
jsdt://localhost:4461/socket/Session/chat_session
Creating session objects
Done
Ready. (HELP for commands)
>
```

The small bracket prompt indicates the server is ready for commands if needed. At this point everything is set and our clients may join as required.

Client   Starting the client code is achieved by calling:

```
c:\code\>java Whiteboard
```

There is no status information printed this time. This should show the main window that you saw in Figure 13-16. For the client you now need two steps to get you running. In the File menu you will first need to Connect to a server. This pops up the familiar server dialog. This establishes the session connection. To join a group you need to use the Join Group menu item. Either select a group name or type in a new name to create a new group. Clicking OK will join you to the group. You should see the confirmation message about your joining in the chat window. If you see this, everything is working correctly and you may now play with your collaborative whiteboarding system.

If you don't see anything, the cause may be some bugs or implementation strangeness. For example, it is known that with a socket-based session, if the client that originally created the group exits the group or the application, then it causes any further action on that group to hang completely. (Sometimes it might throw a `TimedOutException` after a minute or two.) Any attempts to join that server by any client after this point results in hangs and other strange behavior. Swapping to RMI or LRMP sessions does not cause this behavior (because of the server socket exiting in the TCP implementation).

An Exercise for the Reader

The server code that you've received could still do with some improvements. These improvements may be to make it more like commercial systems or to optimize it. This section is devoted to areas where we think the system could be improved, but the execution is left to your imagination and coding time availability.

Client

On the client-side code, there are a number of nice additions possible. One such item would reduce the disparity between the user interface implementation and what the shared drawing API allows you to do.

Alternative Image Transfer Scheme   First on our list of possible improvements is implementing a different scheme of sending the image. At the moment it is assumed that you can suck the entire image file into a single array of bytes. On machines with small amounts of memory, or heavily loaded machines, this can cause memory errors. It might not be possible to allocate a single array 100 K long. Since the channel will only allow a complete array rather than a stream of bytes, we have the potential for problems.

NOTE: *An even worse problem is that, if the underlying transport scheme uses UDP sockets, the maximum packet size is limited to 8 K. Any array longer than this is truncated, but no extra packets are created to send the rest of the data. UDP communications are used in unreliable socket connections and LRMP.*

An alternative to get around this is to divide the image up into small chunks and send it in pieces. The `SharedImageEvent` would then need to contain flags indicating the sequence number (if you haven't already guaranteed ordered delivery) and status information such as end-of-file information. The individual consumers would then write this file to disk as they received the information. Once the last piece of the file was received they would then send out the `SharedImageEvent` to the listeners for the UI to update the picture.

Ignoring Users   A feature commonly found in commercial chat systems is the ability to ignore individual users. There are a couple of different options on how to go about this. We could either implement it internally with the shared API code or keep it completely user interface–based. Both options would benefit from the addition of at least one more method that gives a list of all the users currently joined to the group.

For the first option, we need an extra method that takes the user name and is told to ignore it. Inside the shared data handler, each time an event is received from a user name that corresponds to one of the ignored names, it is dropped immediately. The problem that this approach suffers from is there is the potential in our implementation that a user name may exist on more than one machine. At the time the user interface code deals with the ignore information, the hostname has been lost. Therefore we would be filtering everyone with that user name, regardless of which machine they are originating from.

The second option is to keep the information entirely within the user interface implementation. The UI would need to keep a list of all the user/host pairs that are sent to it through the listener events. Then, when the ignored user sends an event, the UI code detects the sender and drops any further information. Again, this solution also has some problems. User identification information is sent only with the chat events. For the shared drawing event, the sender is not known. While it is possible to filter the chat text, it is impossible to filter the drawing, thus a user can remain obnoxious by scrawling on the whiteboard. This makes the first solution probably the more preferable, as it is easier to work around its potential problem areas.

Server

Suggested improvements to the server have a much lesser impact of the general experience. These changes are aimed more at greater efficiency rather than new or changed functionality like the client suggestions offer.

Controlling the Session   For the security conscious, the current server setup is not particularly good. For example, if the sessions were created with LRMP as the transport layer rather than sockets, potentially anyone in the world could join that had access to a multicast-capable router or tunneling—not a particularly desirable aspect. Neither is the fact that anyone could add objects to the session. Preventing this would require the addition of a session manager like the one you saw in the previous chapter.

A session manager would need to be written for each of the servers to stop nonchannel objects being created and for use in user authentication. For really security-minded people, the user name code on the client side could be modified to extract the user name from the login name. On the server side, a confirmation check with the OS login system would need to be done to check the user identification and, potentially, group privileges.

Security aspects of this application have not really been explored. The above ideas are just some of a number that could be implemented on top of the basic system.

Image Storage   One of the suggestions for client-side improvements was for better transport of the images while they are on the connection. There are also improvements of a different kind that could be made for the server.

When the consumer base class receives the raw image, it saves it directly to disk before passing the event to the derived class. While this is fine for client-side code where the image is accessed only once, on the server that is a really bad idea. Every time a user joins, that file must be read back in from disk before sending it out to the client. This takes time not only for the reading, but also all of the extra array allocation, garbage collection, and other processing.

A better way of doing this is storing the image file data in memory, eliminating all of that costly I/O time. To do this requires modification of the base drawing consumer class. What would need to be done is to pass the raw image file data and the file type to the derived classes and let them deal with it. For the client code (`SharedDrawingConsumer`), the data would be saved as a file; for the server code (`DrawingRecorder`) the array would be held in memory until needed.

Clear Event Handling   There is only one small issue remaining— dealing with clear events. Under the current implementation, if a clear is received after an update thread has been started, that clear might be received before all the updates are complete even with the updates set at maximum priority. That is, the user might clear the screen but later receive some of the update events, which would cause the screen to be inconsistent with the general state of the image.

All sorts of alternative schemes exist for this on both client and server sides of the code equation. For example, the client could buffer all the events until it knows that all the server updates are finished (you can tell this because this is the only time the server Client sends information) and then clear the screen. Alternatively, a separate flag (JSDT

`Token`) could be used to indicate a clear action, the name of which is sent as the first update event. The server grabs the token; when it is released, all of the updates are known to be done and clears can take place.

Perhaps the most acceptable solution is to implement some server-side controls. As the architecture stands today, updates are sent in a separate thread. Once created, the server code does not keep a reference to that thread. Instead we could keep a reference of all the currently active threads. If a clear event is received at the server, it immediately interrupts all the updater threads, causing them to stop. They would then exit without sending any more information. In this case there is now a much smaller window between when a client sends a clear event and when that update is stopped by the server. The window is small enough to be insignificant in light of the problems of the current implementation, and other non-JSDT solutions would not do any better.

JSDT Directions

You've now seen almost all of the things that JSDT can do, and many of the problem areas have been highlighted throughout the text. JSDT, like other Sun APIs, is a rapidly evolving system based on user feedback. The following items outline some future areas of improvements, addressing issues highlighted during our discussions. They also answer some of the more frequently asked questions about how JSDT relates to the rest of the Java APIs and Sun's work.

JSDT 1.5

The current release of JSDT is version 1.4. It is planned that the next version, 1.5, will incorporate a few new features but it will mainly be a bug fix release. The few known new features are detailed below.

Data (Object)   As you have probably noticed throughout the use of the channel, the constructor for the data object takes only an array of bytes. If you wish to send a full class you need to perform the serialization yourself. This array is referenced internally to the data object, which then undergoes a second serialization onto the underlying networking stream. The setup time for serialization is quite large, so having to do this twice for every transaction adds quite a bit of overhead.

Alleviating this problem will be a new constructor to be introduced in JSDT 1.5 that takes a serializable object as the argument. This allows you to directly place the object in the data representation and have only one hit for serialization.

To maintain some consistency, the ByteArray object also has a new `setValue()` method that takes an `Object` instance. It functions in the same way as the Data object variant, allowing a serializable object to be written directly to the array. To read the value back from the array, there is a new method, public `Object getValueAsObject()` that returns the deserialized object.

Checking the Managed State   Earlier in the chapter, it was noted that there was no way of determining whether a shared object was managed without first joining it (if you were even permitted) and calling the `isManaged()` method of the `Manageable` interface. Another new feature will be the ability to check all manageable objects (Session, ByteArray, Channel, and Token) first to see if they are managed without having to join them. The check for the session will be in the session factory, as in the `checkExists()` method. For the shared objects, the Session class will have `isXManaged()` methods.

Working with Other Java APIs

No Java API can ever work alone for any real-world application. Quite often there are questions about how JSDT fits into the rest of the Java philosophy. JSDT is not part of the core APIs, nor is it classified as an extension API. In its past lives it was first a research project and then has turned into a commercial product for Sun. As such, it is something that is sold by the Java Software part of Sun rather than a core part of the Java development efforts.

Java Messaging Service (JMS)   If you have looked at the documentation for the two APIs, you might notice that one of the contributors is the same guy that wrote JSDT and hence wonder what is going on. Like JSDT, JMS is a collaborative-style set of APIs. However, the problem area they seek to address is very different. JSDT is designed for use on the low end for developing collaborative applications where many people are using the same application and seeing the same output simultaneously.

JMS is at the other end of the scale. It is designed for groupware applications like Lotus Notes and similar systems. You may create groups and share information in a single application or many applications. It makes use of higher-level protocols like SMTP for delivering mail and message delivery capabilities that are based on TCP/IP. JSDT uses raw TCP/IP as its core delivery mechanism. Messages delivered through JMS are like email—non-real-time information passing. JMS is much more reliable, and some degree of persistence is also inherent in the system that can deal with network outages.

At the lower levels of JMS is another set of Java APIs called the Java Transaction API (JTA). JTA is a lower transaction–based API for interacting with database style services on each end. In comparison to JDBC, JTA provides many more authentication and security features. For example, it deals with cryptography-based authentication schemes as part of the basic APIs, where this is not even considered with JDBC (unless of course you create your own socket factories as JDBC uses standard sockets).

Generally speaking, you would not use JSDT and JMS in the same application, as they are targeted at two different audiences. There is no reason why you could not implement JMS using JSDT because it contains most of the important aspects such as reliability and message selection.

Serverlets   An interesting question is how JSDT relates to the use of serverlets or can be incorporated into a serverlet. Serverlets are designed for use in the processing of requests and creating dynamic content for a web server. JSDT, in contrast, as you already know, allows dynamic sharing of information.

Because JSDT applications can run either as a standalone item or inside a browser (with the appropriate permissions and signed JAR files), there is no reason why a serverlet would be prevented from hooking a JSDT shared object and generating output based on that information. Conversely, a request being processed could always send information to the shared objects too.

Silly as this might sound, there are some good reasons why this might be worthwhile. Say you have a bunch of people designing something collaboratively on some shared CAD tool. There's plenty of grunt to drive the Java application. However, there are other members of the team or the management who like to check in on the progress. Using JSDT the machine acting as the server would store a copy of the plan as people are updating items. The serverlet is also watching this session. Every so often a user wanting to watch proceedings would query the web browser and this could dump a two-dimensional picture and accompanying information on the current state of affairs. This is much quicker since all transaction processing of querying a database and processing results is no longer needed, the serverlet being delivered live information as it changes. Another slightly weird use might be to keep several serverlets in sync with information by using JSDT as the sharing mechanism.

Further JSDT Information

If what you have read in this book has gotten you sufficiently interested in JSDT for further investigation, there are a number of places to find more information (apart from emailing the author). The developer community surrounding JSDT is quite active. Also, unlike its approach to some other products, Sun is very responsive in working with the developers to build a better API for JSDT. The forthcoming features we've discussed are all driven by developer requests rather than any internal motives of Sun.

Mailing Lists   The first place for both technical questions and suggestions for improvements is the mailing list. Sun hosts the mailing list as part of the Java Media Framework site. You can subscribe to the list by sending email to

```
javamedia-request@sun.com
```

with the body containing

```
subscribe jsdt-interest
```

Once you see the confirmation you can join in the discussions.

FAQ   The homepage for JSDT can be found under those devoted to the Java Media Framework at http://java.sun.com/products/java-media/jsdt/

In standard *netiquette*, before asking any questions that you might have, please check the FAQ. The author maintains a JSDT FAQ under his homepage. You can find this at

http://www.vlc.com.au/~justin/java/jsdt_faq.html

Feel free to contact the author about adding extra items to the FAQ or items that are not clear enough.

Custom Implementations   For those interested in adding other transport mechanisms for JSDT other than the four available (JSDT 1.5 will include an HTTP-based implementation as well as the three you've been introduced to in the book), an implementers' guide is available. This guide shows you how to write a new transport mechanism. You can find this guide under

http://java.sun.com/products/java-media/jsdt/techinfo.html

Summary

That concludes our look at JSDT and the book. As you can see, JSDT can be quite a powerful API for quickly creating collaborative applications. Don't just get stuck on the whiteboard analogy. There are many different ways of using JSDT to make your applications much more interactive when used in group environments. It certainly makes development time much quicker for these types of applications. The example in this chapter took about a week to write from scratch and hopefully will present you with enough parts and ideas to try out your own system.

In conclusion, the world of Java networking is extremely vast. There are so many things to be covered that you can quickly lose track of everything that is happening. Hopefully you now have a good understanding of not only the fundamentals of Java networking programming, but also an appreciation of the relative strengths and weaknesses, enabling you to make the right choice in your real-world application.

INDEX

About the Author

Justin Couch is a well-known name in the Java community, a leading Java programmer, a Sun insider, and the author of *Java Unleashed* and *Web Publishing Unleashed*. He works with Australia's largest defense contractor, ADI, and with the Oz Army Battle Simulation Group as a team leader/system architect on mission-critical controls. Justin has a background in electrical engineering and computer science, with a focus on networking, communications systems, and visualization. He is an independent contractor with expertise in both VRML and Java networking.

SOFTWARE LICENSES

9. **Governing Law.** Any action related to this Agreement will be governed by California law and controlling U.S. federal law. No choice of law rules of any jurisdiction will apply.

10. **Severability.** If any provision of this Agreement is held to be unenforceable, This Agreement will remain in effect with the provision omitted, unless omission would frustrate the intent of the parties, in which case this Agreement will immediately terminate.

11. **Integration.** This Agreement is the entire agreement between you and Sun relating to its subject matter. It supersedes all prior or contemporaneous oral or written communications, proposals, representations and warranties and prevails over any conflicting or additional terms of any quote, order, acknowledgment, or other communication between the parties relating to its subject matter during the term of this Agreement. No modification of this Agreement will be binding, unless in writing and signed by an authorized representative of each party.

For inquiries please contact: Sun Microsystems, Inc. 901 San Antonio Road, Palo Alto, California 94303

JAVA™ DEVELOPMENT KIT VERSION 1.2 (JDK) and
JAVA™ SHARED DATA TOOLKIT VERSION 1.4 (JSDT)
SUPPLEMENTAL LICENSE TERMS

These supplemental terms ("Supplement") add to the terms of the Binary Code License Agreement ("Agreement"). Capitalized terms not defined herein shall have the same meanings ascribed to them in the Agreement. The Supplement terms shall supersede any inconsistent or conflicting terms in the Agreement.

1. **Limited License Grant.** Sun grants to you a non-exclusive, non-transferable limited license to use the Software without fee for evaluation of the Software and for development of Java™ applets and applications provided that you: (i) except as provided in Section 2 below, may not re-distribute the Software, in whole or in part, either separately or included with a product; (ii) may not create or authorize your licensees to create additional classes, interfaces, or subpackages that are contained in the "java" or "sun" packages or similar as specified by Sun in any class file naming convention; and (iii) agree to the extent Programs are developed which utilize the Windows 95/98 style graphical user interface or components contained therein, such applets or applications may only be developed to run on a Windows 95/98 or Windows NT platform. Refer to the Java Runtime Environment Version 1.2 binary code license (http://java.sun.com/products/JDK/1.2/index.html) for the availability of runtime code which may be distributd with Java applets and applications.

2. **Java Platform Interface.** In the event that Licensee creates an additional API(s) which: (i) extends the functionality of a Java Environment; and, (ii) is exposed to third party software developers for the purpose of developing additional software which invokes such additional API, Licensee must promptly publish broadly an accurate specification for such API for free use by all developers.

3. **Trademarks and Logos.** This Agreement does not authorize Licensee to use any Sun name, trademark or logo. Licensee acknowledges as between it and Sun that Sun owns the Java trademark and all Java-related trademarks, logos and icons including the Coffee Cup and Duke ("Java Marks") and agrees to comply with the Java Trademark Guidelines at http://java. sun.com/trademarks.html.

4. **High Risk Activities.** Notwithstanding Section 2, with respect to high risk activities, the following language shall apply: the Software is not designed or intended for use in on-line control of aircraft, air traffic, aircraft navigation or aircraft communications; or in the design, construction, operation or maintenance of any nuclear facility. Sun disclaims any express or implied warranty of fitness for such uses.